From humble beginnings as the daughter of a Clerkenwell milliner, Emily Soldene rose to become a leading lady of the London stage and a formidable impresario with her own opera company. The darling of London's theatreland, she later reinvented herself as a journalist and writer who scandalised the capital with her backstage revelations.

Weaving through the spurious glamour of Victorian music halls and theatres, taking encounters with the Pre-Raphaelites and legal disputes involving Charles Dickens in her stride, Emily became the toast of New York and ventured far off the beaten track to tour in Australia and New Zealand. In *The Improbable Adventures of Miss Emily Soldene*, a life filled with performance, travel and incident returns to centre stage.

PUBLICITY: Helen Richardson
Helen.RichardsonPR@gmail.com

SALES: Daniel Scott
daniel@allisonandbusby.com
020 3950 7834

Allison & Busby Limited
11 Wardour Mews
London W1F 8AN
allisonandbusby.com

First published in Great Britain by Allison & Busby in 2021.

A CIP catalogue record for this book is available from
the British Library.

First Edition

ISBN 978-0-7490-2657-8

Typeset in 11.5/16.5 pt Adobe Garamond Pro by
Allison & Busby Ltd

The paper used for this Allison & Busby publication
has been produced from trees that have been legally sourced
from well-managed and credibly certified forests.

Printed and bound by
CPI Group (UK) Ltd, Croydon, CR0 4YY

The Improbable Adventures
of
Miss Emily Soldene

Actress, Writer and Rebel Victorian

HELEN BATTEN

This text is an early unedited version of the manuscript.
Further editorial changes will be made and any errors
corrected for the final edition.

To Amber, Scarlett and Daisy
An ancestor to inspire you

Contents

Emily as King Chilpéric in Herve's operetta *Chilpéric*

Introduction

Every family has their own myths and legends: the tales of supposedly famous and infamous ancestors, passed down through the generations to bring out at the annual gatherings of the tribe, the weddings and the funerals; to intrigue grandchildren or amuse new partners.

Among our forebears we allegedly had a notorious actress. According to my nanna she was grand and slightly risqué – her name was Lady de Vries. Other than that she knew no more; just that she was grand.

'What? A real lady?' I asked her.

'No dear, not a lady, not a real lady at all I imagine,' she said.

Rather prescient of Nanna as it turned out.

At the time there was no evidence for the existence of this Lady de Vries, and we had no idea how we were supposed to be related to her. She was dismissed by the family as another example of my nanna's dramatic imagination.

However, years after Nanna had passed away and the theatrical lady had slipped from the family memory, I happened across her while doing a piece of research into our family history. I had been asked to write a book about a more contemporary set of female ancestors. I made a phone call to a local historian of the ancestral village in Hertfordshire. He told me that I had a famous actress in the family, that I should talk to a renowned historian of musical theatre who lived in New Zealand. He gave me Kurt Gänzl's address. There followed a flurry of emails, and two monumental volumes of a thousand words each, kindly given by Kurt (because I'm family), which were sent halfway across the world and landed on my desk.

It seems we did indeed have a theatrical ancestor. In fact, she was my first cousin three times removed; my great-great-grandfather was her favourite uncle. She was a singer as well as an actress, and Nanna was right – she was no lady. She had several names (none of them de Vries) but the one she used most was Miss Emily Soldene.

With one Google click I found a photograph. Emily Soldene, singer, born in the year after Victoria became queen and dying just two years before the beginning of the First World War – a woman who had truly lived through an entire era. She was dressed in curious silk boy-britches, a low-cut kimono-style jacket revealing a fulsome bosom and thigh, a floppy pastry cook's cap slipping off a tumble of blonde ringlets, and a face tipped heavenwards, eyes hopeful, expectant; her mouth wide in a secret smile as if communicating with a celestial friend in the firmament. Cheeky and yes, probably no lady, at all.

But what I read next really caught my attention. Not only had Emily been a star of the music halls, moving up in society to become the leading lady in light operas, but she had also started to produce and direct the productions she starred in. Then she had set up her own theatrical company. She had bought the tenancies of London theatres like the Lyceum and the rights to popular operas. Emily had even brought *Carmen* to the British provinces for the first time (with herself in the role of Carmen of course).

And there was more – like today, if you really wanted to make it big you had to go to America. Emily took her productions to Broadway, then across the Wild West to a gold-booming San Francisco and back again several times. And then she couldn't resist hopping on a boat and going across to Australia and New Zealand. These trips were long, dangerous and expensive; only a few very wealthy, adventurous ladies or actresses would have made them. These trips were Emily's biggest triumphs and her biggest disasters.

But perhaps the most surprising development in Emily's full life was her second career as a journalist. In an era when the lady journalist was a new and distrusted phenomenon, at the age of fifty-two, Emily managed to get herself a weekly column and a byline in one of Australia's largest newspapers, the *Sydney Evening News*, sending dispatches from London on anything that took her fancy. Emily had that most rare of things for a woman from a working-class background – a public voice.

There was also an understudy to Emily's main role. A few more Google clicks revealed the existence of another doublet-clad ancestor, dressed in velvet knickerbockers, pantomime tights and high heels. Emily's sister, Clara Vesey, joined Emily on the stage when she was twenty years old. There is less written about Clara, although plenty of photographs – she was one of the most photographed actresses of the nineteenth century. Eleven years younger than her half-sister, Clara was rarely allowed to play lead roles – these were reserved for Emily, despite the fact that Clara was supposedly an excellent singer (and was definitely considered prettier). It seems Clara was destined to travel with her big sister's company as Emily's understudy.

At first glance it seems Emily was the main player and Clara tagged along in her slipstream, a passenger on board for the often-bumpy ride – but the story is more complicated. Sisters can be the best of friends and the biggest of rivals. Eventually Emily and Clara made different life choices, but these choices and their consequences seem to say something not just about the sisters themselves, but also about women in nineteenth-century society in general, and perhaps even women today.

Emily has faded from the limelight now, but in Victorian Britain she was a star, and together with Clara, the sisters were regular celebrities, invited to parties for their wit, gossip and general bonhomie. The people they called friends included Pre-Raphaelites, peers of the realm, maharajahs, Rothschilds, Dickens, Gladstone, Oscar Wilde and the Prince of Wales. They did the Season with impunity, drank champagne, ate oysters and gambled on horses, somehow working exhaustive social lives around their theatrical commitments. They had close friendships they shouldn't have had, with grand men. Emily claimed to have been stalked by Jack the Ripper. I know this because Emily also wrote a book, *My Theatrical and Musical Recollections*. It was one of the bestselling books of 1898 and scandalised society. As one reviewer said:

> *She has had the good fortune to know many of those whom*
> *the world calls smart people, and many of those whom the*
> *world calls smart people have had the evil fortune of meeting*
> *her. One and all these she 'gives away'.*

It's a great read. Emily has an icy wit and a literary twinkle in her eye, with plenty of mischief and just a sprinkling of spite for her few bêtes noires.

But one of the secrets of Emily's success was her awareness of the Soldene brand – and the memoir, fun as it is, doesn't tell the whole story. In fact, like too many autobiographies, truth has been sacrificed at the altar of image. The real-life adventures of Miss Emily Soldene are darker, and actually more heroic. I think she left some of the best bits out.

So I've put them back in.

Emily on her great American tour as the pastry cook, Drogan, in
Geneviève de Brabant

Chapter One

BROADWAY

Stage fright (noun): Nervousness on facing an audience, especially for the first time (*Oxford Dictionary*)

On the same night Emily Soldene made her debut on New York's Broadway, news of the death of her little sister, Clara, had been telegraphed back to England.

As it turned out this telegraph was slightly premature, although as Emily left her and Clara's suite at the Fifth Avenue Hotel for the theatre on a dismal night in November 1874, she was taken aside by doctors and warned that this was probably the last time she would see her sister alive.

This was difficult for Emily, not least because she always suffered from nerves before she went on stage, and today the stakes were particularly daunting. She was about to perform the lead role in a new opera to a theatre full of critics she knew were waiting for the much-hyped English upstart to fail. Of course, the one person who always managed to calm Emily was her sister, Clara; but now that Emily really needed her, Clara was not by her side. Although it probably occurred to Emily that Clara could have said the same thing.

Emily was a great believer in omens, and from the start there were signs that this trip was going to be difficult. As the White Star ship, the *Celtic*, sailed out of Liverpool on a sunny autumn morning, Emily's business partner and mentor, Charles Morton, discovered that he had left his umbrella behind. Everyone had laughed and teased him about what a bad portent this was. Less than forty-eight hours later no one was laughing:

> 'What horrors! what suffering!' Ah! if the ship would only be still for five minutes! Neither the ship nor anything else would be quiet for five minutes. All the company were prostrate, and my sister Clara soon dangerously so. The wind for days blew and howled . . . Every now and then the ship took a header, then sprang up with a sickening bound, skimmed the tops of the waves like a swallow, shook, shivered, vibrated, and, shaking the water from her shining sides, down she went again. In a moment of confidence a gentleman kindly informed me she would certainly "break her back one of these days"'

The stormy seas were relentless for eleven days. When they finally arrived in New York Harbour it was clear that every member of the cast was severely depleted, exhausted and weak. But the worst was Clara. Always fragile, now she looked hollowed out and frighteningly pale. Her blue eyes seemed bigger as her face got smaller, like a tiny and frightened woodland creature with bones that could snap. Clara had to be carried onshore, and then instead of getting better, she got worse and developed what Emily described as 'gastric fever'. She became low and tearful; Emily couldn't remember the last time she had seen her sister smile, and the worst thing was Clara's terrible insomnia. The doctors tried everything, but the more sleeping draughts she took, the less she slept: 'there she lay, always wide-awake.'

At first Emily worried that Clara might not be well enough for the opening night. Clara was supposed to be playing the impudent servant boy Oswald. Her costume had been specially designed to please the largely male audience, with provocative tights, a doublet short enough to expose nearly all of her legs, a short cape and feathered cap styled to sit at a cheeky angle on her mass of curls. Emily never underestimated the need to captivate, some might say titillate, the erotic imaginations of their gentleman fans. Without Clara on stage, Emily was missing one of her greatest assets. But this worry was soon eclipsed by the greater fear that Clara would never take to the stage again. All the doctors that Emily had summoned to the Fifth Avenue Hotel had given the same prognosis – that if Clara didn't manage to get some sleep soon, her body would give up and she would die of exhaustion and starvation. Of course, sleeping pills had yet to be invented.

A primary cause of insomnia is fear, particularly when the nervous system is triggered into fight or flight mode. If this happens, it's difficult to fall asleep, and you wake at the slightest disturbance. Something about the voyage must have put Clara into a state of terror that could not be turned off or reassured, even now that they were on dry land. This had been Clara and Emily's first ocean voyage. They had only ever been to sea once before, and that was a day trip with a group of young parliamentarians who had taken them out from Portsmouth across to the Isle of Wight. The trip nearly ended in disaster when on their way back they were surrounded by deep fog and found themselves in the path of an ocean liner. They were only saved by a young politician shouting, 'Shove her along like h—l!' When Emily now stroked her sister's forehead and kissed her hand, it was terror that she saw in Clara's eyes.

As Emily was helped into her costume by her trusted wardrobe lady, Mrs Quinton, she must have wondered what on earth she had done – gambling not only her finances and reputation, but the very life of her sister. And she might have wondered whether she should go back to the hotel and stay with Clara, she might have considered that no performance could ever be more important than the life of the person she was closest to in the world. She was probably facing the most dreadful dilemma.

In the end Emily must have decided that the show had to go on, because suddenly she was standing backstage waiting for her cue. Luckily, she was playing one of her favourite roles – Drogan, the pastry cook, in Offenbach's *Geneviève de Brabant*. It was the role that had settled Emily's fame, and had run for an unprecedented three hundred shows in London the year before. It had been met with thrilled appreciation from the capital's opéra bouffe fans. Unfortunately, *Geneviève de Brabant* had already premiered in New York and proved less than popular. Emily believed this was because it was performed in the original French without any cultural adjustments. However, she knew from others' experiences that what was popular in Britain didn't always translate to the States, and she had also been set up for a fall.

Emily's promoters were an ambitious couple of young men called Maurice Grau and Carlo Chizzola, who had just started out and decided to specialise in opéra bouffe. They had taken the lease of the old French Theatre in Fourteenth Street, renamed it the Lyceum, and hired Emily and her Soldene Opera Bouffe Company to be their star offering for the Christmas season. As well as planning the tours and negotiating the venues and ticket prices, the promoter's job was to handle the publicity. In this, Chizzola and Grau had surpassed themselves, blitzing the city and the press with the following notice:

Messers Maurice Grau and Chizzola experience much pleasure in being able to introduce to the New York public Miss Emily Soldene the reigning Queen of the London Stage whose lyric and dramatic talents have raised her to an enviable position and rendered her a universal favourite with the public . . .

The novel entertainment known as English Opera Bouffe must not be regarded in the light of a mere imitation of the French, but rather as a clever adaptation which, without losing the lightsome grace and champagne sparkle of the original, fashions the dialogue and its scintillating wit to the taste and humour of English speaking audiences.

Miss Soldene has labored successfully to assemble around her a company of marked ability in which will be found the same harmony of action and perfection, of ensemble characterizing the troupes of leading comedy theatres.

The bar had been set high for the Soldene Opera Bouffe Company, not least because they were facing an American press that had already made up its mind about British theatrical imports. Lydia Thompson and her 'British Burlesque Blondes' had arrived on American shores in 1868, performing a set of burlesque musical numbers. In the nineteenth century burlesque had not yet evolved into the erotic dancing that we know today. The word *burlesque* originally meant to make fun of, and Victorian burlesque consisted of women playing male roles in tights. The shows were full of jokes and the British Blondes were expert at improvising witty repartee with the male audience. They were as scandalous as they were popular. Thompson was the darling of the New York newspapers, but outside the city the press were more conservative and she faced disgust wherever she went. However, Thompson revelled in the publicity. During a run in Chicago, the owner of the *Chicago Times*, Wilbur F. Storey, attacked her so ferociously that she made her troupe post notices calling Storey 'a liar and a coward'. Then Thompson and her husband horsewhipped Storey at gunpoint. Thompson told a reporter that Storey 'had called her by the most odious epithet that could be applied to a woman' and she could stand it no longer. Despite being fined and jailed, Thompson said she was glad she did it. Sales of tickets soared and Thompson made $370,000 – the equivalent of nearly $7 million today.

However, by the time Emily arrived six years later, the novelty of the British Burlesque Blondes had worn off, and the press were lamenting the arrival of yet another indecent British import – which was unfair because, although a Soldene production always contained a splash of sauciness, it was a much more subtle, classy offering, with more talent on stage. Emily was producing an opera with integrity.

This view from the press was not helping Emily's state of mind. In common with some of the greatest performers in history, Emily suffered from nerves. Stage fright causes the blood vessels in the extremities to constrict. The performer's body reacts like an animal under threat. As normal digestion closes down, there is a feeling of butterflies in the stomach and the body instinctively tries to assume a foetal position, which is unhelpful if you are about to go on stage. The definition of courage is not an absence of fear, but feeling the fear and doing it anyway, and by this measure Emily had a lot of courage. Because, despite feeling sick with dread and having no voice to speak of, Emily walked out of the wings on the night of 2nd November, into the bright, blinding lights to confront a full theatre of not entirely friendly faces.

As Emily opened her mouth to sing the first note, nothing came out. Her voice was barely a croaky whisper. But as so often happened, from somewhere came some sort of sound, and once she could hear herself, in a kind of torturous virtuous circle, she seemed to be able to make more noise, and the louder it got, the more she seemed able to relax and slip into a familiar groove. Her spirits and her notes started to soar, and she may even have started to enjoy herself, although it must have been a difficult moment when Oswald the page came on stage and she remembered Clara lying on her deathbed in the Fifth Avenue Hotel. The cast, despite being weakened by the journey and dreadfully nervy, followed their leading lady and began to recapture a bit of the sparkle that had so thrilled the London audiences a few months before.

The performance came to an end, and the applause was enthusiastic but not overwhelming. Emily knew how important it was to leave everyone with the impression of a hit and so she harnessed a trick she had picked up over the years. She had learnt to bow in 1866 from a leading lady called Madame Sherrington:

A charming artiste, but artificial and perfect to faddish in deportment. From her, by close observation, I acquired the effective stage curtsey. When you find your audience flabby and not inclined to rise to the occasion, this is how you manage them. You finish your aria, you bow slightly. They, rather bored, applaud slightly, you bow somewhat deprecatingly right and left, then a little lower full front. They applaud more, you repeat the manoeuvre, but show no signs of going off. They applaud rather vigorously, you convey by gesture how utterly unworthy you are of so much distinction. They appreciate such delicacy of feeling, and applaud vociferously, loudly, continuously, rapturously. Now is your time to retire, you bow and bow, and, always keeping your face to the audience, slowly exit, kissing your hands and overcome. Thunders of applause and acclamations – 'Brava,' 'Brava,' 'Bravissima,' 'Bis,' 'Bis.' Of course you take your call and your encore, you have earned it.

That night Emily earnt her standing ovation. It was not perhaps her longest or loudest, but it was an ovation of some kind. A good sign, but she would have to wait until the morning and the press reviews to find out whether she had a hit. But first Emily faced an even more daunting prospect – going back to the hotel and seeing whether Clara was still alive.

She opened the door to their room to find the maid laying out a supper for her:

'My sister?'

She nodded. 'Resting ma'am. But not asleep.'

Emily was overcome first with relief and then a feeling of almost terminal exhaustion from the day's events. She couldn't go in to see Clara, not yet. She sank into a chair and forced herself to eat a little supper. In the quiet, by the light of the fire and flickering candlelight, Emily read a book – probably a novel; it may even have been Dickens, as he was a favourite. She waited until her body and mind had quietened a little. Then she crept into the bedroom to find Clara, awake, of course, and just as pale. Emily lay down on the bed they shared:

> *Taking her in my arms, I held her close and petted her and patted her like a baby, and 'hushed' her, and prayed in my heart, as I had never prayed before, that she might sleep. And after a bit she dozed for five minutes, then woke up wondering, 'where was she?' 'Hush,' said I, sharply, 'Go to sleep,' and she did; slept for six hours. When she awoke I was exhausted, stiff, cramped, all the strength had gone out of me, I could not move, but she was saved.*

From that moment Clara got better. It took a few weeks until she could emerge, but when she did, she looked 'lean and rather like a young stork', but she had survived.

Occasionally in the press Clara was referred to as Emily's

daughter. Although there were many interesting grey areas in matters of marriage and parentage in the Soldene family tree, it seems unlikely. Clara's birth certificate states her year of birth as 1849. Emily's birth certificate has yet to be found. It took historian Kurt Gänzl twenty years just to find the first official mention of her. In the 1841 census she is two years old, called Emily Lambert, and is living with her mother Priscilla and a man she is recorded as being married to; a clerk named Frederick Lambert. In other official documents the given date of her birth varies slightly, but not by much. Gänzl has settled for her date of birth as 30th September 1838. This means Emily would have to have been an eleven-year-old mother. Not impossible, but still, rather implausible. Siblings, particularly sisters, can be attached to each other in such a way that the older sibling becomes the mother figure, particularly in families where the mother is otherwise engaged; and the strongest attachment comes when they both realise that they must band together against the parents. There were plenty of good reasons for Emily and Clara to be close.

When the notices came out the next day they were broadly favourable, with plenty of admiration for the leading lady herself. This is the one, from *The Play*, Emily picked out to put in her memoir:

The brightest anticipations in respect of the immediate and marked success of the Soldene English Opera Bouffe Company have been realised. Miss Soldene and her artists have won a victory of which the results are destined to be enduring . . . So rare a grouping of excellences in one entertainment is seldom, if ever, brought about, and as a consequence, the immediate decision of the French 'nerve' of the acting, the charm and beauty of the singing, and

the magnificence of the stage costume, was of the most
favourable kind.

Of course, Emily omitted from her memoir the less ecstatic
reviews which show that her attack of nerves had not gone
unnoticed, such as this from *The Clipper*:

> *She had sung but a few notes and spoken a word or two,*
> *before a feeling of disappointment spread, as her voice was*
> *almost inaudible both in song and speech. As she warmed*
> *up to her work, however, she improved considerably and the*
> *fact was soon realized that the new star of the burlesque*
> *hemisphere was not only a refined and cultivated artist in*
> *acting, and one very graceful in action, but also that she*
> *possessed a voice of marked sweetness and purity in tone,*
> *though ordinarily of much power.*

It seemed as if Clara had survived and so (narrowly) had Emily's
Broadway adventure, but it had been a huge gamble. What had
led Emily to risk launching herself on a Broadway stage in the
first place or indeed to become an actress at all? For an answer,
the first place to look might be to her mother, Priscilla Swain.

Emily's grandmother's pub, The Horse and Groom, in Preston,
Hertfordshire, where she spent much of her childhood

Chapter Two

THE BIGAMIST BONNET MAKER

Such a fuss about two wives, when lots of people have three or four and nobody says 'nuffin'! How do I know? Oh well – because – well, I just know, don't you know (Emily, 1903)

Emily's mother, Priscilla Swain, was unconventional, but then she came from an interesting family.

Priscilla's grandfather, Stephen, was a person of renown in the town of Hitchin in Hertfordshire, not least because he had a wooden leg, which he had acquired after fighting the French in Canada. He was in the 19th Dragoons, and came back from the Americas with some choice military songs which were passed down the generations; my mother remembers her grandfather singing them. Stephen obviously had a talent for leadership (or at the very least liked being in charge) because at various times, as well as running a shop on Hitchin's high street, he was a special constable, surveyor of the highways, receiver of the assize returns and the master of Hitchin's workhouse. Perhaps Emily and Clara had inherited their love of theatrical clothes from him – he put the purchase of some plush new crimson velvet breeches on expenses, after his pair was stolen by an inmate of the workhouse.

When Stephen's son, Priscilla's father Charles, got into trouble for making a young lady pregnant and refusing to marry her (he was taken to court and ordered to pay maintenance), Stephen knew just what to do with him. Charles was sent off to join the 19th Dragoons and once again an ancestor found themselves fighting through a freezing Canadian winter, although this time he was battling the Americans and he didn't lose a leg. On the way the dragoons stopped in Ireland and it was here that Charles finally did get married, not to an Irish woman, but to a local Hertfordshire girl, Catherine (Katie) Young, who sailed all the way across the Irish Sea in 1811 to get wed. Charles must have been quite compelling. Nine months later Katie was back in Hertfordshire and gave birth to Priscilla.

It was five years before Katie saw Charles again. Was this a blessing or curse? At first glance it seems that it must have been very hard for Katie, essentially a single mother, with no idea when, or if, this compelling new husband was ever going to come home. He didn't have a track record for constancy and his father hadn't set a reassuring example of coming back unharmed.

However, Charles's presence may not have made things much easier. The family tree reveals that when Charles did return in 1817, Katie had nine more children over the next twelve years – all but one of whom survived into adulthood. In fact, Katie only stopped having children when Charles died, presumably because he was an alcoholic, because by this time he ran an alehouse in a small village outside Hitchin called

Preston, and the cause of death on the certificate is liver failure. It's not known why Priscilla decided to leave the security of her Hertfordshire village and run away to London, but things might have been a bit fraught in the Swain household. It could also be that Priscilla was quite ambitious. What is known is that at some point in the early 1830s, whilst still a teenager, Priscilla decided to walk out of her village inn home and take the road south down to London. She made it as far as Clerkenwell and then stopped.

This was an intrepid move – nineteenth-century London was not for the faint-hearted. The American novelist Henry James called it a dreadfully delightful city, 'the biggest aggregation of human life, the most complete compendium in the world.' It was a gathering of fortune seekers and chancers, buying and selling in its narrow, dark streets, full of filth, literal and metaphorical. According to the philanthropist Charles Booth, three-quarters of the population lived in poverty and it was poverty on a scale that is difficult to imagine today. Not even in our most deprived, hidden corners do people now live in the conditions that most did in Victorian London. It was normal for a large family to live in one small room with cracked or paneless windows, sleep on lice-infested mattresses or straw on the floor, use pots as toilets, and be surrounded by vermin and cockroaches, and smoke from a fire, if they were lucky enough to buy a piece of coal. There was no welfare state, no sanitation, no healthcare, no education, no protection from unscrupulous landlords or employers. Even if you were managing to live above subsistence level, the precariousness of life meant that you could lose what little you had very quickly. The threat of the workhouse must have felt very real.

This meant that nineteenth-century London was edgy. People lived unconventional lives with chaotic domestic arrangements that country-bred Priscilla would never have encountered before. One can only imagine what effect the sights, sounds and smells must have had on our nineteenth-century Dick Whittington. The closest thing she'd experienced to a metropolis was the market town of Hitchin.

But Priscilla must have known that London offered more opportunities than anywhere else in the world, and Priscilla had a highly marketable skill – she was a bonnet maker. Millinery was one of the few occupations open to an upper-working-class lady. It was a relatively respectable profession requiring a four- to five-year apprenticeship, technical skill and some creativity and fashion sense. Hundreds of women in Hertfordshire and Northamptonshire made a relatively good living from it and the Swains were no exception. Millinery was a tradition passed down the female line – the last person in my branch of the family to make hats for a living was my great-aunt Alice in the 1920s. Most women worked from home and sent the hats down to London, but Priscilla must have sensed the greater opportunity just forty miles down the road. London was the greatest clothing and accessory manufacturing centre in the world, full of small self-employed enterprises. It was the one place where it would be relatively easy for Priscilla to start her own business.

At first she rented a room in Clerkenwell, but Priscilla must have prospered because by 1841 she is recorded in the London Trades Directory under the name of Mrs Priscilla Lambert, renting a warehouse down the road in Aldersgate and owning a hat shop. This means that before she was even thirty years old she was running her own business in the heart of the capital. Her premises were in a busy street which has now been replaced by the Barbican. It was not the most exclusive shopping street in London, but it was arguably on the edge of three of the busiest shopping areas – Holborn to the west, Cheapside to the east and the Strand to the south. During the day it thronged with people and at night the large glass shop windows were lit up with gaslight, twinkling through the London fog.

How Priscilla did this, and where she got the money from in an age where there were significant legal impediments to women owning their own business, not least because they had no legal right to property or ability to borrow money, is a mystery. But, somehow, Priscilla did manage it and she was doing well, achieving that extraordinary feat of being a single, financially independent young woman and business owner in the 1830s.

Priscilla was part of a new breed of young women coming into the city from the countryside to work in the clothing, retail and hospitality sectors. They were known as working girls and considered not quite respectable, making a living without the help of a man, sometimes living alone and walking the streets unchaperoned. Newspaper columns were written about them. Nevertheless, these bold young women were usually defiant, flaunting the ultimate symbol of their independence – a key to their own front door. A music hall song of the time ran: 'She could look after herself, knew her own mind and had her latch key, and was too worldly wise to be taken advantage of or got around.'

But was she?

In 1838 Priscilla found out she was pregnant. Emily was born on 30th September 1838 at 101 Claremont Square in Clerkenwell. The identity of Emily's father is a mystery; however, it seems likely that he was a man named Frederick Lambert. Certainly, in the 1841 census Priscilla calls herself Mrs Lambert (although there is no evidence that she had married). She is living with Mr Frederick Lambert (occupation, clerk) and two-year-old Emily Lambert. Also living with them was fourteen-year-old Caroline Swain, Priscilla's youngest sister, who was presumably brought down from Preston to look after baby Emily, while Priscilla went off and did the necessary job of earning money making bonnets. What happens next is a mystery. There is no trace of Frederick Lambert after this; he vanishes completely.

In contrast with the candid way that Emily writes about her life in the theatre, she is discreet about her childhood. The public are only allowed the briefest glimpse into a sugar-coated world, where the city of her youth is lined with tall trees full of singing sparrows with glossy feathers and bright eyes. There is a delightful fruit seller with a big basket full of 'ripe, rosy, juicy cherries', and the New River ran 'bright and sparkling' through the Terrace – which must be an outright lie, because a river running through to central London would have been more like an open sewer, with all the detritus of human existence flung into it.

Clerkenwell was not the poorest area of London – Whitechapel just next door and Bermondsey across the river competed for that prize. However, alongside Southwark it was a close runner-up, with pockets of the destitute mingling with the poor working class and even a few lower-middle-class streets.

When Charles Booth conducted interviews for his poverty maps of London, a policeman described Clerkenwell as 'the melting pot' of London 'where all the stolen silver or jewels come to be melted or disassembled'. Some contemporaries might have put the unmarried mother, Priscilla, into that category.

In the fictional childhood of Emily's memoir, however, there is a strict God-fearing mother (a career as a bonnet maker, or in fact any suggestion that her mother worked at all, is never mentioned), and there is also a father whom we are told is a barrister. Frederick Lambert was certainly never a barrister, nor was the man whom her mother did eventually marry and whose name Emily would take, Edward Soldene. He did work in the law, but only as a much lowlier legal clerk.

Moreover, Emily places herself squarely in the middle of the middle classes:

When I was a little girl, nurse told me if I was not an exceedingly good girl and did not do exactly as I was told a big dragon fly would sew up my eyes with an unbreakable multi-coloured web.

Emily would never have had a nurse – an auntie maybe, but not a nurse. There was also talk of governesses taking her to chapel, being sent off to an academy for young ladies in Islington, and housemaids taking orders from her mother. If Emily didn't eat dinner her mother would allegedly say, 'All right Mary, put it in the safe for Miss Emily's tea.'

However, it does not seem likely that Emily grew up with her mother. Her descriptions of youth are mainly rural – a picture of a bucolic, timeless childhood running across fields, picking fruit in orchards, hiding in woods surrounded by cousins and being chased by aunts, a world away from the dangerous muddle of Clerkenwell.

Like so many children born out of wedlock, Emily seems to have been sent away to be brought up by her maternal grandmother, Katie Swain, and the large extended family that lived in the villages surrounding Hitchin in Hertfordshire. Katie was now a widow and the landlady of The Horse and Groom Inn in Preston. Emily's aunts ran the rival pub in the village, The Red Lion, and her uncle, Charles (my great-great-grandfather) ran a pub in Langley Bottom down the road. Priscilla's other brothers were blacksmiths and farmers, and her last sister had married a shop owner in Hitchin. There were plenty of family members to look after and absorb another small person without anyone noticing, and Emily had a tribe of young cousins as playmates. Sending Emily to the countryside left Priscilla free to run her business, keep her reputation and perhaps find a man who would marry her.

Amidst her childhood reminiscing, Emily also fails to mention that her grandmother Katie was a landlady. Female publicans were not uncommon in the early nineteenth century, but they inhabited a grey area of lower-middle-class respectability. Like working girls, inn-keeping was not quite decent. It was a habit of the Swain women to inhabit this grey area, which must have made it easier for Emily herself to get into a less than respectable profession later on.

Instead, Emily's childhood stories are of the vicar falling asleep in her grandmother's parlour after lunch, and picking flowers in her grandmother's greenhouse, which she puts inside the Bible to take to church with her aunts. She tells of being caught by her grandmother reading a copy of *Don Juan* which she had found in an attic, inside a truck marked Mont Réal (the old name for Montreal, a souvenir from someone's Canadian soldiering), and getting a good smacking in the orthodox manner with the slipper because 'the authorities' did not approve of ladies reading. It's all very respectable. She paints a picture of a rural ideal: kisses behind haystacks, secret dells to lie down and daydream in on a hot summer's afternoon, being sent out to gather snow to put in the big bowl of pancake batter for Shrove Tuesday, maypole-type rituals and ancient country festivals that at the beginning of the twentieth century Emily laments having disappeared. These are hardly the scribblings of a child brought up in inner-city London.

But all this was to change in 1849 when Priscilla gave birth to a little girl – Emily's sister, and her closest friend and companion, Clara Ann Soldene, later to become famous as the actress Clara Vesey.

While Emily was picking cherries in orchards, back in London her mother had somehow uncoupled herself from the mysterious Frederick Lambert and struck up a special friendship with another clerk in a lawyer's office, called Edward Soldene. How and why she married him is a mystery, but on 4th May 1848, at the age of thirty-seven, Priscilla finally walked down the aisle. Clara was born a year later, and eleven-year-old Emily was brought back to London and became part of a family unit with her mother and the man whose name she adopted, Edward Soldene. The new family moved into the top half of a small mews house in Islington just off the City Road.

However, things were still not quite what they seemed. Edward Soldene was a bigamist. He already had a wife. In fact, he'd had another wife for nearly twenty years, and five other children too. Priscilla must have known this because Sara Soldene and her children lived (conveniently or inconveniently, who knows?) just around the corner from them in Islington. And it wasn't as if Edward had left his former wife and moved in with Priscilla and his new family. Seven weeks after Clara was born, Edward Soldene had another baby with Sara, a little girl called Sarah Ann – a half-sister for Clara. On the night of the 1851 census, when Clara was two years old, Edward chose to be at home with his first wife Sara and the six children they'd had together. Priscilla, Emily and Clara are recorded as living in the mews house on their own, and all three of them are given the surname of Lambert. Priscilla even calls herself Mrs Lambert, which would make her a bigamist as well as Edward Soldene. Given the prevailing moral climate, it's not surprising that Emily doesn't dwell on her parents in her writing.

To be fair to Priscilla, the Victorians may have portrayed themselves as morally conservative, but the reality was more complicated, especially in the capital. Amongst the working classes, the older custom of couples living together without being married, often breaking up and recoupling once or twice in a lifetime, was still operating. Serial monogamy was quite normal. Things only changed at the beginning of the twentieth century when the introduction of state pensions and benefits meant that arrangements had to become more official. In an age when divorce was not an option unless you were very rich and prepared to see your petition debated in the Houses of Parliament, it was simpler not to get married, just in case. Everyone accepted this – if you said you were married and behaved as if you were, you were treated as if you were. Even bigamy was not unusual. It was such a problem that in 1861 the government voted to make bigamy a Class One indictable felony, which in theory meant it could be punished by death. Men made up the majority of bigamists in court, and forty-two per cent of them were, like Edward Soldene, aged from thirty to forty. It seems it was a dangerous age for men inclined to roam. In the days before social media and the internet, it was quite easy to hide and people just disappeared to start again.

However, whilst living together may not have been unusual, it did leave Priscilla and her daughters vulnerable. A man could walk away from cohabiting and suffer no ill effects, but a woman, having less earning potential and possibly children to feed, might quickly end up in the workhouse. Even if Edward Soldene did stick around, after he had paid his first family's housekeeping expenses from his clerk's wages, there would be little money to spare for his second family. So Priscilla had to carry on making bonnets to feed them, and Emily was probably brought back from the countryside to help look after her baby sister, Clara.

Mothers can provide daughters with a great example of what to do, or, perhaps more importantly, what not to do, and the consequences of Priscilla's complicated love life were almost certainly not lost on her eldest daughter. For the next nine years Emily lived with her mother and baby sister in their small flat in Islington. She would have observed the comings and goings of Edward Soldene between her family and his other family round the corner. She would have been a witness to Priscilla's attempts to pay the bills and extract financial help from this less than honest man.

These observations may well have played a part in the next

big event in Emily's life. On St Patrick's Day 1859 Emily slipped out of the family house in Islington and made for a house in Cleveland Street W1, an address that would later become famous as the lodgings shared by William Holman Hunt and Dante Gabriel Rossetti, and the headquarters of the Pre-Raphaelite Brotherhood. Emily had decided to elope.

Over the years Emily would say, 'I ran away when I was very young, but old enough to know better.' However, there were good reasons she might have been tempted to marry twenty-four-year-old lawyer's clerk, Jack Powell. He was the right age and had a good enough job; in fact he was more senior in his law office than Edward Soldene. And he was willing to get married. The 1851 census had revealed that there were between 500,000 and a million more women than men in the country, and the ratio was particularly disadvantageous in London. A quarter of twenty- to forty-five-year-old women were unmarried. The newspapers were full of columns of hand-wringing anxiety about a phenomenon known as The Surplus. Who was to financially support all these wallflowers? Women did not earn enough to support themselves, largely because they weren't paid enough. The Surplus were potentially a massive drain. No woman wanted to be seen as part of this demeaning Surplus. Basically, a single man, of the right age, with an income and his health, could not be allowed to get away. Especially when her mother's willingness to compromise herself without a ring on her finger seemed to have left them so vulnerable.

But Jack Powell had an added attraction – he had connections. His father was the journalist John Powell, a close friend of Charles Dickens, an association that was to have consequences for Emily later. But in the late 1850s when Jack started courting her, a whole world opened up to Emily of which no innkeeper's granddaughter, or bonnet maker's daughter, could have dreamt. John Powell had worked alongside Charles Dickens as a political journalist in the lobby and was then appointed the deputy editor of the newspaper launched by Dickens, the *Evening News*. They were both friends of the journalist George Hogarth; in fact Emily claims that Charles Dickens met his future wife, Hogarth's daughter Catherine, while having supper at her father-in-law's house. Nineteenth-century journalism was a louche, bohemian profession that gave access to the highest echelons of politics, arts and the aristocracy and also permission to mingle with the worst criminals and prostitutes. Armed with intelligence, wit and confidence, you had a rare social mobility. The Powells had a beautiful house on the banks of the river Thames in west London. Years later Emily wrote:

I was always 'Oxford' in my young days, when I used to see the race from the 'Lookout' of an old house on the Mall, Hammersmith – an old house, with an old garden, and an old and champion mulberry tree; in the season the grass beneath black with fallen over-ripe mulberries.

Bumping into the new Master of the Mint, a certain Macdonald Cameron, at a party in Sydney in 1893, Emily recalled a conversation:

'How do you do Mrs. Poo-ell? So many years since we met. Don't you remember? I used to come up to the Poo-ell place at Hammersmith on Sundays and have a whiskey and soda,

and a pull on the river with the boys, and sit under the big
mulberry tree in the garden and talk nonsense with you'.
'Why of course', said I, 'and we called you "the baby"
because you had such big, white arms'.
'Jolly times those' sighed the M.C.

Jack's two brothers also had interesting friends. Both artists, they specialised in stained-glass windows and were part of the Pre-Raphaelite movement. The Powell boys mixed with the most exciting artists, critics and poets of the day, on the fringe of the secret society set up by William Holman Hunt, the Rossetti brothers and John Everett Millais, called the Brotherhood.

The Powell brothers were always welcome at Cleveland House, and Holman Hunt and Rossetti seemingly didn't mind Jack turning up too with his witty, pretty girlfriend. Years later Emily was to recall the Brotherhood with fondness:

The Cleveland House always seemed to me a shrine, full of saints with their haloes in various stages of development, full of virgins carrying sheafs of lilies, full of the Divine One carrying little lambs. To me, always full of devotion and art, these things were lovely, and the to-be-brothers-in-law, friends of the Brotherhood, would often take me across to the studio of the then obscure but eminent ones. Regular Trilby business.

Once Emily had had a taste of this urbane life, it is understandable that she might have wanted to hang on to it, even though Priscilla took a dim view of Jack. But there was a problem – according to the laws of the time, at the age of twenty, Emily was still a minor and needed her father's consent to marry (whoever her legal father was). This consent was not forthcoming. The Brotherhood sympathised with Emily and Jack's predicament, and suggested they used Cleveland House for their wedding breakfast. They could be married in the church opposite, just about far enough away from the Soldene parish in N1 that they wouldn't be recognised.

When Emily arrived at the church, Jack was waiting at the altar with a stranger stood beside him and his little sister sitting in the front pew: 'At my wedding (runaway one – Langham Church, Langham Place) the best man I think was the pew opener, and of course he couldn't be entrusted with the precious ring'.

Afterwards they retired to Cleveland House and had a celebration with the Brotherhood, which must have made it seem a bit more special, decadent and quite romantic. However, the honeymoon only lasted as long as the wedding breakfast. The reality was that they had nowhere to live. Emily had probably hoped that once they had presented Jack's parents with a fait accompli they would find space for them in that big old grand house in Hammersmith Mall. But the Powells seem to have been as impressed with the match as Priscilla, and they were not offered any accommodation.

Emily was forced to go to her mother and not only announce that she was married but that the newly-weds had nowhere to live. One can only imagine the row. Nonetheless Emily and Jack did move in with Priscilla and Clara, and within a year Emily had given birth to her first daughter, whom she named Katie, after her inn-keeping grandmother. And less than a year after Katie's birth Emily found herself pregnant once again.

This household of three generations of women and Jack may well have been relatively harmonious, but there was a threat hanging over all of them – not only did every new baby mean less money to share around, but if Jack didn't bring home a wage packet for whatever reason, Priscilla's bonnet making couldn't possibly support them all; within a couple of months they wouldn't have enough money to pay the rent. If Emily was to keep on having children at this rate, she needed to get a job. But doing what? The options open to her were hardly appealing. At the age of twenty-two, Emily must have felt as if her life, which had looked so promising, was over already, and the best she could hope for was that things remained the same. Emily might have been determined to do everything to avoid her mother's predicament, and in that she had succeeded. However, she was probably beginning to wonder whether she hadn't found herself somewhere worse.

But then Emily had a moment of true epiphany. It was also a moment of pure envy. One morning in 1861 Emily opened her paper to read how an unknown singer called Adelina Patti had appeared at Covent Garden in *La Sonnambula*. According to the review, the audience had been somewhat 'frigid' to begin with, but before the opera was halfway through they had warmed up considerably. By the end Adelina had received a standing ovation; overnight it seemed a star had been born. This caught Emily's attention; she could just picture the scene, and it appealed to her. Later that day she was standing waiting for a bus to Chelsea. The stop happened to be next to a music shop, and in the window was a poster of the Diva herself.

Emily examined it carefully. Despite having fine eyes, this new bright star was not pretty. Her face was long and thin.

Her chin was, in Emily's opinion, 'underhung'. She wore her hair in plain bands. At this Emily felt an arrow of fury hit her right in the middle. Instead of catching the bus to Chelsea, she caught a bus to Soho and marched right up to the front door of the country's greatest singing teacher Mr Alfred Mellon, and gave it a determined knock. When it opened, Emily demanded an audition but was told by the slightly alarmed maid that her master was not at home, and so Emily had to return to Islington, a disappointed and 'sad faced girl'. It was probably for the best. Emily was eight months pregnant with her second child and Mr Mellon might not have been able to see past the bump.

However, this ball of envious fury did not go away. It would lie dormant for days at a time and then something – perhaps a conversation, a review, walking past a certain theatre, a crying newborn baby or an irritating husband – would bring it bubbling back up, and all that frustrated ambition would return just as strongly, if not stronger than ever before. So a couple of months later, after her daughter Nellie had been born, when the fury was screaming so loudly (louder than her two children combined) that it could no longer be ignored, Emily had another go at finding a singing teacher. She walked into the rooms of Mr Howard Glover, who was less eminent than Mr Mellon, but still well regarded and well connected. Mustering every inch of her nerve, Emily asked if he would teach her how to be a singer.

The young Miss Emily Soldene: concert soloist by day, Miss FitzHenry by night

Chapter Three

Miss FitzHenry

Fame is the spur that the clear spirit doth raise (Milton)

When Emily strode into Howard Glover's studio, it likely wasn't just about earning some money or becoming a singer – Emily wanted to become famous. She wanted to meet the most interesting people, go to the best parties and wear fabulous clothes, to travel not just the country, but the world. Emily's desire to eat the best food and drink champagne is also not to be underestimated. Fine dining was her greatest pleasure, and her magnificent figure bore witness to that. Today Emily might have become a reality TV star, a model, an internet influencer or a blogger, but in the mid nineteenth century there was only one way that a woman from Emily's background could have a chance at the celebrity lifestyle, and that was to go onto the stage.

At least Emily had talent. Singing was a thing in the Swain family – it still is. Generations of tenors, baritones, sopranos and mezzo-sopranos singing in our homes, all together loudly in rounds and harmonies, alongside pianos, in cars, at Christmas, in amateur theatricals and choirs, until we drop dead. Emily recalls fondly her uncle, perhaps my great-great-grandfather Charles, singing at Christmas with a drinking horn brought back from one of those wars in Canada. He would bring it down from its peg on the wall, fill it with ale, toast the room and sing lustily:

> *The Nineteenth Light Dragoons my boys*
> *Are men of high renown*
> *They're a credit to their country*
> *And an honour to the crown . . .*
> *Oh (molto lungo e forte e sostenuto) –*
> *The Nineteenth Light Dragoons me boys – are men . . .*

Even the Swain aunts used to carry Emily home from the harvest singing the song of the 19th Light Dragoons with a sprinkling of Irish ballads. Early on, Priscilla had noted Emily's talent for singing and took pride in her ability:

> *I must tell that I could always sing. It was a dreadful thing*
> *when people came to drink tea at our house. My reputation*
> *had spread, and I would be asked to favour the company.*
> *'Now Emily be a good girl and do as you are bid'. And so,*
> *behind my mother's black silk apron, I sat, a tiny trembler,*
> *and trilled out my little stave, and many kisses and caresses*
> *(which I hated) were my reward.*

However, Priscilla was not so taken with Emily's theatrical proclivities. At an early age, having secretly devoured any book she could lay her hands on – the *Arabian Nights*, *Robinson Crusoe*, *The Pilgrim's Progress*, Gibbon's *Decline and Fall of the Roman Empire* – sitting locked in a cupboard with a palpitating heart (all fiction being seen as the work of the devil), Emily embarked on a career as a playwright. Her first attempt was based on the story of Henry II's mistress and called *Rosamund*. Emily was author, stage manager and cast combined. She constructed a maze out of bedroom chairs and stole a reel of Priscilla's bonnet silk and, as Queen Eleanor, followed the thread to the centre and stabbed Rosamund through the heart. Unfortunately, Priscilla found the manuscript, tore it up, and gave Emily sharp slaps to her bare back and arms, 'low bodices and short sleeves offering no protection'. Later, when Uncle Charles was visiting, Emily was caught with a rushlight behind her, dancing to her own shadow on the wall. 'Good God, Priscilla, you have let that child go to a playhouse,' he said.

Priscilla most certainly had not. What Priscilla had done was allow Emily to see the most famous English baritone of the Victorian era, Charles Santley, sing in a concert. The effect was instant: 'Never shall I forget it. I felt I would give the world to sing, to study, to be an artist.' Of course, if it was Santley that planted the idea, it was the envy inspired by Adelina Patti that finally turned the idea into action. I can't imagine how Emily managed to get around Priscilla's objections to going on the stage (not to mention how her husband, Jack, must have felt). Emily says in her memoir that she 'attacked the home authorities with vigour and demolished all objections triumphantly'.

Female performers did not have a good reputation – to most people they were little better than prostitutes. They were paid to perform in public, in costumes that broke all the codes of Victorian decency. To succeed, an actress needed to be assertive and flamboyant, intellectual and emotional – all qualities that were seen as deeply suspect in a woman. Actresses postured in front of men, they acted with men, they flaunted an outrageous knowingness. They worked at night, walking round the streets in the dark in notorious areas. Many starred in popular pornography as well as on the stage; sexual harassment and financial offers in return for physical favours were endemic. The very nature of theatrical life meant that actresses lived and worked beyond the bounds of decency. In the 1880s the editor of *Punch* fulminated, 'Would any one of us wish our daughter to go on the stage? There can only be one answer to this, "No!"'

However, it was common knowledge that if a woman wanted or needed to earn her own living, especially after marriage, no other legitimate occupation could potentially offer a better wage, and women were entering the profession in ever greater numbers. If you were talented and lucky, and you succeeded, the theatre offered an unrivalled world of financial independence and agency. It was a choice between independence and respectability and it seems Emily valued independence more.

In a sense, Emily was only following in her mother's and grandmother's footsteps; just in a literally more dramatic way. Katie and Priscilla had sacrificed a good deal of their respectability when they became a publican and a working girl. Perhaps this is how Emily eventually brought Priscilla round to her way of thinking, or at least enough to let her go to an audition. She had almost certainly said, however, that she was going to be an opera singer and would not appear in music halls. All women who worked on the stage were suspect, but those who worked in music halls most of all.

A career in the music hall was almost certainly not what Howard Glover had offered Emily when she walked into his studio, either. Howard Glover had not been Emily's first choice of maestro, but he was still a good choice. Until recently the stage had been a closed shop and almost all lady performers had come from theatrical families. However, in the early decades of the nineteenth century an explosion in outlets for popular entertainment, most notoriously the music halls, ballets and pantomimes, meant that there were new opportunities for outsiders to come in. But to get their first job they still needed the help of someone who had knowledge and connections. For a fee, the aspiring performer could not only get musical and theatrical tuition, but also an agent.

At this point Emily's ambition and courage should be noted. Mr Glover was not as musically talented or renowned as Mr Mellon, but he came from an impeccable theatrical heritage. His mother was the most famous actress of her generation – Julia Glover – and it was to her old studio, located above Jefferys, the famous music shop in Soho Square, that Emily went for her audition. She displayed pluck just turning up on the doorstep of such an illustrious name, without any introduction or connections. Emily was definitely aware of Howard Glover's famous lineage: 'My master was very fond and proud of his mother and often talked about her, and what a wonderful artistic life hers had been, though from a domestic point, it was a failure.'

Julia Glover had led an interesting life. Her father had

sold her to her husband for £1,000 in 1797. She ended up financially supporting not only her own family but also her husband's other 'unofficial' family down the road, her distressed brother, her father and her orphaned grandchildren. She had five children; Howard (christened William Howard) was the last and was rumoured not to belong to the errant husband, but to the American actor and writer John Howard Payne (the clue might be in the name). All her children went into the theatre in some capacity or another, except for Howard, who decided on a career in music. Glover never managed to write anything spectacular, but he knew everyone, was well liked and respected, and he was the music critic of the *Morning Post*. That, together with his maternal heritage, meant Howard Glover could open doors for an aspiring young singer.

When young Emily trotted into the room, Glover must have seen something in her. He engaged her on the spot for a two-year apprenticeship in return for £200 cash and half her earnings while she was with him. At £12,000 in today's money, this was quite an investment and it is a mystery where Emily found the cash – certainly not from Jack or adopted father Edward's meagre clerk's salaries. That would be a lot of bonnets for Priscilla to make and sell too. The answer might lie in a legacy from her grandmother, the property-owning publican. Katie had died the year before. Whether she would have approved of how Emily chose to spend it is another question, but Emily must have believed in herself to invest this amount of money in a singing career.

The training was comprehensive. It was not just about learning music – Glover made Emily read, recite and think about the meanings of the words before she was allowed to look at any of the notes. He was very particular about pronunciation, consonants and sounding the ends of words. Musicians tend to be perfectionists and Glover was no exception. He made Emily's hands tremble: 'With all his goodness, he was impatient, and when I sang a wrong note at one lesson, and was corrected sharply, at the next (though knowing it perfectly at home) I would repeat the error through sheer fright.'

But he must have liked Emily, because he gave her the press tickets that inevitably came his way due to his position. He insisted that she watched and learnt from the professionals. Every night of the season, Emily was at the two London opera houses – Covent Garden or Her Majesty's – or the second-best options. She saw the world's greatest singers at some of the most vibrant years in the history of opera. New works were coming out of Vienna, Paris, Milan and London. Emily was starting out just as opera was entering a golden phase, and she caught the excitement:

Then for the first time I heard Mme. Tietjens, that grand singer to whom time has brought no successor, before whose greatness I could have fallen down to kiss the hem of her garment; Trebelli, Mongini, Guiglini. and Mario. Mario was then beginning to sing out of tune, but five minutes of perfect music, which we got now and then, was compensation for all the false intonation.

. . .

And Delle Sedie, there was a singer! When he sang 'Eri Tu', big tears tumbled out of my eyes, I could not help it.

Such moments are impossible to describe. They can only be remembered. When I listened to all this passion, and pain, and joy, and ecstasy, a sort of despair came over me as I realised that such heights were only for the divine few.

Emily was inspired and overwhelmed, although not so overwhelmed that she was above being mischievous about these musical legends. For example, she describes the moment when Mme. Ilma di Murska made her London debut – looking, apparently, 'painfully thin, undecided, and straw-coloured':

She had a huge crinoline, and as she came down the rake of the stage the crinoline wobbled, and her skirt being rather long in the front, she stepped on it and stumbled forward in the most awkward embarrassing manner.

Emily reports that she got no welcoming applause and was a half a note sharp, 'making the audience shiver'. And as for Mme Artot – she was perfectly adorable as the page in *Ballo in Maschera*, but she had the longest fingernails Emily had ever seen before or since, 'except on the fingers of a Chinese bank-teller in the Shanghai Bank, San Francisco, or an American millionairess of the first generation.'

But these little details aside, Emily was swept away:

All these things filled me with impossible ambitions, producing sometimes an exaltation of feeling positively painful. This was the sort of Fool's Paradise I dwelt in when I went to 'Have my voice tried' at the Canterbury – such sublime imaginings, such sordid realities.

The problem was Emily's career was rather slow to get off the ground. Her first public appearance was six months after starting with Howard Glover, on 7th June 1862. By 1862, Queen Victoria had already been on the throne for twenty-five years, Prince Albert was dead, and Emily was over twenty-three years old, which by Victorian standards was quite old to be making her debut.

It was at the St James's Hall, a small but select venue for people with discerning musical tastes, and a respectable engagement for a novice. Not only was the now great Adelina Patti top of the bill (something that Emily might have seen as a bit of an omen), but the concert featured many of the fine foreign artists who were in London for the season. Now Emily had to fulfil her part of the bargain and sing the piece Glover had chosen for her – one of his own composition, 'The Strain I Heard in Happier Days' – and sing it in a way that would be a credit to her teacher.

It was unfortunate that Emily had been put at the top of a long morning's programme – people were still getting into their seats. Emily walked onto the stage with Glover. She looked out at the audience and was perhaps startled by the wall of strangers' faces. Glover started playing the introduction, which was rather long, and just at the point where she was supposed to come in, she froze. Emily simply could not force a sound out of her lips. With barely suppressed rage Glover hissed, 'Go on' and pinched her, and the shock of it all sent the notes tumbling out.

Emily had a fine, strong mezzo-soprano voice and even better musicality – she had a particularly striking ability to convey her emotion in the music. The audience gave her generous applause and the notices were good. Emily had been successfully launched; singing in front of Adelina Patti had turned out to be a good omen after all. The near-disaster of a career finishing before it had even begun was averted, and Emily's ambition lived on. Or, at least, that's what Emily tells us in her memoir. In reality she only received one review and this was in Glover's own paper, the *Morning Post*. No surprises then that it was a good review for the pupil in whom he had invested so much, but even the reviewer could not ignore her stage fright.

> *The only unknown performer in the programme was Miss Emily Soldene, a young lady possessing a very beautiful mezzo-soprano voice and a genuine musical feeling, as exemplified in her execution of Mr. Glover's ballad 'The Strain I Heard', despite the extreme nervousness against which she was evidently struggling. Miss Soldene was unanimously applauded, as she well derived to be, and is destined, we believe, to become an ornament to the concert room . . .*

Nerves, especially first-night nerves, were to be Emily's constant shadowy companion, and it was a full six months before Glover felt confident enough to put his protégée back on stage again. He gave her a better slot this time – number three in the running order – which meant the audience was concentrating and she had time to compose herself. Emily sang a gloomy ballad titled 'Regret', but she was followed by her hero Charles Santley and then she was allowed to sing a Rossini duet with the respectable baritone, Lewis Thomas. This time Emily was more composed and Glover put her forward for two more concerts in the following month. Emily must have been rather large by then because ten days afterwards she gave birth to her third child, a boy, Edward Charles Soldene Powell.

Just a month later she was on the stage of the Drury Lane Theatre performing in another Glover concert, and so it carried on for the next year. Emily was getting excellent experience and appearing with the finest singers – Pyne, Parepa, Tietjens, Trebelli. But she was only getting these opportunities because Glover was giving them to her and, as yet, she had not earnt a penny. The truth was Emily's career was stalling. This is not something she admits to in her memoir. Emily plays with timings so that it looks as if her rise was meteoric, and she omits the two and a half years when nothing much was happening.

There were three singing career options open to Emily – she could be a concert artist, or an opera singer, or an entertainer in the music hall. She'd been dangled in front of the concert world for a while now and, so far, no one had taken the bait. So next Glover sent her off for an audition at the Haymarket, which was staging light, popular English-language operas. It would be an obvious first step into the highly competitive, oversupplied opera scene. Unfortunately, Emily didn't impress the management and was not taken on. She must have been devastated. If she was determined to be a singer, there was really only once place left to go.

In her memoir Emily describes her music hall debut as Glover's inspired attempt to rid her of her nerves once and for all: a kind of immersion therapy where nightly exposure to the heckling of the rough music hall audience would kill or cure her. In reality it was a last chance to get her singing career off the ground.

Emily was furious at being sent to audition at the Canterbury. She had never been in a music hall before and felt it was well beneath her; it hurt her artistic pride. For a start she had to go south of the river, to the badlands of Lambeth. She was horrified by the greasy pavements, the muddy gutters full of dirty babies, the commonplace public house; and she hesitated at the door, hardly able to bring herself to go in. However, after a bit of walking past a couple of times and hovering about the threshold, she took a deep breath, and stepped in. She was shown upstairs to a long picture gallery, at the end of which a rehearsal was taking place. Of course, Emily appreciated the pictures (as we know she was a lover of art), but she was revolted by the smell of beer and stale tobacco.

I have since been told that on that day I carried my head very high, and by my manner conveyed the utmost scorn for the Canterbury and all its surroundings. 'Why what's this Ferdy?' asked Mr. William Morton as I appeared in the distance and proceeded to sail up the gallery. 'Dashed if I know,' said Ferdy (Mr. Jongmanns), 'sent on by der governor; but it's all right if it can sing.'

Luckily this haughtiness didn't seem to affect her performance. It turned out that 'it' could sing, and Emily was engaged to perform nightly, not at the Canterbury, but at the new music hall in the West End, the Oxford.

Music halls had begun with singalongs in pubs at the beginning of the nineteenth century and developed into organised nights in special rooms, with professional performers. The line-ups consisted of well-known songs, adaptions from the new light operas, madrigals, choruses, comic songs, sometimes even a circus act. In some ways music halls were the precursor to the cinema – mass entertainment for the lower orders, reflecting their everyday lives and concerns.

Charles Morton (the older brother of the William Morton who auditioned Emily) is seen as the father of the music hall. In 1838, the year of Queen Victoria's coronation and the year Emily was born, Charles Morton converted the upstairs room of his wife's pub, and hired professionals to come and sing selections from popular operas. Soon he was running musical pubs all over London. Eventually he bought the Canterbury Arms in Lambeth, with a patch of derelict land at the back, and started building. In 1862 he opened a brand new, bespoke concert venue that could seat 2,000 people, complete with a long picture gallery. He renamed it the Canterbury Hall and it was an instant success, and a veritable contagion of halls sprung up. By 1866 there were thirty large halls seating 2,000 people or more, and nearly 300 small ones.

The middle classes and the God-fearing hated this new invasion. Music halls were seen as encouraging all the wrong moral values and distracting from the right ones. They were situated in risky areas, facilitated the drinking of alcohol and were beloved of prostitutes looking for work. But more than anything it was the nature of the performances – the risqué costumes and suggestive lyrics – that upset the moral majority. Music hall acts were subversive and had a relentless sprinkling of innuendo. They championed the underdog, while making fun of the people in charge and the socially ambitious. Love was always a big theme and was either rose-tinted or a comic disaster. Marriage was always a disaster. In the music hall, sex was not a taboo but celebrated. It was not surprising that Emily refused to perform under her own name.

When Emily had announced her ambition to become a singer, she had been thinking Covent Garden, not variety. However, Emily had invested a lot of time and money and it seems she wasn't prepared to walk away from it yet – the alternative must have seemed too dreary. A death of hope, a drowning in maternity with the threat of poverty a constant companion, her survival reliant on a husband she had married too young, a life just too dull. The timeless attraction of fame – a life extraordinary rather than ordinary, to be someone rather than no one. If this was the only way she was going to get herself noticed, then she was prepared to stoop that low.

Emily adopted a pseudonym and accepted a contract at the Oxford Music Hall. For reasons best known to herself, she took the name of Miss FitzHenry, and for the next five years this is how the world knew her. And the money was good. Starting at £6 a week and rising to double figures, her salary was the equivalent of £600 a week today. Not a fortune, but in those days, it would have taken a skilled workman fifty days to earn this amount. Emily's new salary financed three young maids taken from the extended family in the Hertfordshire villages, a move to a whole house in Islington, and Jack giving up his job and becoming her manager. Just as today, the popular generally paid better than high art.

Located at one end of Oxford Street, the Oxford had the advantage of being in the West End, and it was the newest, smartest venue. Its clientele included not just working- and lower-middle-class men, but journalists and politicians – the bohemian men about town. This also made it a notorious venue for prostitutes, and the Oxford managed to lose its licence several times.

> *I went to the Oxford in the autumn of 1865, and 'Up the Alma's Heights', a declamatory song, written by Capt. G. W. Colomb, was my first real hit. All the military men in London came to hear it. 'Launch the Lifeboat' by Alfred Plumpton, was the second. All the naval men in London came to hear that. I soon got used to the people, the place, the management, and the manager.*

The Oxford was typical of large music halls – it consisted of a long room with a stage at one end and a bar at the other, and in between there were tables at right angles to both. It was smoky and rowdy. To try and keep some sort of order, there was a master of ceremonies, the chairman, who was immaculately turned out in evening dress. He commanded proceedings by sitting at the top table, mimicking the upper classes with his exaggerated manners and accent, and introducing each act with a big wooden gavel. Unlike the St James's Hall, performers were not welcomed by polite applause from a silently expectant audience. They had to work hard, and if they didn't, they were hit with jeers, hisses, and hails of eggs and vegetables.

Frederick Stanley, lawyer for the London Music Hall Proprietor's Association and Charles Morton's personal lawyer, described the scene that would have faced Emily:

> *A dazzling blaze of gas; the sharp clink of pewter pots and glasses; an incessant babble of voices, male and female talking, shouting and laughing, blended with the loud din*

of a stringed and brazen band; an army of hot perspiring
waiters, napkin on arm, and laden with bottles and glasses,
perpetually running to and fro, between a liquor bar and
an audience of impatient tipplers; an insignificant looking
creature standing in the centre of a large stage and lustily
stretching his lungs in the somewhat vain endeavour to
make himself audible above the general clamour; – such is
the appearance of a musical hall upon entering.

However, Emily had spent much of her childhood in a pub
watching her grandmother manage the customers. It was in
her genes to rise to the challenge of rowdy behaviour. It might
not have taken as much getting used to as Emily suggests. And
being on the stage of one of the most prestigious music halls
every night did mean that Emily became famous relatively
quickly. She became a household name, in London at least,
achieving a level of notoriety that would have taken her years to
achieve otherwise. Emily had also found herself plunged into a
culture of worldly-wise prima donnas and showmen who lived
by a very different moral code to the rest of society. Her fellow
female performers in particular were vivid personalities who
had had more experiences than most of their contemporaries
would in several lifetimes. They were free to say things and
do things, in fact encouraged to say and do things, that most
Victorian women didn't even have knowledge of. There was a
boldness and glamour to backstage life.

One of the singers was a pretty lady called Miss Crouch. She
had a very passable soprano voice, but an even more attractive
figure. She went on a visit to Paris and never came back. Instead,
she became Cora Pearl, the most celebrated *demi-mondaine*

of the Second Empire: 'That was in the sixteen button boot days, and though Cora's name was pearl all her buttons were diamonds.'

The ladies of the ballet were always the most controversial:

I can always remember Tessi, with the wonderful hair. It was not golden, but it was 'hanging down her back.' 'In the front row' were two beautiful girls, Miss Alice Dunning, afterwards celebrated (particularly in the States) as Miss Alice Dunning Lingard (Mrs. Horace Lingard); and Miss Wilson. subsequently known to fame as 'Lardy' Wilson.

And then there were the fans – the men who loitered around the performers. Actresses were the only women (along with prostitutes) with whom men could have a natural conversation, unhampered by the purdah created by society's conventions; they were the only women that they could playfully get to know. Some men found this compelling. Fans would come multiple nights, sometimes every night, hanging around backstage after the performance, offering to provide their carriages to transport actresses to and from work or their other theatrical commitments; they'd take them for supper, to exclusive private rooms, often little select parties. Sometimes the more attractive and charming actresses would be taken to balls, and mix in the highest circles of politicians, businessmen and aristocrats – 'the Ton' (although they were never befriended by any of the upper-class ladies). 'Gifts' of expensive clothes or jewellery were the perks of the job. Access to the lady performers was granted according to the size of a gentleman's wallet, or their position in society. Only the most influential got to linger in the wings during the performances. The eminent Victorian theatre critic Clement Scott was of the belief that: 'It is nearly impossible for a woman to remain pure who adopts the stage as a profession . . . There is no school on earth so bad for the formation of character.'

The actresses also got to know the prostitutes who hung round the halls.

Of course there was a certain amount of 'gay' society, the 'Chappies' and 'Johnnies' of that period. And the 'Daughters of Joy' were not conspicuous by their absence. No doubt most good people think that an excess of fortune and lots of drink may induce ossification of the heart and memory in these poor girls. They are wrong, and many a night have I, 'by request,' sung 'Home, Sweet Home,' because 'I made 'em cry.' I daresay these were 'off nights,' but there is the fact for what it is worth.

It was a hectic, 'candle burning at both ends' kind of existence. Emily can't have spent much time at home. Most popular music hall artists were expected to not just perform at one theatre, but two, or even more, in one night. London was full of carriages dashing across the city, taking fully costumed and made-up artistes from east to west, north to south and any permutation in between. Emily was unusual in only being contracted to the Oxford, but sometimes Charles Morton did ask her to go and do a turn at the Canterbury afterwards, and Emily felt obliged to agree. If they got caught in a traffic jam the driver would shout 'Make way, I have Miss FitzHenry in the back due to go on at the Canterbury any moment' and the carriages would pull over so she could speed through. It was surely more fun than making bonnets, or indeed looking after her children.

The operatic selections sung at the Oxford were carried off bodily to the Canterbury in broughams, where, when we arrived, being 'called over the coals' was not an expression but a fact; for over the coals, through a long ill-lighted underground cellar (the original old Hall of 1850) we had to go.

One of the many things the Oxford introduced to Emily was gambling. Emily loved a wager, and it was to remain an obsession for the rest of her life. It was something that came naturally – an attraction to risk.

The Oxford was a great rendezvous for racing men . . . On the eve of, or after a big race, the busy hum of the betting men was nearly as loud as the voices of the singers. Down would come the hammer of the Chairman, 'Order, gentlemen, order.' To do the gentlemen justice, they did order, and much business was the result. So you see, music was not the only thing heard at the Oxford. Sometimes one got the 'correct tip' and 'pulled it off.' But it was not always so.

One morning Emily was leaving the theatre after a rehearsal and an 'exceptionally big' man opened the door for her and asked her what horse she was backing in the Derby.

'Nothing,' said I.

'Put your money on Hermit' said he.

So she did.
She told Charles Morton and everybody else, and they

thought it was hilarious – Hermit was running at a hundred to one. It must have been playing on her mind because she had recurring dreams that people were shouting 'Hermit wins! Hermit wins!'. On the day itself she was on the bus to the theatre in a snowstorm. It stopped at the Mother Red Cap in Camden Town and she asked the conductor who had won the Derby: '"'Ermit," he said dismally. Why! I'd got a bit on and felt like finishing my journey in a cab.'

Working in the music hall also offered Emily her first opportunity to travel. Morton took her to Glasgow to sing at a 'Total Abstainers' Saturday night concert. Absolutely refusing to ever wear the crinolines that were the height of fashion, Emily captured the audience's attention by coming on stage dressed in diaphanous white satin with no petticoats underneath. Afterwards she was informed that the committee of the city fathers had approved her singing but thought she had displayed her figure too much.

In Glasgow Emily found herself singing with a certain Signor Foli:

> *It was the first time I had met him, but we soon became good friends. When I told him I was married, he looked at me with the greatest astonishment, and said, 'What a pity.' He did not explain whether it was a pity for my husband or myself.*

Of course, Emily was a wife and a mother of three children under the age of eight. It might be thought that such amusements as travelling around the country and flirting with tenors wouldn't be open to her, and yet her family never seemed to get in the way of her extracurricular activities. She hardly ever mentioned Jack in print, but the one thing she did say was, 'he never let the space of the green room get between us.'

Years later, in one of her articles, Emily wrote:

A woman lecturing the other day on the 'Emotions' said 'a woman could only love once.' Such a feeble person, such limited horizons. Evidently no experience. She's wrong. I know. Have been there, haven't you? Why, of course you have. Don't say another word.

Just over two years after Emily arrived at the Oxford, in October 1867, she was reported as being 'unwell' for a few weeks and did not appear on stage. There was nothing wrong with Emily – she was just having a baby, her fourth and final child, John Arthur Powell. Unlike her other children, Emily never mentions this son except one sentence reporting his death in San Francisco thirty years later. John Arthur Powell is something of a mystery.

This sick leave was to prove problematic. A new singer was brought in to cover for Emily and became one of her greatest rivals. Emily was a fun, open, witty girl, who rarely took herself (or others) too seriously; she liked people and they usually liked her. But occasionally she did make enemies – Kate Santley was one of them. Born in Virginia, USA a year before Emily, she appeared in 1864 playing a small part in a pantomime in Liverpool under the stage name of Eva Stella. Within three years she had changed her name to Kate Santley, and made her debut as a soloist at the Marylebone Music Hall with cheeky numbers such as 'Not for Flo' and 'Can anyone tell me where

Peter's gone?' The London audience loved her, and as soon as Emily went on maternity leave, Charles Morton employed her to cover for Emily. But when Emily came back Kate was kept on, playing a star billing at both the Oxford and the Canterbury every night. It can't have been much fun to come back from maternity leave and find there was a new act in town – especially one that, though practically the same age as Emily, appeared younger and was still single with no children. Santley had lots of sweet top notes that Emily couldn't hit, a tiny waist, and a reputation for saucy songs rather than pathetic ballads. As Emily says in her memoirs: 'Miss Kate Santley – ah! So slender and slim – bewitched all beholders.'

Fortunately, Kate Santley didn't hang around for too long – a few months later she took a job in musical theatre and became one of its biggest stars for the rest of her long, successful career. Emily still had not managed to be in a theatrical production of any kind, although she had auditioned many times. It must have rankled. Emily and Kate never liked each other and years later this dislike was to explode in print and end in near-bankruptcy.

Celebrity is often likened to a drug – it's addictive, it releases adrenaline and it changes the chemicals in the brain; and, like all drugs, you become used to a certain dose and then need more to keep the high going. The problem is a performer can get used to a certain level of fame, but when they look around there will always be someone richer, someone prettier, someone more famous. Emily might have started to see the limitations of where she had found herself.

Emily's closest female companion was Morton's lead

singer, Charlotte Russell. Many felt Miss Russell's clear, pitch-perfect, natural yet powerful soprano voice was the greatest in England. She was a big factor in the success of the Oxford and Canterbury – not just pulling in the ordinary crowds, but also world-famous opera singers like Mario and Griso, who made a pilgrimage to the music halls to hear her. Most importantly, high-class performers joined the Oxford and Canterbury to share a stage with her. Miss Russell had plenty of opportunities to graduate to opera, but she always stayed in the music halls, Charles Morton's to be precise, probably because she was married to his little brother, William, the one who had auditioned Emily. Miss Russell was also not blessed with the best of health – she had terrible rheumatism and suffered from gout which eventually killed her. She was in a train accident and kept having children. These factors may well have limited her ambitions.

Emily's relationship with Miss Russell was a bittersweet thing. Emily had enormous respect for Miss Russell and appreciated what an honour it was to share not just the programme with her, but the stage sometimes – they frequently were asked to sing duets together. But Miss Russell's ability meant she was generally given the best music to sing. There were new operas pouring into London but Emily was not often given the chance to perform them – Miss Russell had that honour. Emily was stuck as the singer of pathetic ballads. While they were very popular, and Emily's powerful mezzo and ability to transmit the tragedy were superlative, they were only showing one very particular aspect of Miss Soldene. There was a whole side of Emily that hadn't had its moment on stage.

Meanwhile Emily was invited to the annual party thrown by an American impresario, Pony Moore:

> *He handed me on to the table and begged as a great favour that I would sing a song, 'Happy be thy Dreams.' I said I would. Then he sent for all his minstrels to come and take a lesson in ballad singing. When I'd finished, Pony addressed the crowd. 'Great God,' said he, 'if that gal 'ud only sing that song in New York, in Wood's "Muse-um," she'd knock 'em. Great Caesar's ghost she'd knock 'em!' This was not very refined, but, all the same, Pony Moore's ball was one of the features of the London season, and everybody, who 'by hook or crook' could, went.*

Pony had planted a tiny acorn, innocently, in a throwaway moment of fun. But it probably took root and took hold until it grew into something so big Emily couldn't ignore it. Emily decided she needed to up her game: 'So many people at this time thought me dreadfully dramatic, and said I ought to study and go on the stage.'

At the beginning of 1868 Emily went for a trial with the stage manager of the Queen's Theatre, Mr John Ryder. He gave her Portia's speech 'The quality of mercy' to read. After Emily had finished, Ryder walked back and forth for a couple of minutes deep in thought and then said, 'You have tears in your voice. Are your tears near the surface? Can you cry easily?' Emily said she didn't know.

> *'Look at me,' he said, smiling, and, reciting a few lines, the tears ran down his face as freely and as miserably as possible.*

Of course, I was astonished. 'Come to-morrow, same time,'
said he; 'we will have a serious lesson.'

Emily had earnt herself a chance to enter into a new world of theatre and to expand her career. But Emily never went back to see Mr Ryder. All her dreams of becoming an actress, never mind going to New York, were about to go up in smoke, literally. The very next night the Oxford Music Hall burnt down and Emily found herself out of a job.

Britain's premier music hall: the Alhambra, Leicester Square

Chapter Four

KING SPARKALETTO

Shakespeare spells ruin, but legs means dividends (*The Era*, 1862)

No one knows how or why one of the country's most prestigious music halls burnt down. Arson was suspected and fingers were pointed at the proprietor himself, Charles Morton.

At 3 a.m. on 8th February 1868, a fireman employed to watch the theatre noticed seats in the corner of the gallery on fire. Almost immediately flames burst through the roof, and in less than an hour it had all come tumbling down. Morton was quickly on the scene, too quickly some felt, and it was suggested that more could have been done to save the Oxford. Although the hall had been a success with the public, behind the scenes Mr Morton was not making as much money as before. He had sensed an opportunity, floated the business under the name of the Oxford and

Canterbury Company and made a nice profit, but now the share price had dropped, and Morton was finding he didn't like other people having a stake in the business. Morton might have felt he'd be better off starting over again.

However, with all the tobacco, gaslight, wood and velvet, theatres often burnt down; and when a theatre started to burn, it was usually pretty catastrophic. Only a few months earlier, on one of those late-night dashes from the Oxford to the Canterbury, Emily had witnessed Her Majesty's Theatre in flames: 'the carriages were stopped at the Trafalgar Square end of Parliament Street, and we saw a magnificent sight – the burning of Her Majesty's Opera House. To me it was dreadful, I had been there so much.'

Emily's feelings on the burning down of the Oxford must have been of an entirely different order; this was her livelihood in flames. In her memoir she simply states: 'In the middle of the night the Oxford was burned. I sang the last song sung in it, and that song was, "Launch the Lifeboat."'

This final song, unfortunately, turned out to be quite apt.

Overnight Emily found herself without a job, with four children and a husband to support, not to mention the wider circle of dependants – the three servants from the Hertfordshire villages, and Clara and Priscilla too. Also, Emily's contract with Howard Glover had run out the year before and she couldn't rehire him because he had since moved to America. The Soldenes lived in a world where there was no safety net, no benefits, no unemployment insurance, state or private. They rented their house, which of course was expensive in London. There were many mouths to feed. The difference between success and destitution was just a matter of a couple of months' missed rent. Emily must have been wondering if that original £200 gamble with Glover had been a monumental mistake.

The obvious place for Emily to look for a job was the Alhambra. By the end of the 1860s it was the most famous (and infamous) music hall in Britain. Situated in Leicester Square, it was constructed like a great Moorish palace with minarets, a turnip-shaped dome, and a huge fountain at the front. Its programme was similarly exotic, concentrating very much on dancing and legs – ballet was its speciality. It had a long gallery at the back that was perfect for prostitutes to loiter in. This was its second claim to fame. It made terrific business, and if Emily managed to get a permanent slot there, she would make more money and be even more famous, although her reputation in 'right-thinking' society would slip even further. However, as dancing was the focus, there was only room for one singing diva – and the day after the fire, Charlotte Russell was offered the job and accepted it without hesitation.

Within a couple of weeks, it had become apparent that Emily was not going to be thrown an instant lifeline. Over the next few months, she kept the family fed by singing in one-off concerts. She put two adverts in *The Times*: 'MISS FITZHENRY is at liberty to accept engagements for concerts, public and private dinners &c.'; and 'MISS EMILY SOLDENE is at liberty to accept ENGAGEMENTS at military concerts &c to sing "Our Own Brigade", Captain Colomb's new patriotic song, and other favourite songs.'

In anxious times doing something is better than doing nothing, even if it doesn't lead to results. Emily probably felt better having placed those adverts, even though it was humiliating. She is unlikely to have been cheered at the thought of the likes of Kate Santley reading them.

In the end an engagement came not from the adverts, but from her mentor. Charles Morton had decided not to rebuild the Oxford, but instead leased a sixteen-acre plot of land in the Royal Gardens in North Woolwich. He constructed pleasure gardens that would open during the summer months, from 3 p.m. to 11 p.m., to 17,000 people. There were two dancing halls, an orchestra, a pavilion and a lake with a grand picture of the 'March of the English through Abyssinia' at one end. There was croquet, bowls, brass bands and trapeze artists. At the end of each evening there was a fireworks display and the launch of a hot-air balloon.

On top of the regular entertainments, Charles Morton announced a series of 'monster festivals'. The highlight of these was a full-length production of John Gay's *The Beggar's Opera*. Written in 1728, *The Beggar's Opera* was a light-hearted British romp involving thieves, fences, whores and venal officers from the lower reaches of London life. The musical numbers were drawn from a wide number of sources – dances, traditional airs, popular ballads and French vaudevilles. It was satirical and burlesque. Morton asked Emily to play a leading role – not, however, as the heroine, Polly Peachum, or even the coquettish vixen Lucy Lockit, but as the hero of the piece, the cheeky, fast-living highwayman, Captain Macheath. Emily's first full-length proper stage role was as a man.

This is not as unusual as it might sound. In the nineteenth

century women frequently played men on stage. There was a name for these parts – breech roles. Victorian men loved legs; they found them so exciting they had to put long tablecloths over tables to stop their minds wandering. A show of a live lady's ankle was the height of provocation. When women played men in Victorian theatre they generally wore a short doublet or knickerbockers. Thighs would be revealed, covered only in flesh-coloured tights. Male costumes were designed to highlight every feminine curve. To the repressed Victorian male this was catnip, and a full audience was secured. Emily's low, rich voice and full curves did not suit the coquettish, faux-naïve, youthful female roles in *The Beggar's Opera*, but, with rather fine legs, she made an excellent Captain Macheath. She was funny, ironic, suggestive, knowing; very different to the earnest, tragic passion that was required from the pathetic ballad that was her hallmark. Who knew? A whole new side of Miss FitzHenry had been unleashed. It seems that Emily had the unusual talent of being both tragic and comic.

Emily only played Macheath once, but it was enough to earn her a part for the winter season. She was approached to take a starring role in a pantomime at the new East End Hall in Whitechapel. The music halls in the East End of London were rougher than those of the west, but they were full. With 4,000 working-class men and women turning up every night, they were extra lively and whatever her feelings about starring in a Whitechapel music hall, Emily wouldn't have to worry about paying the rent for at least another six months. Emily accepted the job. The pantomime was *Aladdin*, but there was no obvious role that quite suited Emily's talents, so they created a new one – King Sparkaletto. *The Era* reported:

> *And when Miss FitzHenry, the popular singer from the*
> *West End of London entered, beautifully 'made up' as King*
> *Sparkaletto, the applause was loud and long continued.*
> *If we mistake not, this was Miss FitzHenry's debut as a*
> *pantomimist, and if this is so, we must congratulate her.*
> *She has made, in taking to the stage, no mistake in her*
> *vocation, or, rather she has mistaken it hitherto in holding*
> *to the less ambitious career of a singer . . . the applause*
> *which greeted the essay was such as to make one think*
> *that a revolution had broken out, for pit and gallery were*
> *almost unceasing in their demands for an encore, and*
> *the cries were only stopped by a sudden change of scenery*
> *. . . The singing it should be mentioned induced a tumult,*
> *which seemed little short of an emeute . . .*

Victorian pantomimes were even rowdier than their twenty-first-century equivalents and Emily, the landlady's granddaughter, was in her element. She conveniently forgets about these moments of lowbrow triumph in her memoir, but it was these two parts – Macheath and King Sparkaletto – that were crucial to her finally getting her big break on the stage. King Sparkaletto caught the attention of the manager at the Alhambra, John Hollingshead, and as soon as Charlotte Russell's one-year contract ended in February 1869, Emily was offered the prima donna role at Britain's most famous music hall. Miss FitzHenry's career and her family were safe for now.

Meanwhile, across the Channel, events were taking place

in the world of musical entertainment that were to prove even more significant for Emily's career trajectory. In 1855 a German Jewish immigrant called Jacques Offenbach walked away from a promising career as the musical director of the Comédie-Française in Paris, to buy the lease on a small wooden theatre off the Champs-Élysées. Offenbach believed he had spotted a gap in the opera market. His goal was to create a new style of musical entertainment that would offer more fun than grand opera, while retaining a high degree of musical sophistication. The Théâtre des Opéras Bouffes-Parisiens opened in July 1855 and started showing Offenbach's short, quirky, comical operettas. In traditional opera the music was the priority, but Offenbach wanted the words and the music to have equal value. On the surface the plots were crazy, but they were actually satirical, poking fun at the rulers and society of the day, but in such an obtuse way that Offenbach stayed out of trouble. There was plenty of sexual innuendo, but it was relatively refined, so that women could still come along and watch. The music was light, with deceptively catchy tunes. People often refer to the 'Offenbach bounce' as the sonic equivalent of drinking a few glasses of champagne without the hangover the next day.

Offenbach's music was cleverly constructed: deceptively simple and required a high level of vocal training. Opéras bouffes were not musicals, but modern productions like *Oklahoma!*, *A Chorus Line* and *Hamilton* are seen as their direct descendants. Offenbach was famously prolific and, with his librettist Halévy, wrote a stream of hits like *Orpheus in the Underworld*, *La belle Hélène*, *Barbe-bleue*, *La vie parisienne*, *La Grande-Duchesse de Gérolstein* and *La*

Périchole, which delighted Parisians.

News of these continental hits were of great interest to impresarios like Charles Morton. He had introduced anglicised (some would say bastardised) segments from these new Offenbach operas into his music hall programmes from 1864. Unfortunately for Emily, Charlotte Russell was generally given them to sing, with one exception which was well noted by the critics. This was 'The Laughing Couplets' from *Orpheus in the Underworld*, in which Emily was allowed to sing as Venus. It was a huge success, the popularity no doubt helped by the 'Galop infernal' and the cancan dance following fast on its heels.

Once at the Alhambra, Miss FitzHenry was back to singing the pathetic ballads for which she was so famous. But her comic turns were not forgotten. Just as Emily was giving birth to her mysterious fourth child, one of Offenbach's greatest operas was premiering in Paris. *La Grande-Duchesse de Gérolstein* was seen as a send-up of the Russian tsarina, Catherine the Great, but it was really aimed at the sexual excesses of sovereigns of either gender. It was the story of a female ruler of a fictional German duchy who has a weakness for men in uniform. She declares a needless war in order to find new male prospects. 'Ah, how I love men in uniform,' she declares, and sings in her signature tune:

Ah how I love the military!
Their cocky uniforms,
Their moustaches and their stiff plumes.

The Grand Duchess promotes Fritz, a handsome private, to the rank of general. When he fails to respond to the Duchess's romantic overtures, she allows her courtiers to humiliate him. Fritz returns to his peasant fiancée, and the Grand Duchess has to marry her long-term betrothed, the limp Prince Paul. She accepts his offer of marriage with the wry observation, 'When you cannot have what you love, you must love what you have.' Emily may well have agreed with her.

La Grande-Duchesse had originally been put on at the Covent Garden theatre, and then was toured round the country by its manager, John Russell, with Miss Julia Mathews playing her eccentric highness. As Emily says: 'Miss Julia Mathews was Mr. Russell's prima donna, and I think pulled the prima donna string somewhat too tightly.'

There was something about the role of the Grand Duchess that seemed to go to the heads of leading ladies. Ruling the country, starting wars and enjoying a penchant for men in uniform – that level of female emancipation didn't happen very often. The first Grand Duchess, Offenbach's muse Hortense Schneider, was once stopped from going into Versailles. The guards told her that on that day it was closed to all but royalty.

'How dare you! I am the Grand Duchess of Gérolstein,' she declared. They apologised profusely and she swept past in her carriage into the gardens.

Miss Mathews had also taken her method acting rather too seriously, and while a hit with the audiences, offstage she was infuriating Russell. She had fallen out with her onstage love interest, Wilford Morgan, and was demanding that a replacement be found, or she would leave. Instead Russell decided to try and find a replacement Duchess, and understandably thought that Emily Soldene could well fit the bill of the lusty, imperious, yet ultimately pragmatic heroine. He approached her discreetly. 'Of course I jumped with joy;' says Emily, 'anything to get out of the music hall into a theatre, a real theatre, with no smoke, no varieties, no – well never mind.'

The problem was Emily was only five months into her year-long contract with the Alhambra. She went for the difficult conversation with the Alhambra's owner, Frederick Strange. He absolutely refused to release her. She cajoled, she used her feminine wiles, she got cross, she pleaded, she tried to bargain, but nothing made him budge. Poor Emily, as she said: 'It was like death losing such a chance.'

But she wasn't going to give up that easily. She had made an unlikely ally.

The premiere danseuse and therefore the biggest star at the Alhambra was a lady known as Mme Pitteri. She bathed in warm milk every day and had two maids – a French one and then an English one to wait on the French one. Emily was most impressed by her toilette service of solid silver and the many presents she had received, some of them from princes. Emily knew that Mme Pitteri had great leverage with the management.

I went to Mme. Pitteri, whose word was law, and begged her to get me off, and she, like the lovely, kind, splendid,

*big-hearted woman she was, did it, and I was free to take
my step. Years afterwards, asking an agent who had made
much money out of the danseuse (and who licked the dust
from her feet in the days of her prosperity) for news of
her, he told me indifferently "she was dead". Dead in
poverty and distress; died while filling an engagement in
a low dance house among the sailors in Marseilles. She
had spent all her money; the presents were gone, so were
the princes.*

A salutary tale for any lady performer.

Emily was released from the Alhambra, but things didn't
go to plan. The provincial theatre managers had hired the
production on the basis that they were getting the much-lauded,
bankable Julia Mathews as their leading lady. Emily may have
been a music hall star, but she had not proved herself in the
theatre. They refused to have her, and Russell had to go and
persuade Miss Mathews to come back. Emily was distraught.

*Ah! What tears, what snubs, after I had begged out of
the Alhambra, and learned the Opera in six days. For
some weeks I had a dreadful time of despair; and began
to think that after all there were worse things than music
halls and regular salaries.*

To have to beg for work when she had just managed to
find a relatively permanent and prestigious position must
have been soul-destroying, not to mention the humiliation
of being publicly snubbed by all those provincial theatre
managers. And underlying this was a bigger issue: Emily

was thirty-one years old. In the nineteenth century, actresses had an even shorter working lifespan than they do today. At thirty-one Emily was running out of bankable years. Women performers were objectified, their bodies displayed to the maximum degree; talent was less important and experience more or less irrelevant. Moreover, the attractions of relatively easy money meant that supply was greater than demand – all the time new, younger, attractive, willing and hungry recruits were coming up behind Emily.

Emily had never been a beauty. She had slightly heavy features, a mouth that was surprisingly large and an imposing décolletage which, by the time she had had four children, distracted – not necessarily in a good way. Emily also liked her food, and she was now of a formidable matronly cut, although her legs were still deemed acceptable in tights. Attractive certainly, but her beauty was not her main asset. At thirty-one Emily would have known that this was probably her last chance to make it in the theatre.

Early on Wednesday 24th November 1869, the Soldene Powell household was woken by a frantic knocking at the front door. There was a cab waiting outside to take Emily to the Standard Theatre. Miss Mathews had had another argument with her leading man, and was refusing to turn up, pleading sickness. With a full house booked for that evening and no understudy, there was only one person whom John Russell could find to be his leading lady at such short notice. Emily was the only mezzo-soprano besides Julia Mathews who had learnt the songs.

When Emily arrived, the theatre manager, Mr Douglas,

was most unimpressed and 'pooh-poohed' her, but worse was the obnoxious Morgan whom one would have thought would have learnt his lesson:

The tenor refused to rehearse with me. But my temper, unbroken, was up to concert pitch, and I went through it without him. Then came the costume question. I had to wear Miss Mathews' dress; the skirts were considerably too short, so bands of velvet were sewn on. In the middle of the lap of the pale-blue satin military dress was a huge and highly descriptive grease spot. 'Lor,' says the dresser, 'that hain't nothin', onny w'ere Miss Mathews puts 'er fried fish at night; she 'ave hit hafter hevery hact; nobody 'ull see hit from th' front.' In the delicate 'business' of the second act, Fritz, lying back in my lap, made many piano and extraneous observations calculated to break me up with either rage or tears. But he might as well have tried to disturb Lord Nelson on top of his Trafalgar Square column. I made a success, converted Mr. Douglas, and delighted Mr. Russell. I know I sang and acted remarkably well, considering the circumstances, and after four days the tenor (I was not his 'Sweetheart when a boy' – but no matter), knelt on the stage, kissed my hand, and begged the Grand Duchess to forgive him. I am glad to say her highness, taking a lenient view of the case, pardoned him on the spot; but Miss Emily Soldene has consistently disliked him ever since.

Perhaps Julia Mathews was not being such a prima donna after all, and the tenor, the troublesome Wilford Morgan, was just ghastly.

Emily was not exaggerating when she said she was a hit. The reviews were excellent, such as this one from the *Standard* on 28th November: 'Miss Soldene makes a captivating and exalted-looking Grand Duchess, and sings the sparkling music with an amount of spirit and abandon that brings down the hearty applause of the audience.'

Russell was so pleased with her that when the ten-day run of *La Grande-Duchesse* was finished, Emily was engaged to play the lead role in Offenbach's latest offering, *Barbe-bleue*. Not everyone was convinced by Emily's transformation. The journalist John Plummer noted in his journal:

> *She made a magnificent Duchess, and her large mouth and robust figure were soon forgotten in the charm of her singing and the excellence of her acting. I mentioned this to Mr. Clement W Scott, the dramatic critic of the London Figaro of which at the time I was the associate editor but he ridiculed the idea of her being more than a clever serio-comic. 'I know her well', he said 'she is only Miss FitzHenry of the Oxford and Cambridge Music Halls.' Nettled by Scott's remarks, I wrote to Miss Soldene, complimented her on her performance, comparing her to that of Theresa, the famous singing comedienne who I had seen in Paris a few weeks previously. A note in reply invited me to revisit the theatre.*

It has to be said that Plummer, as a result of a childhood illness, was profoundly deaf. However, most people agreed with him, and Miss FitzHenry, having served her purpose, went into instant retirement. Miss Emily Soldene had finally succeeded in her ambition to become a real opera star and was on the stage for good.

Clara Vesey as the Duke's pet page, Oswald, in *Geneviève de Brabant*

Chapter Five

The Perfect Pair

It was perfectly lovely for us two to be alone on tour; independent, with nobody to contradict or control us . . . there is no other word for such a state of things but 'lovely.' (Emily, 1898)

The first time Emily mentions Clara in her memoir is when she describes Clara accompanying her on her tour around the south of England with John Russell's opéra bouffe. Emily had the excitement of seeing her name in large letters at the top of the bill: 'No matter whatever direction I went for a walk, my willing feet always led me past the bill – "Benefit of Miss Emily Soldene – The Grand Duchess"'.

It must have been such a thrill after everything she'd been through. But it was even better that Emily had her sister Clara with her, witnessing it. They had escaped the domestic yoke of prim, judgemental mothers, husbands and children. They were free and having the sort of fun few Victorian women ever had – an all-expenses-paid road trip. Emily had gone straight from childhood to the role of wife and mother. Maybe there was a feeling of making up for lost time:

> *How we did enjoy ourselves. Came home from the performance at such hours, 10.30 at least; had hot coffee and toast, and raw tomatoes, and onions sliced in vinegar; sat up reading novels as late as we liked, stopped in bed, reading novels as late as we liked; read novels at breakfast, dinner, tea and supper, a proceeding which, at home, was much discouraged and attended with penalties.*

All younger children are destined to grow up in the slipstream of their older siblings, watching and learning what to do and what not to do; they are born with a template and a yardstick already in place. From the moment baby Clara gained consciousness she would have been aware of Emily's presence. And what a presence it was – Emily was not only eleven years older, but a prima donna long before she hit the stage. She must have filled every room with her exuberance. Clara grew up with a ringside seat to her sister's battles with her mother – Emily's elopement, awkward pregnancies and questionable career choices; her scales and arias probably filling their small dwellings, threatening to break glass. Her costumes taking up all the space.

Siblings have a unique ability to either validate or invalidate, they know each other from the beginning: what makes the other happy, what makes them sad; they know which buttons to press. Sisters share the same stories and memories and yet often interpret them differently – they have the power to disrupt narratives, a person's very sense of who they are. Siblings are direct competitors for their parents' attention, resources, approval and love. A sister's triumph can feel as if it is at the other's cost – when one is more, the other is less. There is a reason why there is so much intensity and ambivalence in sibling relationships.

For the older sibling, a new baby's arrival is always a moment of trauma. Their existence is threatened by the new baby who now takes their place. But there was an added complication for Emily – her own probable father, Frederick Lambert, had disappeared from the scene years before. This new baby had a father who was at least present in some capacity. When Emily was summoned back to London to live with her mother, it was to come as an outsider into a new family unit. She was the outlier. It's no wonder that when she came back from her happy exile in the country alehouse, she made so much noise, no longer out of sight and out of mind, that later on she literally wanted to be centre stage.

Meanwhile it must have been hard for Clara to mark out any space for herself, to find her own voice growing up in Emily's shadow; and as soon as Clara started to become a young woman herself, Emily started to have children, one almost every year. The house must have been even more full of Emily's creative productions, loud crying ones, whom Clara was expected to look after while Emily went off to her expensive singing lessons, and her nights at the opera, dressed up in glamorous creations while Clara was left at home with the babies and the husband. It would have been so easy for Emily and Clara to begrudge each other; they both had good reason. But it wasn't like that at all. Not at first.

Clara seemed to love being around her sister. Emily

was glamorous and saucy, and they could have whispered conversations about topics Clara could never have raised with their mother. It was through Emily that Clara would have learnt about the world, and what a world it was – sparkly costumes, handsome young aristocrats, scandalous actresses. Emily probably promised that one day she would bring Clara into this world and she could see it for herself.

The attachment was mutual. Emily always acted as if Clara were her baby. Some big sisters can find little sisters a pesky annoyance, but Emily seemed to love having a little sister, perhaps because Clara could give her what she had always wanted – a devoted captive audience. And Emily couldn't wait until she could take Clara with her. What fun it would be to show Clara her world. It's one thing to experience something, but someone else witnessing it makes it real. Working in the theatre was fun, but it was also ruthless; you could never quite trust anyone. There had been times when Emily must have felt quite alone. She must have longed for an ally, for someone she could completely trust, who would always have her back. Someone she could be vulnerable with, not have to put on a brave face for at the end of the evening. This must have made having Clara as a companion very appealing.

Emily and Clara were a good fit for each other, the perfect pair. But there was another factor at play that might explain why Emily kept her sister so close. All the time she was touring the country seeing her name in lights, Emily was aware that these days of stardom were precarious and limited. Like the most beautiful days of late summer, that must have made them all the more precious. She knew all the stories of the former stars, so recently brilliant, falling so quickly into obscurity and poverty. Emily had already experienced what happened when the Oxford burnt down and her first engagement as the Grand Duchess fell through at the whim of a few provincial theatre managers. However loud the applause and frequent the encores, her position was temporary. Emily must have known that these leading-lady days could not last much longer than a few more years. Not unless she did something cunning. How was Emily going to find some sort of longevity that would keep her in the limelight and maintain her family's financial security? An idea seems to have come with her next production.

When Emily got back from her tour she went to see the new opéra bouffe, *Chilpéric*, at the Lyceum. Its French composer, Hervé, was playing the main role of Chilpéric, King of the Celts. A few weeks later when Hervé retired exhausted, Emily was offered the chance to play the part herself. Emily did like playing big, powerful men. They allowed her to act and say things that typically did not come with female roles, unless one was the villainess. The female cross-dresser often impersonated heroic men in the prime of life; these roles allowed Emily to have agency in the plot.

Once again, Emily was able to stride out in tights and boots with a big crown on her head. Even more excitingly, she got to ride a horse onto the stage while singing the comic 'Ham song'. 'I rode on the stage in such style,' she says, 'that the men in front forgot I was a girl, and also forgot to laugh.'

They had taken the show to Dublin, and Emily was offered a circus horse, which was pure white and beautiful, but highly spirited. The circus owner told Emily she could have the horse for free if she could mount it on stage in one go. Always up for a wager, on the first night, Emily swung her leg over and leapt on to its back in one dashing manoeuvre which brought the audience to its feet. Naturally she won the wager and got the horse for free. Emily's rural childhood had probably given her some skills as a horsewoman – her grandfather and two of her uncles had been horsebreakers.

The thespian magazine, *The Era*, also approved of Emily's derring-do:

> *[Emily] fulfilled the requirements of the character as efficiently as it is possible for a lady to do, contributing, by the way, a novelty to the piece which is likely to prove a sensation. Miss Soldene, as the huntsman king, crosses a horse in a style which would do credit to the most accomplished follower of the hounds, and cracks the whip with as much gusto as her jokes.*

I think we can allow Emily this piece of self-applause in her memoirs.

> *To play Chilpéric at the Lyceum after Herve was rather an undertaking, but I came out all right, and made a dashing lady-killer. The dresses suited me personally, the music suited me vocally. It was a delightful part, and I had a delightful time. The people in the theatre made no end of a fuss over my success.*

But perhaps the most important lesson from the Chilpéric experience was to confirm to Emily the benefits of being able to tickle the audience with your dancers.

Exceedingly nice the ballet looked in graceful and classical and rather diaphanous draperies, but perfectly proper – the sort of thing one might take one's mother, or, in fact, one's mother-in-law, to see. They were indulging in a wavy, dreamy, mystical movement, when suddenly, "Bing-Bang Boom!" on the drums and cymbals, and to everyone's astonishment four-and-twenty legs shot out on the O.P. side as far as possible, and as undressed as possible, and, before we had recovered from this severe shock, four-and-twenty other legs shot out on the P. side, just as far and quite as nude. The dresses were worse than deceptive, they were slit up to the waist. But if the ballet was fetching, what about the Pages? Such pages! such figures – long and straight in the limbs, and soft and supple and – well, simply darlings. And their costumes! It did not take you long to see them. And one realised that with obvious advantage brevity could be applied to more things than wit.

Thackeray once wrote that seeing a dancer on stage in flesh-coloured tights offered a thrill like 'the thrill of a public execution'. Emily was watching and taking note. Meanwhile the activities of her former boss, Charles Morton, were to give Emily her next cunning plan.

Ever since the Oxford had burnt down, Morton had been looking for a grand project to replace it – the pleasure gardens at Woolwich had never reaped quite enough financial reward. Then in the spring of 1870 a large, low-grade music hall – the Philharmonic in Islington – came up for sale. Charles Morton managed to persuade an 'anonymous' investor (Charles Head) to put in £4,000, and bought it. While Emily was off touring the south of England, Morton had spent the summer turning 'the Phil' into the most fabulous venue, with a new stage and a new bar that extended the whole length of the corridor with, to quote Emily, 'magnificent barmaids'. There were private boxes with crimson silk, blue satin curtains and a wide promenade where people could be seen, and yet still see (perfect for prostitutes). He had created a thoroughly top-grade theatrical establishment that would have a similarly sophisticated musical programme.

How Emily managed to persuade Charles Morton to let her direct his newest and boldest project is anyone's guess; but somehow she did, and this meant that she would not only be the leading lady on stage, but had taken a step up into management. It was a brave but smart move on Emily's part. She must have calculated that a way to increase her longevity in the theatre was to start working on the production side of things as well. Control is power, and that generally leads to more security – as a director Emily was less likely to make herself redundant and more likely to give herself the best parts.

Now Emily was given the job of coming up with a suitable programme. Morton insisted that like the Oxford, the Phil's programme should be musical, relatively sophisticated, and exploit the craze for the new wave of opéras bouffes coming over from Paris. Emily took to the task with characteristic enthusiasm, as if she had been directing all her life – perhaps, growing up with her puppet shows and killing off Rosamund, she had been.

Emily decided the main attraction was to be a condensed performance of the opera she had most recently and successfully starred in, *Chilpéric*, with herself in the lead role. Emily cheerfully rewrote the score with maximum entertainment in mind, putting a pen through the slower moments. What was not to be condensed was the role of the dancers:

From the first moment of going into management – recognising the attractive force of female beauty – I surrounded myself with the best-looking and best set-up girls that could possibly be found. I selected my chorus from the ballet. The result, a minimum of voice, perhaps, but certainly a maximum of good looks and grace. Nobody ever saw my chorus still, immovable, wooden. No, they felt the music, were full of life, and, like a blooded horse, were anxious for a start. Then they understood how to "make up" which is not an accident, but an art.

Emily also made an important addition. While she had been touring with *Chilpéric*, and Charles Morton had been renovating the Phil, there had been a scandal raging at the Alhambra. The Middlesex magistrates had removed the Alhambra's licence because of the arrival of an indecent dancing troupe, the Colonna Quadrille, whose interpretation of the cancan, it was felt, had taken this notorious dance to new levels of depravity. Originally the cancan had been a perfectly demure, traditional French dance performed at social functions. It was usually danced by four men. In the 1820s it was adopted by the Parisian dance halls and had become a platform to show off male gymnastic abilities, all high kicks and splits; acrobatic, yes, but erotic? Not yet, not until women started performing it. The effect on the audience was combustive – not least because in the nineteenth century women did not wear knickers, but pantalettes with an open crotch, which meant that high kicks were quite revealing. The effect on a male audience for whom a flash of ankle was deemed incendiary can only be imagined.

The troupe at the Alhambra had pushed the boundaries of the dance one step further. The Colonna Quadrille was made up of four women. Two of them were dressed as men in sailor shirts and closed knickers. This meant they could kick higher than their heads. They danced with two women in short ballet skirts, pantalettes and flesh-coloured tights. This unique combination was both scandalous and compelling. Pictures of the troupe were the lead story in erotic magazines.

Unlike the Alhambra, which was classified as a music hall, Emily knew that Morton, cleverly, had made sure the Philharmonic was licensed as a theatre. It was therefore under the jurisdiction of the Lord Chamberlain rather than the Middlesex magistrates. The Lord Chamberlain was famously more lenient when it came to dancing girls, and so Emily offered the now unemployed Colonna Quadrille a part in her new opera. The most notorious member of the Quadrille was a young girl called Sarah Wright, who, as Emily said, had shorter skirts and longer legs than most girls. Emily renamed her 'Mdlle. Sara' after the actress whom everyone in New York was talking about, Sarah Bernhardt.

Goodness knows what awful suffering was endured by the Middlesex magistrates, for while the Alhambra languished in outer and inner darkness, making Leicester Square a hideous, howling wilderness, filled with the sighs of the unemployed four hundred, up at the "Little Phil" in merrie Islington, safe under the shield of the Lord Chamberlain's licence, that wicked, wicked dance was danced every night. The theatre was crammed, and "Wiry Sal" was the toast of the London clubs.

Emily had pulled off a bit of a coup. She didn't seem to be afraid of scandal, but rather embraced it, attracted it and used it. She was bad. What made her so naughty? Her family history might provide a clue. For all Priscilla and her family's giving vicars their Sunday lunches and delivering Old Testament punishments, her grandfather had been taken to court for his adultery, her grandmother ran an alehouse, her mother had come to London unchaperoned as a teenager, lived in one of the most notorious districts, had an illegitimate child and then married a man who was already married. Basically, they were respectable when it suited them, and not, when it didn't.

And then there was Clara.

Emily was a thirty-one-year-old married mother of four, who had a low, booming mezzo voice and an ever-enlarging matronly figure which could no longer be hidden. None of these factors taken by themselves could have harmed Emily's career – but when taken together, the prospect of her being a star, in the sense of a mass-appeal sex symbol, the sort of figure that would gain the publicity and adulation that was really needed to be a stratospheric draw, was unlikely now to happen. Or at least Emily was only going to appeal to a niche crowd – the sort that liked their ladies to be big-breasted and commanding in tights. And actresses needed a mass following. Fans meant theatre seats, night after night (because there was no other way to see them).

Then there were the fringe benefits that came with the fans – the meals, clothes, jewels, gifts, payments in kind. They accumulated, or at least might be stored for use on a rainy day, when the work dried up. Fans were an expected bonus of a career as an actress. Of course, there was the ultimate perk of the job – the opportunity to marry one of these fans, who were often from another stratosphere in terms of wealth and class, one that an actress could only have dreamt about joining. Of course, if, like Emily, you were married already, that opportunity wasn't available.

But Clara was different.

She was twenty, unmarried and had never had children. She was attractive, in a different way to Emily – in a pretty, tiny, elfin kind of way. Her voice was a sweet high soprano. In a way Emily and Clara perfectly complemented each other. They would never be rivals for the same parts, their voices were different ranges, they were attractive to different men in different ways. And as Emily's attractiveness waned, Clara's could make up for it. They were a perfect pair.

I don't know when Emily first realised Clara's potential, but she lost no time in using her first management role to promote Clara. She gave her one of the lead roles in her potted *Chilpéric*:

> *On this occasion an interesting young lady made her debut, playing Brunehant. She was pretty, and had a charming figure; her stage name was Miss Clara Vesey – my sister. Mr. Morton was Clara's theatrical sponsor – and selected*

the name of "Vesey" from the comedy of "Money" – a
not inappropriate derivation considering that she soon
developed into a great personal attraction, occupying
a front place in the first flight of photo'd professional
beauties, and proving consequently a financial fact both
to her manager and her photographer.

As the new technology of photography developed, it was quickly realised that photographs had all sorts of interesting potential, including the erotic. A business in suggestive postcards and magazines grew up and flourished. They were delivered by post or sold underneath counters in tobacconists. The most notorious purveyor of erotic material was the Holywell Street Shop just off the Strand which was one of Britain's most infamous streets for picking up prostitutes, and also at the heart of London's theatre district. The photos on these postcards and in the magazines varied in their level of explicitness. Some pictured completely naked ladies, but many of them were merely suggestive, and taken to appeal to the particular quirks of Victorian male proclivities. Victorian men liked voyeuristic scenarios – ladies being surprised in a state of undress, attending to their toilette, being spied upon without their knowing, revealing clothing malfunctions in public places. They liked women who inadvertently showed pieces of their anatomy, flashes of stockings, ankle and cleavage. Naked women holding fishing rods, shepherdesses holding crooks suggestively. All erotic signals if your mind is set that way. They loved women in certain occupations – shop girls, barmaids, milkmaids, strict governesses about to do some punishing. But most of all they liked actresses. Actresses are the most common occupation featured in Victorian erotic material. They were seen as simply the most provocative and sexually exciting young women around.

Alongside this intimate material, legitimate publicity photographs of real actresses were sold as postcards or appeared in the weekly and monthly racy gentlemen's magazines. In theory they were respectable, but taken in context, again if your mind was set a certain way, they were anything but. They transformed the actress into an icon not just of glamour but also of sex. The actress could be purchased and collected and displayed in your own home.

Clara Vesey became one of the most photographed actresses of the 1870s. Although Emily had the bigger roles on the stage, it was Clara's image that was the most widely distributed. Clara was usually in nude tights, with lace-up booties, dressed up as a pageboy in a doublet with an unfeasibly tiny waist. One leg astride a rock or leaning on a chaise longue, a cane or sword in hand, hat with an erect feather pointing skyward, knowing smile on her lips. There are photographs of Emily in tights too. But somehow the costumes are never quite as revealing – she has breeches over the tights that come down to her knee, a long jacket over the top. They are not so conventionally saucy.

Emily had no problem playing with erotic metaphors in her memoir.

Mr Calvert was the Shakespearian manager, and looked upon opera bouffers with a severe, not to say a cold and critical eye. That was in the morning; but in the evening, when I went off my first exit, I saw him examining with much interest the fashion of Miss Vesey's (the pet Page) boots. She wore them particularly high, and had one foot on a stool, so he could make sure, exactly, how they were trimmed. When he saw me, he murmured something about he 'had not noticed anything like that before.' Up to this day I am not certain whether he meant the boot or the wearer.

Emily then goes on to tell the story of her own adventure with a favourite theme of Victorian erotic fantasies:

I was alone drawing on my tights, when I had a strange feeling that everyone has felt, the feeling that there is someone in the room, or someone is looking at you. I turned round, the room was empty, but the impression remained.

As Emily sat at her dressing table putting on her make-up, the impression got stronger. She pushed back her chair and looked beneath the table: 'immediately opposite to me, in the dark shadow, my eye encountered another eye. I could not actually see, but I knew, I felt it.' She turned down the gaslight and saw a faint gleam coming from between the floorboards.

When I was changing for the second act, the man was caught on the other side of the wooden partition, with his eye glued to a gimlet hole. I need not say he was kicked out of the theatre there and then. He was an old hand, and, in the course of years, had probably acquired more knowledge than he knew what to do with.

There was another factor that may have taken part in Emily's calculations. Interactions between sisters were synonymous with lesbians in the language of Victorian erotica. And attractive young women engaging in lesbian activities were highly popular with Victorian men. If they were real sisters acting out on stage, how much more intriguing and tantalising.

Clara proved herself very adept in her role as Brunehant, Chilpéric's jealous vixen sister-in-law, who lures a man into bed in order to persuade him to kill Chilpéric's lover. But for her next project Emily decided to put on a production, not of an opéra bouffe, but a traditional English ballad opera – *The Waterman*. Written almost a century before, it was the popular story of Wilhelmina, the pretty daughter of the passive Mr Bundle and his ambitious wife, and the battle for her affections between the good Thames waterman, Tom Tug, and the bad dandy, Robin. Emily decided to play Tom Tug, and evidently was received well by the audience: 'She deported herself wonderfully like a hearty young fellow of the nautical class, and displayed much tact and humour in the love-making scenes with the coquettish Wilhelmina.'

The coquettish Wilhelmina was played by none other than her sister, Miss Clara Vesey.

Soon Emily and Clara were building up a regular fan base of distinguished admirers. Emily's use of female sexuality, not just her own, but other women's (including her younger sister), might leave us conflicted. Can we forgive her because that was just what it was like in those days? Is it right for us to judge, with all the relative legal, social, educational and financial advantages that we have now? Do we approve of

Emily at this point? I'm sure Emily would have had no truck with any of these ruminations. She would have seen such moral judgements as a luxury – she had to earn a living.

There was no such thing as political correctness in Victorian theatre. The casting couch was alive and well. While Hollywood was still a small hamlet outside Los Angeles, actresses were already prey to predatory audience members and theatre management alike. Although to what extent was it a game in which sometimes both sides were willing players? To be fair to the women involved, though, there weren't many – if any – other avenues open to them.

The opéras bouffes that were so fashionable, being originally French, had to be translated and adapted to the taste of the British audience. The lead player in this enterprise was a Scottish travel and golf manual writer, Henry Brougham Farnie. Emily brightly recounts the casting couch romps that surrounded *Chilpéric*:

The late Mr. Farnie was very constant in his attendance, and was generally to be found in one of the upper entrances very much engaged with the chorus – the feminine chorus. He never allowed anything in the way of a deputy or anything else, if he could possibly help it, to come between him and the chorus. He had a very keen feeling for the beautiful, and most especially affected the Burne-Jones style of beauty, but was not bigoted. Indeed, I may mention, as showing the broad and catholic view he took of these aesthetic differences, that the best-looking girls in the theatre, even if they were a little plump, were never allowed to appeal to him in vain. As a rule their intelligence was not on a par with their physical perfections, but this did not affect the benevolence of his intentions. And he would call a rehearsal at any extraordinary hour, and if the girls were very good-looking indeed would stop with them any length, or even give them lessons privately one at a time; but there his consideration ended, it did not extend to ordering any refreshments.

Meanwhile Farnie had some competition, with the appearance backstage of one of the most successful actor turned dramatists of the late nineteenth century:

Sometimes he would be assisted in the work by the late Mr. Dion Boucicault, who came to the theatre pretty frequently, and was understood to take a good deal of paternal interest in the young ladies' progress; of course, purely from an artistic point of view. But Mr. Farnie must have a real regard for Mr. Boucicault, and would not allow him to be worried with the woes of the chorus, for no sooner did the girls surround this charming author-actor, and most interesting man of his day, than Farnie would clap his hands together violently, and cry out, 'Now, girls, to your places; you'll get your cue in a moment. And, mind! I'll fine everyone that's late. Do you hear?' And they did hear, and fled.

I notice that Emily refers to both the gentlemen concerned as 'late' – they were obviously conveniently deceased by the time of her memoir's publication in 1898.

Almost as important as what happened on stage, was what happened backstage – the culture of well-bred patrons of the theatre. The ability to mingle, intrigue and captivate the rich and influential was all part of the job of a successful actress. One story, which caused a particular furore when Emily's *Recollections* came out, involved a certain tall, gaunt, long grey-haired, pointy-bearded 'gentleman of Israel', as she put it, who arrived at the Alhambra every night around 9.30 p.m. wearing a scarf that glittered with a priceless gem – sometimes a ruby, sometimes a pearl, sometimes an emerald set round with diamonds:

> *He talked (with a nasal accent) to the ballet a good deal, but it was understood always for their good. Indeed, he was looked upon as a regular father to the ballet, but perhaps an irregular one would be nearer the mark. If the girls admired (which they generally did) the emerald, ruby or pearl, he told them gently it should be theirs, but for one thing; It was 'a gift from a dead friend; he could never part with it.' I will not record the subsequent and disrespectful remarks of the ladies . . . [he] was never weary of proclaiming his infallibility in the way of personal virtue (notwithstanding all and many inducements to the contrary), and his faithfulness to his domestic obligations. In spite of which, when unprotected female folk (especially if they were plump), came in a cab to do a 'turn,' he would, when they were through, offer them the accommodation of his brougham and his personal attendance . . . The old gentleman was – Well, now, who was it? Don't all speak at once.*

Emily does not seem too taken with this gentleman, perhaps because she had been one of the plump ladies taken for a turn in the brougham. When her memoir came out the gentleman was immediately identified as Baron Lionel de Rothschild.

At the end of a very successful *Chilpéric* and *Waterman* season, Emily and Clara again went on tour, this time with the company from the Phil. It was a more extensive and gruelling tour, venturing not just to cities and towns in the south, but going up north to Manchester, Leeds, Newcastle, Glasgow and Liverpool. They managed to time their visit to the Theatre Royal in Doncaster with the races. Emily and Clara were thrilled – they had had many a flutter on the horses over the years, but they had never been to an actual racecourse before: 'Every day Clara (my sister) and I asked Mr. Head for a tip, and every day he gave us a fiver instead, which we most successfully lost.'

Then it was the day of the Leger. Emily and Clara couldn't keep still, jumping up and down and shouting with the loudest. They won with the horse Hannah.

After the race, the Baron led her slowly along through the crush, one hand holding the bridle, the other round her neck. The people hurrahed and applauded, and when the Baron, stooping, pressed his face against her soft velvety muzzle, and kissed her, the crowd screamed with delight. And I, like the emotional idiot I was, found the tears were running down my cheeks. I could not help it. Some moments are worth years of ordinary things.

And that, I suppose, is it – a life that is not ordinary, but extraordinary. What sacrifices, what compromises are worth making in exchange for moments that are extraordinary?

Miss E. Soldene

The Merry Maid of. Islington.

Emily attracted attention, not only for the popularity of her productions, but also her ability to make money

Chapter Six

The Impresario

Taking a theatre was a serious matter (Emily, 1897)

About the same time that the Oxford theatre was burning down, Karl Marx published his seminal work, *Das Kapital*, which captured a certain mood of the era. Marx saw that something was very wrong with the world, in particular the misery and poverty of the majority. Marx believed they were condemned to this crushing poverty because there was such a thing as the ownership of property, and power was in the hands of the few who owned the property, or, since the Industrial Revolution, more specifically the means of production. He believed that the working classes would eventually have a revolution and claim the means of production, and that the ultimate aim should be to abolish the concept of property altogether.

Emily was very interested in politics (and politicians)

and kept herself engaged and up to date with the issues of the day. She always had an opinion. I'm not sure she would have read *Das Kapital* itself, though; novels were more to her liking, and I have a strong feeling she might have thought Marx an idiot. In a way, however, Emily reached some of the same conclusions – that is, that power and wealth lay with the ownership of the means of production, and if you weren't one of those owners you were being exploited or, in Marx's words, you were in chains. But Emily didn't think there should be a revolution. She decided that she should find a way to become one of those property owners and join the new class of the bourgeoisie – or put more simply, rather than being an employee, she decided she should become the employer and start her own production company.

This would be a bold move in the twenty-first century, but in the nineteenth century Emily's ambition might have seemed extremely reckless. Emily was not only a woman, but a wife. Since the 1300s, according to the law, a married woman was a *feme covert*, which meant that she was under the protection and influence of her husband and had no legal identity. As Sir William Blackstone KC wrote in his *Commentaries on the Laws of England* in 1765:

> *The husband and wife are one person in law: that is, the very being or legal existence of the woman is suspended during her marriage, or at least is incorporated or consolidated into that of her husband, under whose wing, protection and cover, she performs everything.*

With the exception of a dowry (which Emily obviously never had), a wife's property became her husband's and he could do with it what he liked. The only way for a wife to reclaim her property was for her husband to die. This meant a wife could not legally own a business, or in Emily's case, a production company. Wives basically had the same legal status as criminals and the insane.

The greatest actress of the eighteenth century, Sarah Siddons, said, 'perhaps in the next world women will be more valued than they are in this.' In the end legal recognition on this earth did come – ever since Emily's birth, a movement for change had been gaining momentum. Mary Wollstonecraft had raised it in her *Vindication of the Rights of Women* in 1792, and by 1865 it was high up on the agenda of a campaigning group of women led by Millicent Fawcett, called the Kensington Society. These influential ladies were pioneers in the suffragist movement, but their first success was to change the law regarding women's property rights. Just as Emily was promoted to director at the Philharmonic in 1870, the first Married Women's Property Act was passed. This meant that any wages or property which a wife inherited or earnt through her own work was regarded as her own property. In principle a wife could now own her own business. However, as this law only applied to women who had married after the act was passed, this was no help to Emily at all – although annoyingly for Emily, it would have helped Clara.

It wasn't until the 1882 Married Woman's Property Act that a wife's separate identity was legally recognised and a wife, whenever she had married, was able to own, buy and sell her own property, could own stock and was also liable for her own debts. However, for a wife to have a business in her own right was still fiendishly difficult; for example, a wife could not take out a loan in her own name. Even a single woman or a widow needed to get her father's permission and secure a male guarantor. It was not until 1975 that women could open a bank account in their own names. Actually, it was not until 1982 that women had a legal right to spend their own money in pubs – although Katie Swain and two of her daughters did still manage to run a couple in the early decades of the nineteenth century.

Despite all of this, in the spring of 1874, when Emily noticed an advert for the let of the Lyceum Theatre, she found herself writing to the owner, Mr Bateman, just out of curiosity. The problem is, once one starts flirting with an idea, however outlandish it may seem, it can be difficult to let it go. Emily, not known for her self-restraint, perhaps could not help herself.

Mr Bateman wanted £90 a week, no small amount – the equivalent of £5,650 a week in today's money; and that was just the rent, which would be a fraction of the total outlay of money needed once things like costumes, performers, theatre staff, and publicity had been added in. As Emily said: 'it seemed an immense responsibility to assume, so I played about and fiddled and faddled, and was altogether uncertain and undecided.' But Mr Bateman must have either sensed a sale or been particularly desperate, because he travelled all the way up to Birmingham where Emily was on tour and appeared at her lodgings: '[He] talked to me in so exceedingly practical a fashion, that when he drove me down to the theatre he carried in his waistcoat pocket my cheque for £300, the first month's rent in advance.'

Three hundred pounds in that time is the equivalent of £19,000 in today's money. To put it in context, in 1874 it would have taken a skilled tradesman over four years to earn that amount; quite a sum to commit so abruptly, because a silver-tongued theatre owner turned up outside the hotel room door. And then where did she get the money from and how did she raise it? Perhaps she had a rich patron, a wealthy special friend among her fans. There was one lord in particular whom Emily was close to, renowned for his speculations and had form in leasing theatres.

We do know how she managed to operate as a business – her husband fronted the enterprise. From then on Jack Powell had the position of acting manager, but everyone knew that the theatre was really Emily's concern. This was not unheard of – there had been several famous husband/leading lady management combinations, like Mary Moore and Charles Wyndham at Wyndham's, and Marie Wilton and Charles J. James at the Prince of Wales. It could work well, as long as the husband and wife trusted each other, and had a good functioning relationship and a shared vision. The husband could be the public face of the business, negotiate the loans and manage the bank account, while the real power lay with the showbiz-savvy wife. Basically, Jack could operate as Emily's business beard. Charles Dickens himself could see the advantages. As a young theatre critic he wrote: 'with all that character and taste and propriety which lady-managers seem to have a peculiar talent of imparting to such things. Admirable managers they are, and the influence they possess is really extraordinary.'

But even if Emily had found the means to raise the money,

she still had to find the courage to take the risk. At this point she had been a leading lady for five years, and directing for three; still, it was a huge leap to take on the financial responsibility for her productions, particularly if she didn't have to. Why do it? Perhaps it was because she believed she couldn't fail. And the reasons behind this hutzpah might lie in the production Emily had directed after *Chilpéric*, a new Offenbach opéra bouffe called *Geneviève de Brabant*.

It was the man with a predilection for the chorus girls in *Chilpéric*, Henry Farnie, who first approached Emily with the idea of adapting *Geneviève*. Farnie had a high opinion of his own abilities and was keen on broadcasting it. Other people were less convinced. He did know his audience though, and although his adaptations were lambasted as crass by the more discerning, he had more hits than any other Victorian lyricist, including W. S. Gilbert. When Farnie approached Emily and Charles Morton and suggested he had a go at *Geneviève de Brabant*, Emily immediately saw the potential, but Charles Morton wasn't keen:

> *In the beginning, I had great difficulty in bringing Mr. Morton up to scratch. He jibbed and was financially faddy. Besides, he did not like Farnie – said 'Farnie and Failure' were synonymous, and added many more alliterative and aggravating arguments. But Farnie was finessful – constant dropping wears away a stone – so ultimately matters were arranged, and the work went into rehearsal.*

Geneviève had the usual nonsensical, rumbustious opéra bouffe plot. The pastry cook, Drogan, is at the centre of the play with his magic pie and unrequited love for the Duchess Geneviève. He becomes her page and they are falsely accused of adultery, fleeing death at the hands of the non-cuckolded Duke, and unmasking the villains at the end. It all ends most satisfactorily with the right people ending up with the right people, and all the villains locked up where they should be. Selina Dolaro played the Duchess Geneviève, Clara was the Duke's pet page (an opportunity to show off her legs) and Emily played Drogan, with another chance to put on tights, make love to ladies and be in almost every scene.

The rehearsals turned out to be as farcical as the plot. As this was the first time *Geneviève* had been put on in Britain and it was not under copyright, it had to be done in secrecy, with the cast being given fictitious names. The chorus girls kept fighting for the limelight, which in itself proved rather unreliable, theatres still being a few years off electrification and lit by gas. The light was 'fitful', in Emily's words, as it kept coming and going and fizzing, and then at the critical moments disappearing altogether with an alarming 'swish'. Farnie was not helping by constantly changing the chorus according to his casting couch activities:

A new and handsome girl received with enthusiasm and declared by him to be the exact thing for the part to-day, would frequently (after a private interview) be pronounced by the same authority on the morrow totally unfitted for the proposed position.

Then there was the dress rehearsal – a Continental invention and previously unknown on British shores. Emily was pleased when Farnie insisted they have one. In her experience the costume would only arrive on the day itself, resulting in all sorts of opening-night malfunctions – dresses too tight in the bust, too loose in the waist, shoes always damp and so small it made the artistes limp, or so long they tripped over the toes, actresses unable to turn on stage because a gaping hole in the back would be revealed, and buttons flying off if one breathed out too violently. Emily claimed in her memoir that, 'When the papers next morning noticed that the favourite artiste was "evidently handicapped by excessive nervousness," it would probably be an affair of hooks-and-eyes.'

Or perhaps this was a case of protesting too much? But Emily was soon wishing the dress rehearsal had stayed on the Continent:

Our dress rehearsal was the sort of thing you can remember for a long time – a tale of woe, of disaster, of profane language, of offensive and personal remarks, of bursting buttons, and lost and misapplied and 'impossible to recollect' lines, of wrong notes in the band parts.

The conductor, in a mood, climbed over the musicians and knocked down all the music stands, so that sheets of music went flying in the air and landed all jumbled together. The scenery fell down and a nervous 'Miss Somebody' forgot her cadenza and burst into tears as Farnie shouted expletives from the back of the theatre. Charles Morton, watching on, patted his necktie and whispered to Emily: 'There's nothing in it, simply nothing in it; utter failure. And as for your part, why you do nothing.'

Emily couldn't help but agree: 'No words can do justice to my depression.'

The second act was even worse. The music wasn't ready and the lighting made Emily's Rimmel make-up look hideous, at which point she developed a migraine. At the end of the rehearsal Farnie and Morton had a fight and then Farnie bid Emily goodbye after disrespecting everyone in the production, the management in particular.

> *[Next morning] at ten o'clock there came a messenger in hot haste, with a letter from Mr. Morton. A terrible thing had happened; Farnie had gone – fled - disappeared – packed his carpet-bag for parts unknown, leaving the disconsolate 'Geneviève' to her deserved and dreadful and disgraceful fate.*

With the migraine still whirling around, Emily went down to the theatre to find everything in confusion. With Farnie gone there was no one to manage the production, and he'd left no written stage directions. From 10.30 a.m. Emily had to work, plotting down instructions for everyone. By 7 p.m. she was feeling utterly hopeless:

> *I was sitting on the floor – no, on the green baize stage cloth – cross-legged like a Turk, cross-tempered like a Turk, tired to death, voiceless, hopeless, but going to 'try,' if I died for it, rehearsing in a whisper the 'Sleep Song.'*

According to theatrical superstition a bad dress rehearsal means a good performance. It has a certain logic to it – the performers are shaken out of any complacency and trying extra hard on the night. On this occasion the superstition held true.

The success of that night was a record-breaker. The enthusiasm, the applause, the crowded house! The piece went with a snap and 'vim.' Everybody recollected every word and made every point. The gaiety of the audience was infectious. Every line, every topical allusion was given with dash and received with shouts of laughter…. How Mr. Morton came on the stage and 'took it all back,' and congratulated and thanked and treated everybody. How a certain gentleman, named Clement Scott, sat in the front and was good to us, and wrote a half-column notice, which, appearing next morning in the Observer, made a certain singer famous as Drogan, and grateful for ever.

Clement Scott was, of course, the critic who had been so dismissive of Emily to the deaf reporter, John Plummer. In fact Plummer wrote that after watching the first performance:

Clement Scott was so excited that, forgetting his past incredulity, he gave a cabdriver half a sovereign and told him to drive like Hades to the Observer office in the Strand, near Somerset House, where he dashed off without stopping a moment, half a column of appreciative criticisms which set the theatrical world on fire, and made the name of Emily Soldene famous.

Here is just an extract of Scott's long review:

We question if a better imitation of the opera-bouffe of Paris has ever been given in London than the English version of Offenbach's Genevieve de Brabant played last night to an

116

audience literally wild with delight. It was no fancy success. The opera neatly condensed, charmingly sung, funnily interpreted and containing just that 'go' and ring which we have so often longed for and sighed for in vain.

Having read the good reviews, who should reappear a couple of days later but Henry Farnie, claiming that he knew all along it would be a great success despite the stupidity of the management. Professing shyness, Farnie had not allowed his name to be attached to any advance publicity, but now he lost his timidity and consented to appearing on the second round of publicity material. He also sat in a private box for the second performance and came on stage at the end and took a bow. Five months later Selina Dolaro gave birth to a baby girl and called her Genevieve.

Geneviève de Brabant ran for a year and a half and made the Philharmonic famous. Such was the excitement that every night liveried carriages lined both sides of Islington High Street and duchesses were content to sit in the stalls because there were no boxes left. In 1872 the Prince of Wales, the future Edward VII, went to a cattle show and saw a framed picture hung above a pen of prize pigs. He asked who it was and was told it was Emily Soldene dressed as Drogan, the pastry cook in *Geneviève* at the Phil. He asked where it was and was told it was near the Angel. 'A very good place indeed,' he replied. A couple of days later they were asked to prepare a royal box. Morton ordered a retiring room to be made and bought some of the highest-quality cigars to be placed in His Majesty's box. Apparently, the Prince of Wales was treated with the utmost consideration by the cast and the audience. But Emily's favourite visitor was Lord Dunraven:

Gay, bright, clever, full of life; and who after the opera would walk home with us, cut the cold beef, and open the oysters and stout with the unconventional facility of the man who has been everywhere, done everything, and who had (as he told us) found the most perfect form of happiness when lying on his back, kicking up his heels, and shouting at the top of his voice on the loftiest peak of the Rockies. Such a sportsman too.

Windham Thomas Wyndham-Quin was the fourth Earl of Dunraven and very much a man of his times. Educated at Oxford and finished off in the Life Guards, he owned a large patch of Ireland, fine racehorses, and was interested in Irish devolution. At the time Emily met him he had just taken his seat in the House of Lords and was a war correspondent for the *Daily Telegraph*. He was sent to Abyssinia and then the Franco-Prussian War, at the end of which he witnessed the signing of the Treaty of Versailles (he also saw the second Treaty of Versailles after the Great War in 1919). He went on to be the Under-Secretary of State for the Colonies in successive Conservative governments, fight in the Boer War and come back decorated as a hero. He also had a wife and three daughters back in Ireland. He built boats and sailed several times in the America's Cup. But Lord Dunraven's real passion was big-game hunting. In 1874 (the year before Emily's debut on Broadway) he bought 15,000 acres of the Rockies in Colorado and set up a game park.

Lord Dunraven was handsome with big brown eyes,

fecund Victorian side whiskers, and a fine moustache which suited him. No wonder Emily had a soft spot – he could tell her about all the parts of the world which she longed to see. He also had the means to give her the money to buy the licence for the Lyceum. One might have thought that Lord Dunraven was far too busy being fabulous in a colonising big game sort of way to hang out with showgirls, but apparently not. There is a certain kind of man who can run an enormous variety of things and yet still find the time and energy to pursue extracurricular activities with exciting women who are not their wives. Lord Dunraven was one of these. Despite his many commitments he found time to take trips to the seaside:

> *Dear old Margate – and my mind goes back to dear old times when everyone and everything was gay and the gayest thing in my mind was Lord Dunraven – just back from occidental and outlandish parts – pacing the terrace, and keeping the sun off with a white cotton umbrella, lined with green. People – especially men – didn't walk about in England in those days with white umbrellas – lined with green too. That's nice for one's complexion . . .*

Of course, there is no mention of husband Jack on any of these jaunts. And yet at some point Lord Dunraven was to disappoint Emily, because many years later she wrote in one of her columns:

> *Lord Dunraven, the devolutionist, has written a new book, 'The Outlook in Ireland.' Lord Dunraven is an old hand. Thirty years ago he wrote of Irish emigration, and is always*

of a pretty wit: 'I suppose Parnell died of a broken heart,'
said an American visitor lately to Lord Dunraven. 'Ah, that
is what all Irishmen die of,' was the instant reply. Thirty-one
years ago, his lordship assured me that his heart was broken.
So, you see, Irishmen cannot only die of a broken heart –
they can live with one.

However, when *Geneviève de Brabant* was playing at the
Philharmonic, Lord Dunraven had yet to disappoint her
and, along with a whole coterie of the most fashionable and
interesting young men of the time, was paying her lots of
attention. To hold the fascination of a man as urbane and
accomplished as Lord Dunraven can only have added to
Emily's sense that her star was rising. Emily said that *Geneviève
de Brabant* 'was the sort of success that waits upon one once in
a lifetime'. Perhaps that sort of success, that goes against the
odds and has overcome many difficulties, gives the confidence,
the feeling of invincibility, needed to take the next leap.

Another landmark moment in Emily's rise was her day in
court.

The financial backer of the Philharmonic, Charles Head,
and the manager, Charles Morton, did not like each other
very much. They probably shouldn't have gone into business
together, because even though the Phil was proving to be an
excellent investment for both of them, it wasn't long before
their antipathy began to unravel their business arrangement
rather spectacularly; and as the director and leading lady,
Emily found herself right in the middle.

Charles Head had originally agreed to financially back

the new Philharmonic for three years, on condition that he remained anonymous. But, with *Geneviève de Brabant*'s unexpected triumph, Head started to become visible and involved, hanging around the bar, taking bows on stage, hosting dinners and making speeches trumpeting the Phil's (and his) success. Then he started to invite himself to management meetings, and worse, come backstage and harass Emily, criticising her direction. How much he would have felt able to do this had she been a man, we can only conjecture. When Emily complained to Morton, he backed Emily fully, telling Head that he was not to 'interfere with Miss Soldene or any of my people' and the theatre staff were to restrain Head if he went anywhere near her, which suggests Head must have been quite threatening. Head was furious and stormed down to the bar where he shouted insults, calling Morton a 'bloody scoundrel' and saying, 'he's indebted to me for everything he possesses, but I'll ruin him before I've done with him!' From then on, he propped up the bar and shouted similar abuses night after night.

In the meantime, Morton decided to capitalise on *Geneviève*'s success and booked Emily for a set of matinee performances at the Gaiety Theatre in the West End. Emily refused to do two performances in one day, claiming a weakness in the throat, which meant that the part of Drogan had to be played by a lesser star for six weeks at the Philharmonic. Head immediately served Morton with a lawsuit for breach of contract, claiming that Emily was an integral part of the deal. The judge threw this out of court, accepting Morton's argument that to have Emily playing at the Gaiety was great publicity for the Philharmonic and could only increase their audiences. Then Morton decided to take *Geneviève* on tour. In order to get around his contract with Head, Morton did not own the touring company but gave it to a shadowy architect from Peterborough named Mr King. Head went straight back to court to try and stop the tour, but again the judge threw out his claim and made him pay all costs.

Head was not a man to accept defeat gracefully. Instead he hosted a grand dinner party at the Albion Hotel in Great Russell Street, to which he invited his most heady acquaintances in the arts world, the chairman being no less than Charles Dickens himself. The meal started with Dickens making a humorous introductory speech explaining why they had been gathered. Then Head followed with a statement detailing the course of his business relations with Morton and how he had been mistreated. He was greeted with repeated cheers. Then letters of support for Head were read out, before this resolution was unanimously passed: 'That this meeting having heard the straightforward statement of Mr. Charles Head, desires to express its warmest sympathy with him in the circumstances in which he has been placed.'

A full account of the evening was then passed to the press and Head printed out several hundred pamphlets of his speech, which were sent out to everyone who mattered in the world of theatre.

Charles Morton wasted no time in suing Charles Head for libel and slander.

The case came to court at the Guildhall on 18th February 1873. It caused quite a stir. The barmaid was called to repeat Head's insults, a ticket taker was called to confirm he had been sent out to deliver the pamphlets. Charles Morton provided evidence that Head had actually been complicit in Emily being lent to the Gaiety. However, he did admit that he had transferred ownership to Mr King to prevent Head from stopping the tour. Interestingly, when Morton was asked why, if Mr King owned the company, he had not been to visit it, Morton said that Mr King didn't need to – Emily, 'a good woman of business herself', had been in charge.

Then the main witness for the prosecution, Emily, was called. 'I had a new black velvet cloak trimmed with chinchilla,' she describes, 'and went to the box very satisfied with myself. The counsel argued pro and con.'

Morton had hired one of the Phil's repeat visitors to be his barrister, the dashing QC Sergeant Ballantine, who had even larger whiskers than Lord Dunraven. This must have put Emily at ease. Years later she wrote in one of her newspaper columns:

Sergeant Ballantine was one of my oldest – may I say – admirers. He gave a great supper in my honour at the Freemason's Tavern, Great Queen Street. It was the autumn season, the house sitting, and when it ended no end of MPs trooped into the banquet. I remember the thing that fixed me most was – the large quantity of asparagus (lovely) at that time of year.

Ballantine asked Emily about the merits of touring: 'It is very desirable to go into the provinces during the summer and the autumn as it advertises the Theatre, and provincials come up to renew their acquaintance . . .' This seemed to amuse the onlookers because there was the sound of laughter rippling through the court. Then he asked her about her absence from the Philharmonic.

I bear the principal part in the piece which is very heavy and I played from December 1870 to May 1872 with only three week's intervals. I became ill in May, being very nervous, and at one place in the opera I always felt that I should break down. My doctor told me to leave off playing some time before I did . . . Indeed I'm very nervous now

To which the naughty Ballantine said: 'That is from so many gentlemen looking at you.'

Of course, Emily may have been telling the truth about her nervous exhaustion. Today she might be diagnosed as having chronic anxiety and given some medication to take the edge off this constant private hell she seemed to go through.

Emily's moment in court ended with a pivotal question:

The judge turned to me, standing patiently in the box. "And what do you think, Miss Soldene?" said he. I said I thought the performance given with such success by the Philharmonic Company at a first-class West-end house like the Gaiety was calculated to give an esprit to the Philharmonic. Verdict for Mr. Morton. Mr. Fred Stanley, Mr. Morton's solicitor, thought I was a very first-class witness indeed.

Revenge is a dish best served cold. Head lost the case and had to pay Morton £200 and costs. The next night the theatrical newspaper, *The Era*, reported that Emily was on particularly good form: 'that lady exerted herself with even more than her accustomed success . . . Miss Soldene has rarely been heard to greater advantage, being in good voice and acting with her usual dash and animation.'

In the three years since Emily had taken on the role of director as well as leading lady, she had proved to herself and the world that her show business instincts were good, that she could produce a theatrical hit against the odds with little help from anyone else, and that she could take a big company on tour, managing it in all but name. She had been through a legal process and inflicted a defeat on a powerful enemy. She had also built up a fine following of influential fans and she now had her sister, Clara, at her side at all times. She was ready to take on management at her own risk.

Emily decided to open at the Lyceum with *La Grande-Duchesse*, with herself in the lead role, an appropriate part for a lady who was absolute ruler of her theatrical domain. Clara was given the second lead role of the saucy peasant Wanda, who steals the Duchess's love interest Fritz. It meant that two sisters were fighting over one handsome young man. It was a huge success. This is what *The Era* had to say:

> *Nothing could have gone better with the audience than The Grand Duchess, from the first note of the 'Sabre Song' in the overture to the finale, and the encores were so numerous that it was midnight ere the curtain fell.*

Emily was thoroughly enjoying being in charge of her domain. When she went on to produce another opéra bouffe, this time

La fille de Madame Angot by Charles Lecocq, and put the now 'hot' Selina Dolaro in the role of Clairette, she lost no time in advertising this fact to the papers.

> *Miss Emily Soldene has much pleasure in announcing she*
> *has secured the valuable assistance of*
> *Mme. Selina Dolaro*
> *Who will appear in her original character of Clairette in*
> *'Mme. Angot.'*

However, Emily decided that, never mind the plot, she was going to keep the best tunes for herself:

The concluding verse of the Opera belongs to Clairette, and she ought to sing it. But I, having the might instead of the right, I suppose, had always appropriated it to myself, and brought down the curtain with me in the centre of the stage en tableau, as is the wont of prime donne in power to do on every possible occasion.

Selina and Emily were old friends, going back to the days of the Oxford Music Hall, and both had come up in the world, but when Selina came to rehearse and found that Emily had stolen her best song, she refused to go on unless it was reinstated. 'Of course she was perfectly right,' says Emily, 'and, as for me, I can only say "mea culpa".'

If Emily had behaved badly at least she owned it, and in print too. But she didn't back down. Instead, Emily upped the stakes by taking out another advertisement the next day:

Miss Emily Soldene begs to announce that in consequence of
a misunderstanding

Mme. Selina Dolaro
will not appear in her original character of
CLAIRETTE
in
'Mme. Angot'

It worked.

That afternoon a neat little coupe bowled up to the Lyceum stage door, a neat little tiger threw open the carriage door, and a neat little lady stepped into the theatre and made a neat little speech, and 'was so sorry to upset the arrangements', and next morning the 'ad.' said:

Miss Emily Soldene has much pleasure in announcing that,
the misunderstanding having been arranged,
Mme. Selina Dolaro
will appear in her original character of
CLAIRETTE
in
'Mme. Angot'

Selina Dolaro might have been the bigger star, but ultimately power lay with the owner of the means of production. Dolaro learnt quickly and with months had left Emily and was taking her own touring company around Britain.

Meanwhile, Emily had tasted power and, like her food, she had found an appetite for it. And so, when she was approached by the promoters Grau and Chizzola, and offered a tour of the States starting in Broadway, she jumped at it.

CHILPÉRIC

OPERA BOUFFE IN 3 ACTS.

By HERVÉ.

ADAPTED TO THE ENGLISH STAGE FOR

MISS EMILY SOLDENE

AND HER

ENGLISH OPERA BOUFFE COMPANY.

First performed at the LYCEUM THEATRE, New York, Dec. 9, 1874.

UNDER THE MANAGEMENT OF

Messrs. MAURICE GRAU and C. A. CHIZZOLA.

NEW YORK:

METROPOLITAN PRINTING AND ENGRAVING ESTABLISHMENT
HERALD BUILDING, BROADWAY AND ANN STREET.

1874

Emily launches her biggest hits in America

Chapter Seven

THE LAND OF THE FREE

Liberty (noun): The freedom to live as you wish or go where you want
(*Cambridge Dictionary*)

As Emily now heads off west across the Atlantic Ocean to America, you might be wondering what has happened to her four children, if you haven't forgotten that they exist at all. It's easily done. They are scarcely mentioned in her memoir and they certainly don't seem to intrude into her very full theatrical life (neither does her husband Jack, of course).

She didn't take them to America. On the Celtic ocean liner with Emily were Clara, Charles Morton who was managing the tour, and, according to the passenger lists, husband Jack. He may have been on the boat, but Emily shared the captain's cabin with Clara – and then of course she does let slip that she was sharing a bed with her sister during Clara's insomnia moment in New York.

The Soldene Powell children – Katie now sixteen, Nell

fifteen, Edward thirteen and John ten – were left with Priscilla and a couple of Hertfordshire servant girls. They were living in a house that Jack Powell had bought in the new suburb of Staines to the west of London. Emily, of course, could not purchase a house in her own name. Priscilla's husband, Edward Soldene, had died in 1871 in the home of his first family. His other widow recorded his death. Presumably Priscilla wasn't left anything in his will. This meant that from now on Priscilla was at Emily's disposal, with her own child, Clara, being cared for by Emily.

Priscilla was to live in the substantial house in Staines and then in either Emily or Clara's family homes for the rest of her life, financially taken care of by her daughters – no doubt earning it in trying to keep the four little Soldene Powells out of mischief, while their mum travelled around the globe being fabulous and famous. In the context of the time though, there were worse fates for Priscilla. With no pensions or state healthcare, many working-class people would have been unable to earn enough money to put away any savings for their old age, and would have had to rely on their children or extended family to support them. Many finished their lives in the workhouse. This sense of duty towards family members, whether you liked them or not, was more acute in the nineteenth century; probably because if your family didn't look after you, no one else would. Emily had given her mother a level of financial security for the rest of her life that many would envy. But in this she was just doing what would have been expected of her. Not to have done so, according to Victorian standards, would have been tantamount to wickedness.

But responsibilities went the other way too. It seems to have been something of a Swain family tradition for maternal grandmothers to bring up their grandchildren. Emily seems to have been largely brought up by her grandmother, Katie Swain. There is also a good chance that Priscilla had been brought up by her maternal grandmother too. While her roguish husband, Charles Swain, fought through several Canadian winters, Katie returned to her home village and it's probable that Grannie minded baby Priscilla, while Katie earnt her living. I know that in my own branch of the Swain family, grandmothers continued to look after their daughters' children while mothers went out to work, only stopping with my mother's generation in the 1960s and 1970s, as if childcare kept skipping a generation out of necessity.

Of course, by twenty-first-century parenting standards, leaving four children to go on a perilous journey, for an unknown length of time with practically no means of communication, might be seen as a case for putting in a call to social services. But a mother's job description was very different in the nineteenth century; indeed the whole idea of 'parenting' only came into being in the 1970s. It took first Freud's theories, and then later mother–infant observations from the 1960s onwards, for the importance of the parent–child relationship in the development of the human psyche to be established. It was only when the state and household machinery took over traditional mothering responsibilities that mothers had the time and were expected to invest their energy into building a relationship with their child – a novel concept.

Victorian children could be sent to work down mines, and brought up by nannies and sent away to boarding schools, and beaten to within an inch of their lives, and that was completely acceptable to most people. Instead of childcare, in the nineteenth century a mother's job was to organise the household. For a working-class woman this meant doing whatever it took to keep everyone alive – finding and cooking food, sorting the clothes, negotiating the rent, keeping the family clean, caring for them when they were sick, and of course doing the household chores, all the while very often pregnant or nursing a newborn. A mother usually would have to contribute to the family purse by doing paid work of some kind too. In return for being brought into the world and kept alive, the children would be expected to start contributing to the family income as soon as possible, and then support the parents when they became infirm and old. That was the deal. Parenting was, in a way, turned on its head. For a middle-class woman, all of the above applied, except she didn't do much of it herself – she just had the responsibility for organising others to do it, and she would not be expected (or allowed) to take on paid employment in any form. Middle-class children likewise, except they wouldn't be expected to contribute to the family coffers as soon as physically possible either.

In this sense, Emily was doing perfectly well in her mothering as well as her daughtering role. She had taken herself and her family firmly into the middle-class bracket by earning a substantial wage and had purchased everything that her children needed to survive and thrive.

Another factor to take into account when considering Emily's particular maternal style was the nature of the profession she had chosen. You could be a mother and an actress, but you didn't advertise it. In fact, you carried on as if the children weren't there. Emily was not alone in largely omitting them from her memoirs. The Victorian actress Adelaide Calvert in her memoir says that the early years of her marriage were punctuated by six 'domestic incidents', as if having children was as easy as buying a new bonnet. Yet accommodating a pregnancy and the demands of a new baby must have played havoc with life on the stage – the daytime rehearsals, the night-time performances, the need to be sexually irresistible, not to mention the demands of touring. The acting profession did not lend itself to being a hands-on mother. Performers were expected to rehearse for four hours in the morning, and then be in the theatre for five or more hours in the evening. If they were late, missed a rehearsal or fell sick they were not paid. They often had to make and maintain their own costumes and provide and do their own make-up. Lodgings on tour were often over shops and beds had to be shared. Meals were whatever the landlady provided, or sandwiches and cakes they could carry with them, or cold meat, bread and ale bought at railway junctions. The Victorian actress Catherine Holbrook wrote in her diary:

An actress can never make her children comfortable; ill, or well, even while suckling at the breast, the poor infants, when the Theatre calls, must be left to the care of some sour old woman, who shakes or scolds them into fits: or a careless wench, out of whose clutches, if they are freed without broken or dislocated bones, 'tis wonderful. The mother returning with harassed frame and agitated mind, from the various passions she has been pourtraying [sic], instead of imparting healthful nourishment to her child, fills it with bile and fever, to say nothing of dragging them long journies [sic], at all seasons of the year, all hours of the night, and through every inclemency of weather, frequently on the outside of coaches, in open chairs, etc.

Emily's theatrical and financial success had bought her a kind of freedom. Because she wasn't expected to have a relationship with her children, she didn't have to physically spend much time with them. With the children in a proper home and her mother in charge, as long as the money kept rolling in Emily was free to roam, actually freer than most mothers in the twenty-first century. And what better place for Emily to go than America?

In the days when their home-grown theatrical productions had yet to take off, Americans were still looking to the Old World for much of their culture. This was all to turn on its head in the 1890s with a sudden flowering of native productions on Broadway and then the advent of film. But for successful British productions in 1874, America was like a rather ambitious extension of the provincial tour. New York was a final destination for the brave. Emily had also been brought up on her grandfather and great-grandfather Swain's tales of derring-do in the wars stateside, and with impresario Pony Moore saying that she'd 'knock 'em dead' in New York, and more recently Lord Dunraven's endless tales of the beauty and opportunity of the New World, it was only natural that she'd be keen to see America for herself.

In this, Emily was following in the footsteps of many other British travellers, including her father-in-law's great friend, Charles Dickens. There had long been a tradition among the upper classes to broaden their horizons by undertaking a Grand Tour through Europe, but more recently people had been going to America as well, especially the middle classes. It was seen as an alternative, more avant-garde trip. There were also lots of potential investment opportunities. America's population and economy were expanding on a scale unknown in history and they needed capital and expertise for their industrial revolution. The Old World and Britain in particular were the source of this capital. Many potential British investors came out to prospect. But there was also a curiosity about how the former colony was doing. A hundred years after the War of Independence, and less than ten years after the end of the American Civil War, America was now a united continent. There was an inquisitiveness about this peculiar wayward sibling, with its 'all men being born equal' constitution, and tales of pioneers, gold rushes, cowboys and slaves. The Victorians were great travellers. They approached their forays into the more developed civilisations with the same fact-finding anthropological mentality as they did the jungle. Some of these travellers wrote books about their findings and gave talks to worthy societies when they got home.

Emily approached her American trip with the same anthropological eye. She endeavours to inform her readers and paint a picture:

> The first thing that struck me on landing was the delightful air – brisk, sharp, exhilarating, invigorating. The second thing that struck me (badly, too) was the roads, made of big stones and bigger holes . . . the passengers had to be strapped to the seats to keep them from being hurled out like bolts from a catapult.

Emily was an urban creature, well used to cities. Not only had she spent her years since Clara's birth in London, exploring the streets with an ever-curious eye and then going backwards and forwards across the city to theatres in broughams, she had also travelled to all the major British cities on tour. She had travelled to Paris too. New York, however, was already a phenomenon all of its own. It was the largest city in the Western Hemisphere. As New York was the main US port and trading capital, and the entry point for people emigrating to the US, Emily must have been struck by the sheer volume of different nationalities and languages that she encountered – Irish, German, Italian, Chinese, on a scale that would make traditionally cosmopolitan London seem parochial. There were thousands of two- to four-storey brownstone homes, on streets using a strict grid pattern. New York, quick to embrace the inventions of the Industrial Revolution, had elevated railways and lights lit by Edison's new electric lightbulb (although as she sailed into New York in 1874, Emily wouldn't have seen the Statue of Liberty – that didn't arrive until 1886). Broadway was the main thoroughfare with grand hotels and restaurants catering for the very rich, and Fifth Avenue was full of palaces built by robber barons. Early British traveller Lady Emmeline Stuart-Wortley talked of 'the cosmopolitism of her citizens . . . the heterogenous compounds, and the kaleidoscopical varieties presented at every turn.'

But despite this, New York was less openly a city of dreadful delights than London. The Christian evangelical movement of the 1850s had had an effect. There was a stronger culture of morality, piety and respectability, at least on the surface. Now Emily had arrived, New York wasn't going to know what had hit it. The first target of Emily's observations were the women:

The American lady of 1874 was of an entirely different physique to the American lady of 1896. She was fragile, more than fragile, painfully thin, with tiny hands carried affectedly in front of her (like the performing poodle carries his fore paws when travelling on his hind legs), tiny feet, flat feet, and no instep. She was made up to an alarming extent, not only her face but her figure. Those were the days of the Princesse robe, and the New York elegante, a thin, wiry, contourless being, by the aid of a wash-leather combination, padded and shaped from the neck to the ankle, appeared a thing of beauty, if not a joy for ever. The ladies of New York were aristocratic in features, delicate and refined, with beautiful eyes, fine hair, fine teeth (when not their own). They wore diamonds at the breakfast table, and cut through the vast space of the hotel dining-room with elevated, thin, nasal, metallic voices, that made one's skin creep. They lived on huge under-done 'porterhouse' steaks, roast beef 'rare,' ice-creams, iced water, candies, hot cakes, and molasses. They never drank anything strong, except in the seclusion of their sleeping apartments, and then, with the intelligence of the ostrich, they stood the empty bottles outside the door. They were always chilly, passing their days in rocking chairs, with their feet well up to the stove, and could not venture into the overheated corridors of the hotel without a small shawl over their shivering shoulders. They had a bad habit of looking strange people over from head to foot, and back again, and making audible remarks. 'Mais nous avons change tout cela,' and now there is no more delightful person on earth, than the plump and athletic, swimming, boating, batting, golfing, riding, climbing, bykeing, tailor-clad, trainant-voiced, cultivated, cultured, American lady of to-day. In making these remarks after this long period of time, I am justified. These ladies in those days used to call us beefy Britishers. Of course, at the time we could not retaliate, but some women can wait.

It seems the obsession with women's size was alive and well long before the twenty-first century. Emily's musings sound like she's filing a gossipy report. Being an actress gave Emily more liberty to speak, and she did – it was almost as though she was setting out her stall for a career as a columnist.

Publicity was crucial, particularly when you were new in town, and it was as necessary to be seen offstage as it was on the stage. Emily made sure that as soon as she arrived in New York, she was seen at the most important venues. Clara may have been dying of insomnia in their Fifth Avenue Hotel, but Emily made sure that her first meal was at one of New York's finest restaurants, Delmonico's. The first ever French brasserie-style restaurant in New York, it had imported the latest in Parisian dining and was considered the most stylish eating venue in the city. Emily helped herself to oysters and champagne. She had also cleverly managed to arrive in New York in time for one of the biggest theatrical events of the decade, if not the whole century – the farewell appearance of the greatest American actress of her generation, Miss Charlotte Cushman.

Cushman had had a singular career and lifestyle. She had become a singer at the age of fourteen when her father died, leaving her large family of six siblings and a mother penniless. She was immediately noticed, having a spectacularly low contralto voice, an Amazonian frame, a square jaw and a commanding presence. Unfortunately, she was only seventeen when she lost this voice overusing it in a performance in New Orleans.

Cushman was persuaded to become an actress instead, and she was even more successful, specialising in the tragic. She went on to become the first female theatre manager in the US, taking over the oldest theatre in the country, the Walnut Street Theatre in Philadelphia, in 1842. Like Emily, Cushman specialised in playing men and brought her little sister in to play the heroine roles opposite her. Perhaps it was Cushman who had given Emily the idea. She toured Europe in the 1850s. Her *Romeo and Juliet*, with herself and her sister playing the roles respectively, was a special sensation. Cushman then stopped in Rome and set up a feminist arts colony, with the most famous female writers and sculptors of the time coming to stay. Her sojourn ended tragically when she was diagnosed with breast cancer and returned to America in 1871 to live out her last days at home. Cushman was openly lesbian, polyamorous and fiercely independent; she wore masculine clothes and had a speaking voice as deep as her singing voice. Somehow, she got away with it, perhaps because many people in the nineteenth century didn't realise that women could be sexually attracted to other women – including Queen Victoria, who famously said 'women do not do that sort of thing'.

Emily was well aware of Cushman. Her teacher, Howard Glover, had seen Cushman in her star Romeo role in London and had rhapsodised about her unparalleled fabulousness on many occasions. Perhaps there had been too many occasions for Emily's liking; there was obviously no way that Emily was going to miss Cushman's farewell appearance.

In a country without royalty, Cushman was a good substitute, and the evening kicked off with a parade through the centre of New York, with flowers, flags, bands, bells ringing and cannons firing. All the city's great citizens were there. It was billed as the most spectacular farewell in the history of American theatre. Emily thought otherwise:

I am afraid I was disappointed. I suppose I had expected too much; but anyway, she looked and was a very dreadful old woman indeed. After the performance, Miss Cushman received the Profession on stage, and took leave of the public. What a scene! The vast theatre was crammed; every box was decorated with flags (American), palms and flowers. The people raved and roared themselves hoarse. The band played 'Hail, Columbia,' and the whole audience stood up and sang it. All the ladies of the New York Theatres carried baskets of flowers, which they laid at the feet of this idol for many years. Everybody was trembling, shaking with emotion, tears were plentiful, and in that vast assembly there was but one person unshaken, unmoved – that one was Charlotte Cushman. She walked down the centre of the stage, down the flower-strewn path – an imposing, majestic figure – clad in a plain dark dress, with plain collar and cuffs, her grey hair drawn back in plain bands. She stood firm, composed, not a tremor. 'Ladies, gentleman, and the public,' said she; then, going close to the footlights, extended her right hand, and clenching it tightly as if holding something very precious, her eyes blazed out with the triumph of possession, and in a tone the exultation of which it is impossible to convey in words, she said, 'My Public,' 'My Public!'

Was Emily just a little bit jealous? She was certainly brave, risking the wrath of any American by criticising Miss Charlotte Cushman.

Luckily, the American public seemed to be almost as enamoured of the new British import as they were of their home-grown national treasure. Emily says that in spite of their 'beefiness', the Soldene girls caught on:

Soon everything 'Soldene' was the rage: 'Soldene' shoes, 'Soldene' stockings, 'Soldene' hats, 'Soldene' gloves, 'Soldene' fans, 'Soldene' coiffure. But the greatest sensation was the 'Soldene' girl. Never had been seen such girls, real girls, with fine limbs, complexions nearly all their own, beautiful creamy (Maintenon) white skins, figures perfect, gay, bright, healthy, laughing girls, blonde girls, blonde girls with blue eyes, with demure dreamy grey eyes, soft brown eyes, bright hazel eyes, but they all had black lashes. Then their hair, wonderful hair, running the professional long-haired sisters very closely indeed – yellow, flaxen, red, bronzy, long, wavy, crispy, curling and rippling. I don't think the colour of the hair was warranted, and I don't think people expected it. 'The Boys' simply went crazy over this crowd of imported loveliness.

On 14th November Clara, now recovered from her near-fatal insomnia, joined the cast as the cheeky page, Oswald. Her reviews were favourable. She was described in the press as 'brunette, petite in form, quite pretty, and acts with much archness and vivacity'. The fans followed.

One day a gentleman called at the hotel. I informed him that he could not see Clara: she was out. Presently he electrified me. 'How long has your sister been on the street?'

said he. Then a charming person was introduced to us, a Colonel Somebody. He made several calls, had a box at the theatre, and sent flowers &c., and he was an exceedingly nice man. After a few days the 'Colonel' came to say 'goodbye.' 'Would we allow him to send us each a little present as a remembrance of a very pleasant time?' We were 'delighted.' In due course the present arrived; two boxes full of 'collars,' 'cuffs,' and 'dickeys.' Our Colonel was a wholesale collar manufacturer of Troy, N.Y.

In America all men might be born equal, but as in the Old World, there was a distinct hierarchical social system, less based on birth and more on money, but still very much in existence. The richest Americans were very much preoccupied with social prominence and extravagant displays of their wealth. They lived a life of luxury, easily matching the European aristocracy with their exclusive clubs, private concerts, dinners in the city, receptions, balls, and holidays on Long Island. There was a very definite New York season, and the Soldene sisters were only too happy to join in:

New Year's Day used to be great business in New York. All the ladies stayed in and received the gentlemen; everybody went everywhere, and everybody was 'so glad' to see them. On the big tables stood bowls of punch, cake, sandwiches, pie and fruit of all kinds. All the men one knew brought all the men they knew, and people got pretty lively by the evening. I received of course.

The Soldenes were so popular that Grau and Chizzola sensed an opportunity and threw a grand ball in their honour at the Academy of Music. Tickets were selling at $5 each, the equivalent of $120 today. They made over $5,000 that night or $120,000 in today's money. Emily met a well-known actor there called Mr Charles Thorne, 'a handsome man, a charming artist, and an impertinent person, but his was an impertinence that could be forgiven'. What she doesn't say is that the party got so rowdy that the police had to be called. It made the *New York Times*. After commenting on the remarkable preponderance of men, it reported:

About 1.30 o'clock the wine began to take effect. It manifested itself during a lancers. A ring of men was formed in the middle of the floor, and four couples began to dance the can-can in the centre. They had hardly got under way, however, when the committee followed by the Police, broke through the ring and dispersed the crowd. In a few minutes another ring formed, the dancers this time being a tall youth of much agility of limb and a woman in a short dress of blue silk with black velvet stripes and a red apron. They danced for some minutes. The lady threw her leg several times the height of the gentleman's nose, and afterwards kicked a silk hat off his head with apparent ease three times. She was roundly applauded. The police again interfered, and the disgraceful exhibition was broken up. Capt Gunner collared the man dancer and hustled him off the platform amid the hisses of the spectators.

In the end Emily's trip to New York turned out to be almost everything she could have wished for. She now set off for a grand tour across the States, hoping to repeat her success. Her travel log reads like a brilliant road trip with all the attending highs and lows, but it must have been even more astonishing for the sisters considering that they had had no access to even pictures of these places before they went; all they would have had as preparation were a few eyewitness accounts from the likes of Lord Dunraven.

Here are some of Emily's highlights:

In Philadelphia Emily got pneumonia and, when Charles Morton was sent to find a physician, all the doctors refused to treat a lady of the theatre. However, for the first time Clara was allowed to step in to replace Emily as the leading lady.

In Boston they pulled in the largest audiences that the Globe Theatre had ever seen. Harvard students poured in every night and were rusticated by the university for sending barrels of beer to the Green Room.

In Washington they played at the Ford's Theatre where Abraham Lincoln had been shot.

In Baltimore Emily delighted in tucking into the kind of oysters Charles Dickens had enjoyed (he had told her they were as big as babies), and very much appreciated her first taste of chicken Maryland.

In Buffalo they visited the Niagara Falls. It was absolutely freezing, an ice bridge had formed over the river, there was a hundred-foot ice mountain, the spray froze as it flew, and there were hundreds of tiny rainbows and icicles glistening like diamonds hanging from the trees. They drove across the border into Canada, drank lots of cheap brandy and soda, and sang God Save the Queen, probably to keep warm.

In Cincinnati the rats were as big as cats and filled the gutters squealing.

In Chicago one of the chorus girls poisoned herself and had to have her stomach pumped, for love of the male lead.

Emily and Clara amused themselves by visiting the museum and taking a look at the Fat Lady, the Living Skeleton, the man who fasted for a fortnight, the man who ate two quails a night for a month, the boy who lived on nails (ten-penny ones preferred), a Mormon with his six wives, and two Aztec young men who according to Emily were harassed by women kissing them.

In St Louis the programme seller got his ears boxed for staring at the Soldene girls, and Emily was so ill with a fever and an inflammation of the soft bones of her head that when it was time to leave and head south, she had to be carried onto the train.

From the train they saw cowboys riding along the plains lassoing live cattle and, there being no dining car, had to fry sausages and make tea on spluttering little alcohol stoves, which occasioned much 'unparliamentary' language. Within twenty-four hours they were surrounded by flowering peach trees, summer sun and roses; and at night, the call of the bullfrog and fireflies.

In Houston they were given a breakfast of steak as thick as a boot's sole and just as tough. Emily appreciated the aesthetics of the loafing Texan men, 'tall, nearly too tall, with long legs, graceful figures, dark blue eyes, black hair, and big slouch hats – sombreros, I suppose'.

In Galveston they stared at the ocean and marvelled at the warm breeze, very different to the promenade at Margate. Emily was so superstitious about the number thirteen that the theatre manager painted a fourteen on the door of her hotel room, and the theatre was so dilapidated that nettles blocked the stage door. The reviews were not great either: 'The Press, rather chaste and faddy, found us "improper," which we were not; also "beefy," which perhaps we were; everybody can't be as fat as a stoat nailed on a barn door.'

But still the theatre was full every night, and when it was time to leave the whole town processed to the harbour to see them off, the brass band playing 'God Save the Queen' very badly.

One of the fans that came to the show in Galveston was the famous fighting sheriff of Texas, Tom Ochiltree. Colonel Tom was a legend, not just in the States, but across the Western world. He was a red-headed son of a Texan judge, who had trained as a lawyer, then worked as a journalist, and then become a soldier, fighting against the Apache and Comanche tribes. He went into politics and then rushed off to join the Confederate Army, earning several decorations for his courageous/foolhardy antics during the Civil War. At the end of the war, Colonel Tom went into exile in Europe, but lasted only ten months, before he came back and settled in New York, working as a reporter for the *New York Times* and becoming friends with his former enemies – as Emily says, 'now a New York Dude'. Later on, there would be a hit Broadway musical based on his life called *Colonel Tom*. He travelled the world promoting Texas, and entertaining Bismarck, Napoleon, Clemenceau, Gladstone and Disraeli. When Colonel Tom met the Prince of Wales, he famously slapped him on the back and said, 'Wales, let us have a drink', and then shocked Queen Victoria by performing the Civil War marching song 'John Brown's Body' – which had risqué lyrics, but may also have had more interesting private connotations for her Majesty. It's no surprise that Emily enjoyed his company: 'He told us stories, and everybody knows what steep stories Tom Ochiltree can tell.'

Judging by Emily's account of this trip, she seemed to have an extraordinary amount of fun. She had escaped any of the obligations of motherhood; as the director and leading lady she had a great deal of agency, and yet she had taken none of the financial responsibility or risk for this tour. Charles Morton had done that. She did have her husband Jack with her, but his presence didn't seem to curtail any of her mingling opportunities. Clara, too, very definitely finally away from her mother, and now much more established as an artist in her own right, was still single, and could openly take advantage of the opportunities available for a young, attractive actress on tour.

One of the great differences between America and Britain in 1874 was that America was still recovering from a violent civil war, while Britain had had over two centuries of relatively stable government, to the extent that it was able to turn its attention elsewhere, fighting wars and subjugating large swathes of the globe. America's civil war had ended nine years before, but such was the division and devastation that the wounds were still there to be seen, and none was more obvious than the state of race relations. The 13th Amendment passed in January 1865 had proclaimed that all slaves were free, and America was now in the Reconstruction era – an effort to reintegrate the southern states with the north and the four million newly freed slaves into society. However, the southern states had their own ideas about what this meant and had brought in repressive Black Codes to restrict the freedoms of African Americans. By 1874 tensions were rising as the South slumped into economic depression.

Of all the issues that preoccupied British visitors to the States, the position of African Americans was of the greatest interest. Most of the Britons expressed some dismay and shock at the state of race relations they found there. It was less than a hundred years since slavery had been abolished in Britain and less than fifty since it had been abolished in the rest of the British Empire, and yet the British reporters were already looking at the issue as if Britain's part in the slave trade had never happened. Knowing the interest of her audience in race relations, Emily reports back:

I asked a bright-eyed black and laughing wench which she liked the best, these times or the old ones. She showed all her white teeth an' guessed 'she like the de ole times best – berry nasty missie, but berry nice massa.'

The Soldene Opera Company got caught in the middle of the tensions:

When we got to Louisville, the law conferring on coloured people equal rights with white people had just come into operation. Previously to this, no coloured person could ride in the same car or eat in the same restaurant with a white person; no coloured person could take a room in any hotel. In the theatre coloured people had to sit in the place (a top gallery) set apart for them. All this was now to be changed, and white Louisville was in a ferment of fury and rage.

148

*Dreadful trouble was expected. There was a rumour that
some coloured men were coming into the 'Parquet' (stalls),
and the white gentlemen swore that if they did they'd shoot
them 'on sight'. The trouble came one evening – I was on
the stage – two fine-looking, well-built, coloured men in
evening dress walked down the aisle, when up rose the white
men, and covering them with their revolvers, said one word,
'Git.' They went, and there was not shooting till they got to
the street, but we had no more coloured men in the stalls.*

After a brief foray into Canada, playing in Toronto and
Montreal where the sisters may have had thoughts about their
intrepid grandfather and great-grandfather, it was time to go
back home. Grau and Chizzola had squeezed in one last week
at the Lyceum in New York, and then Emily and Clara raced
straight from their last performance on the Saturday to board
the SS *Queen*, which departed for England that night. However,
there was a clue that this was not so much a goodbye as an *au
revoir*. Hidden in a brief line in a New York newspaper was
the following: 'Miss Soldene contemplates returning in the fall
with a newly organised company.'

The sisters had come a long way since an early night tucked
up in bed, reading racy novels in a hotel room in Bath, seemed
the height of decadence. Their travels had given them a dose
of itchy feet, and London followed by a tour round the Home
Counties was now going to seem a little pedestrian.

Sisters: Emily as Mademoiselle Lange and Clara as Hersillie in *La Fille de Madame Angot* at the Gaiety

Chapter Eight

THE BATTLE OF THE DIVAS

Never regret thy fall
O Icarus of the fearless flight
For the greatest tragedy of them all
Is never to feel the burning light
(Oscar Wilde)

There comes a moment in most famous people's lives when a seemingly infinite upward trajectory isn't quite so upward any more. Sometimes it happens with a very precise event – with a first flop or a clanging indiscretion. Sometimes it's only clear that a star was on the wane with hindsight. Fashion, by its very definition, changes, and what is 'hot' at one moment, invariably cools down; unless, of course, you manage to reinvent yourself frequently, always managing to sniff out the zeitgeist accurately and stay one step ahead. But how many people have managed to do that? Sometimes when a star wanes, they do rise again eventually, but they have to sit out their time in the wilderness. Emily did not have the financial means to sit quietly until such time as she might become fashionable again. She didn't have any savings and she had four children, a husband and a mother to support.

When Emily had left England for America in September 1874, she had been the queen of opéra bouffe, with the superpower of turning every production that she starred in into a box office hit. But when Emily arrived back in England nine months later, things had changed – already, subtly. Audiences abhor a vacuum and when a gap is left, someone else inevitably jumps in. There had always been other opéra bouffe companies around, but none had been able to rival the size, quality and professionalism of a Soldene Opera Company production, not to mention the charisma of its leading lady. But while Emily was away eating Maryland chicken and chatting up lanky Texan cowboys, Emily's oldest rivals, having seen her success, had decided to start companies of their own, namely Selina Dolaro of the spat at the Lyceum, Lydia Thompson of the British Burlesque Blondes which had caused such a stir in the States, and, most galling of all, Kate Santley, Emily's bête noire. In fact perhaps nemesis would be a better word, because Emily seemed to have a bit of a dangerous blind spot when it came to Santley.

Emily had toured America, with Charles Morton taking the financial risk. When she got back, she was determined to have another go at being the sole owner of her own company and they went their separate ways. Emily already had a provincial tour planned and the showpiece was to be a new Offenbach opera, *La jolie parfumeuse*, with herself in the starring role of Rose Michon. This was a curious choice. Rose is a sweet, innocent soprano, with no ballast, and so was neither one of those heroic men, nor one of the imposing tragic/comic formidable and lusty lady roles that Emily had historically excelled at. It seems that Emily had allowed her competitiveness with Kate Santley to cloud her judgement. Because while Emily had been in America, Kate Santley had enthralled the West End with her own Rose Michon. But as Emily should have known from her earlier experiences at the Oxford, Kate had talents that Emily simply couldn't reproduce (and vice versa).

Emily's *La Jolie Parfumeuse* opened in Birmingham and then went to Manchester, but the lukewarm reaction forced Emily to quickly bring back the old favourites *Geneviève de Brabant* and *Chilpéric*. At the end of the tour it was dropped for ever. Emily then took the lease of the Park Theatre in Camden for the winter season, headlining with the safe choice of *Geneviève de Brabant*; but she was now in direct competition with Charles Morton, who was at the Royalty Theatre with his own opéra bouffe offering of *La Périchole* and *Trial by Jury*, with Selina Dolaro as his leading lady. It must have hurt. Morton opened a week earlier, and Emily and Clara went along to his opening night, sitting in a box, determined to show they were up for the competition. She says the audience 'turned their attention to me. "Hall right, Emily, we're cummin' a Saturday night", alluding to my forthcoming engagement at the Park Theatre.'

In the end both Morton and Emily managed on their own, but only just. Emily didn't make the Park in Camden a cult success like the Philharmonic in Islington, and Morton couldn't get on with 'Dolly' Dolaro in the way he got on with Emily. In fact Dolaro walked out halfway through the run.

Suddenly a notice appeared announcing that Miss Soldene and Charles Morton would be back together again in the new year at the Opéra Comique, putting on *Madame l'Archiduc* as the main offering and *Trial by Jury* as the finale. Emily was to play Madame l'Archiduc and Clara the lead role of the jilted bride, the Plaintiff, in *Trial by Jury*.

However, Morton's condition for taking Emily back was that she would have to share the stage with the dreadful Kate Santley. In fact, while Emily was to be Madame l'Archiduc, Morton insisted that Santley was to play Emily's love obsession. Did Charles Morton have a dark sense of humour? Anyway, seemingly with her eye on her brand, Emily writes: 'Miss Kate Santley was engaged for Fortunato, and though people prophesied we should not get on together, we did, excellently, and sometimes talked over the "Bell Goes a-Ringing for Sarah" and "Up the Alma's Height" days at the Oxford.' Morton's brother William recalls it somewhat differently:

> *The general excitement was not a little increased by the fact that two of the chief ladies concerned, Miss Soldene and Miss Santley, were from time to time scarcely as harmonious in their relations as could have been wished. So much so that manager Morton was in constant expectation of one or the other 'walking out of the theatre' as the well-known professional locution hath it. In due course this diplomatic impresario contrived to smooth the two favourites, and they swore eternal friendship – for a time.*

Perhaps Morton had insisted that Emily and Kate play lovers because he thought that the rivalry between them would produce a special spark of electricity on stage or induce a bit of a sing-off, each one trying to outdo the other's applause. In which case it was a rare misjudgement from Morton.

Late on the night of 14th January 1876, Clara was waiting nervously backstage at the Opéra Comique dressed as the

Plaintiff in a full wedding dress and veil. The atmosphere of an expectant theatre about to launch into action was threatening to overwhelm her: the sounds of the orchestra warming up, scenery shifting, an audience shuffling to get settled into their seats, the expectant hum. Unfortunately, Clara knew that it was now so late the audience were in danger of slipping into rowdiness.

The lead role of the Plaintiff, Angelina, required a sweet, high soprano who could look convincingly young, blameless, vulnerable and virginal in a wedding dress. This was obviously not the part for Emily. Although Clara had stepped in for Emily when she had been indisposed, this was the first time she was starring in her own right. It was a big moment for her, and her nerves were not helped by the fact that her grand debut was supposed to be the night before, but there had been such a fiasco that Clara had never even made it onto the stage. The new adaptation of Offenbach's *Madame l'Archiduc* which had preceded it had just gone on and on. There were complaints of pointless dialogue and the audience hissed. Kate Santley had lost her voice, and according to a review in *The Era*:

> *The whole affair began to flag, and comments more emphatic than flattering began to be heard from an excited and noisy audience which spent the intervals between the acts chanting such popular refrains as 'Tommy make room for yer Uncle' etc. The depression increased, and when Miss Soldene, who had worked very hard indeed, sang the 'Alphabet Song' . . . there were many dissentients when a repetition was demanded.*

By the time it reached eleven o'clock, there was still one more act of *Madame* to go, and so Charles Morton walked on and suggested that they might skip *Trial by Jury*. The audience reacted by hurling obscenities at him, and it looked like there might be a riot. The cast struggled on and *Madame l'Archiduc* finally finished at midnight to a rather subdued and reluctant round of applause. Morton then came on again and begged that, for the sake of the performers, they be allowed to finish now, and the audience agree to go home with an offer of free tickets for another night. The disgruntled spectators slowly dispersed, and Clara was left waiting backstage like a jilted bride at the altar.

Trial by Jury was Gilbert and Sullivan's second ever collaboration and the opera that launched their historic partnership. It is probably the most successful British one-act operetta of all time, slotting in nicely as a lively, life-affirming finale to a night out at the opera. In the nineteenth century a man was still legally obliged to pay compensation to his fiancée if he refused to marry her (something of course that Emily and Clara's grandfather had learnt to his cost, and which had propelled him to five years fighting in the Canadian wilderness). *Trial by Jury* is the story of a breach of promise lawsuit which goes awry when the beautiful, jilted bride turns up in court in her wedding dress and the judge falls in love with her. The part suited Clara perfectly with meaty numbers for her to sing like 'Comes the Broken Flower', 'That She is Reeling is Plain to See' and 'I Love Him, I Love Him, with Fervour Unceasing'.

Madame l'Archiduc was never popular and Emily's reviews were unusually tepid. As Emily says: 'Madame l'Archiduc did not "catch on" to the amount expected. The real success was Trial by Jury, in which Miss Clara Vesey sang the Plaintiff with much distinction'.

At this point Emily was thirty-eight years old, while Clara was just twenty-six. For the first time in their careers, Emily was not supporting Clara's career, but Clara was buttressing hers; the tectonic plates had shifted. Since the beginning of time older sisters have had a dread of being overtaken by younger sisters. Along with love and pride, there is an inbuilt tracking device constantly monitoring the younger sister's progress and assessing whether she has been supplanted. Clara's relative success must have shaken an already worried Emily.

It was her success as the Plaintiff that brought Clara to the attention of the son and heir of Lord Lismore. To Emily's extreme excitement he asked Clara to marry him – perhaps seeing her night after night looking charming in a wedding gown had put the idea into his head. To Emily's incomprehension, Clara had said no. But then he asked her again and again, and each time Clara refused. Lord Lismore was Anglo-Irish aristocracy, he was going to be the Lord Lieutenant of the County of Tipperary, his wife would be mistress of her very own castle called Shanbally, and their eldest son would automatically have a seat in the House of Lords. Years later in her newspaper column Emily was to say of Clara's rejection of Lord Lismore's proposal of marriage, 'Such a pity she didn't, I think' – which was an uncharacteristic understatement. Because, even though it must have secretly tormented Emily that she herself had been married so young to a man who would never advance her or her family's prospects in any way, at the same time she wanted Clara to make the most of the opportunities she hadn't had – not just for Clara's sake, but for all of their sakes. Having a sister married to a lord would have opened all sorts of doors and social opportunities; it would also have provided some sort of financial insurance against total destitution for the Soldene family, if and when things went awry in the theatre.

Clara looks somewhat ahead of her time in preferring to work rather than be a wife, in deciding she was not prepared to give up the freedom and excitement of the theatrical life, however rich or noble a man he might be. From a twenty-first-century perspective this seems progressive and even moral. To Emily it probably seemed downright stupid and, moreover, selfish; one can only imagine the heated rows this might have caused between the sisters. It must have been difficult for Emily to believe that her little sister would not take her advice – like experiencing a teenager rebelling for the first time. Emily had been Clara's mother in all but name, but Clara was perhaps seeing her sister for the first time as an ordinary human being, who wasn't always right. It might have meant that Emily had fallen off the sibling pedestal.

As soon as the Christmas season had finished, Soldene and Santley went their separate ways. In fact, they went out on tour in direct competition with each other, both with rival productions of *Madame l'Archiduc*, Kate under her own management and this time playing Madame l'Archiduc herself, and Emily under the management of Morton. Dolly Dolaro was also going out under the management of the rapidly ascending D'Oyly Carte company. It should have been possible for the three companies to sit down and coordinate their engagements – there were enough cities in Britain for them not to have to end up in the same town on the same night, putting on the same show. That would have been the sensible thing to do. Instead, the three companies chased each other up and down the country, almost as if they were doing it on purpose to spoil each other's fun and prove who was the best.

The inevitable clash came in Liverpool when Emily turned up at the Royal Amphitheatre to play Madame l'Archiduc, while on the same night Kate Santley also opened her own *Madame l'Archiduc* at the Royal Alexandra theatre. On this occasion the critics seemed to give the prize to Emily:

> *Miss Emily Soldene has few equals in her particular line and her representation of Marietta was about as crisp, piquant and dashing, both vocally and histrionically, as could be conceived . . . Miss Soldene's fine, full voice had due weight and the encores during the evening were as plentiful as leaves in July.*

This must have been a sweet victory. A month later and Emily's company was again pitched against Kate Santley, this time in Edinburgh – but on this occasion, it was Clara's performance in *Trial by Jury* that clinched the victory, helped by the author himself, Sir Arthur Sullivan, allegedly turning up. Emily does not waste the opportunity to do a bit of name dropping:

> *Sir Arthur Sullivan was on a visit to Lord and Lady Rosebury at Dalmeny; he used to visit the theatre every night. One evening a large party came from the Castle to see the show, and amongst their impedimenta was a basket of beautiful peaches for me. A delicate attention much appreciated . . .*

But however many victories Emily was winning, they were becoming increasingly hollow. The takings pie was being divided up into smaller and smaller pieces. Exhausted after three months' hard touring, by the time the company reached Leeds Emily pleaded illness and retired for the last few weeks of the tour, leaving Clara in charge, happily singing Madame l'Archiduc. Secretly Emily was not just recovering from a sore throat, but also negotiating with Chizzola (now separated from Grau) to go back to the States. Emily needed a much larger potential audience.

She decided there were going to be three important differences to this American tour.

First, she was going to take the company at her own financial risk. Emily was always gambling literally and metaphorically, but this was one of her greatest speculations yet; not least because Charles Morton had famously lost £8,000 on their previous critically successful short American tour and had had to declare himself bankrupt when he got back to the UK. The theatre world had gossiped about it and it had caused Morton all sorts of headaches, not least because of the legal tautology he had to perform in order to carry on putting on productions. Even when playing to packed theatres the cost of taking a full company across the States made it very difficult to break even. Emily knew this full well and yet she went ahead anyway.

The second difference was that the tour was going to be open-ended. Emily was going out with the intention of making as much money as she could for as long as she possibly could, and therefore had not bought a return ticket home.

Lastly, Emily had decided to bring along her old companion, the unfeasibly high-kicking and wiry 'Sal', or to call her by her official stage name, 'Madame Sara'. Wiry Sal was now controversially copying Tchaikovsky's *Black Swan* that had premiered that year. She had gone gothic and was dancing in an all-black tutu with black eyeliner matching her black hair. This was deemed to be, at the very least, provocative.

On 19th November 1876, the Soldene Opera Bouffe Company opened in Boston at the Globe Theatre, playing *Madame l'Archiduc* and *Trial by Jury*. The Boston audiences set the tone for the American reaction in general.

'Trial by Jury' was a sensation in Boston . . . Boston simply went wild, and every night 'Trial by Jury' was played twice, every number being encored and repeated. What havoc the bridesmaids created! and there was a movement all over the house when the fair Plaintiff appeared.

Havoc is the word for it. The theatre was packed but the moral majority were in uproar at the sight of the Soldene girls, in particular Sara the kicker:

The Soldene party are making an enormous success at the Globe Theatre, Boston; but the papers are excoriating them fearfully. The house is crowded to the doors every night, and the moral journals of the moral Hub have had their columns filled with indignant letters and equally exasperating editorials. The buxom Emily and her fair hordes, however, laugh at the criticisms, pocket the greenbacks, and accept the homage of the Harvard College students who flock in large numbers to see them.

Wherever the troupe landed, Clara in her white virginal wedding dress and Madame Sara in her black tutu were the hits, but Emily was getting mixed reviews for her singing and the remarks about her age and appearance were becoming increasingly cutting. For example, this from Chicago under the headline 'HERE'S DIVERSION: THE AGED BUT FRISKY SOLDENE AND HER GIRLS ARE KICKING UP THE DUST AT HAVERLEY'S'.

There is vastly more muscle than music in the party, but the demands of the work, being musically light, were fairly met. A few numbers were exceedingly well rendered. Among these

161

*might be mentioned the hurdy-gurdy trio and the duet in
the last act 'He is the nicest of the three' in which Soldene
herself sung with exceeding sweetness – a most unusual thing
for her ordinary singing is simply distasteful. Heretofore, she
has given evidence of merit only in the few upper notes, the
rest of her voice being uncertain and horribly liable to trip
over the palate and rattle about in a very painful manner
through a series of notes not down in the score.*

Is all publicity good publicity? Emily had to suffer constant
jibes about the size of her mouth. Though she herself attempted
to make a joke of it:

*During this engagement, the Chicago Times came out one
morning with a column about my mouth. My mouth was so
big, they thought it would take 'two men to kiss me.' That
night I had great fun and an immense fan. I was playing the
'Grand Duchess.' Every time I had anything to say or sing, I
said or sang it, then up over my mouth went this large fan.
The people soon caught on, and the opera went with screams
of laughter from beginning to end. There was a nice article
in another paper the next morning, saying if I had a large
mouth, I had also a good temper.*

The *Washington Post* said that Emily would 'try the jetty system
in the improvement of her mouth'. The *St Joseph News* joked:

*We congratulate nature. She sometimes does capricious
things, but she was engaged on Soldene's mouth she was
evidently in her state of mind. Soldene ought to be under*

162

obligations to nature, for nature has given her a feature which distinguishes her from the normal run of comic opera singers.

The *Kansas City Times* excelled itself with:

Here is a long, square-cut mouth, but not only is it phenomenal in size, but also phenomenal in its workings. It's capable of more posing and posturing and contortions than any similar orifice in the world. It does not simply open and shut; it chases the other features all round the face.

Was Emily really laughing, or was there a bit of her crying inside? When a reporter from the *Pittsburgh Dispatch* said that 'Miss Soldene's mouth was suggestive of the Mammoth Cave', he was barred from entry at the box office and told there were no more tickets for the Mammoth Cave. Did Emily feel or at least tell herself that it was all right as long as the money kept coming in? It's interesting that Emily's mouth only became a feature of fun when she was no longer in her youth, as if there's a licence to poke fun once women reach a certain age. Although, to be fair, Emily was not above dishing out these sorts of comments herself.

While the press were proving rogue, events on the ground were equally as random and dramatic. Emily had taken a strange dislike to Brooklyn on her first trip – the freezing ferry trip across from Manhattan, the grubby streets and the dark, echoing theatre; and she was quite superstitious. With some sort of sniff of doom, Emily unusually, and at the last moment, cancelled a potentially lucrative booking at the Brooklyn Theatre for 5th December and went to Providence, Rhode Island instead. Chizzola then offered Brooklyn to her friend the actress Kate Claxton, who was travelling with a play called *The Two Orphans*.

On the night of 5th December the Brooklyn Theatre burnt down in the worst theatre fire, and indeed one of the worst fires, in the whole of American history. The 900-seat theatre was filled to capacity when a gaslight set fire to some scenery backstage. There were no buckets or hoses, and the flames spread with the play going on and the audience unaware that the fire was raging. When someone finally shouted 'Fire' there was a stampede, and with no fire escapes and only a few narrow staircases, Kate's leading man, Harry S. Murdock, tried to calm the crowds. Tens of people were crushed to death, and many more died of smoke inhalation or were burnt to death. In the end it was estimated that 295 people died and many more had suffered terrible injuries. Murdock tried to escape from his dressing-room window, but it was too narrow and he died. Kate Claxton did manage to escape, but unbelievably was haunted by people shouting 'Fire!' at her wherever she went afterwards. As Emily says: 'For months during that tour by some mysterious chance Kate Claxton and I continued close together, and wherever she went, "Fire! Fire!" was the cry. They called her the "Fire Queen," and we got afraid of her.'

Emily's instincts were once again proved right. At the Christmas Day matinee in Washington, someone shouted 'Fire!' and the audience ran; luckily no one was hurt in the crush. But then in April, in the Southern Hotel in St Louis, Claxton was sleeping on the third floor when a fire actually did break out. Rushing to escape, she fell down the staircase, but made it out alive with nothing left but the nightdress she was wearing. A month later she was declared bankrupt, having just got divorced. Touring the States in 1876 was a risky business.

However, Emily's instincts failed her when it came to the wife of her lead tenor, Mrs Knight Ashton. She arrived and joined them in St Louis and at first Emily was impressed:

> *A tall handsome, distinguished-looking woman. She brought her husband the most wonderful presents: a gold-mounted dressing-case, a diamond ring, diamond studs, &c., &c., I am sorry to say this magnificent lady turned out to be the notorious Mrs. Gordon Bailie [sic], who escaping (with much spoil) from London, left her faithful female servant to suffer three years' 'hard' in her stead. 'The presents' were part of the loot.*

Mrs Gordon Baillie was in fact born Annie Sutherland-Newborne, the illegitimate daughter of a Dundee laundress. When she wasn't being an actress on the stage, Mrs Gordon Baillie travelled the world committing fraud, including passing fake cheques in Paris and pretending to be the disinherited child of the Earl of Moray. In Australia she introduced her husband as Baron White of Birmingham, and defrauded an elderly baronet, Sir Richard Duckworth King, for which she served five years in prison.

Emily had an anthropological-like interest in native peoples, which was very much of her time. There were human zoos in cities all across the Western world including Paris, Hamburg, Barcelona, Milan, London and New York, showing people (generally from Africa) in what was seen as their 'primitive' state, as a means of displaying the West's relative 'civilisation'. So when the most famous Native American tribe leader, Chief Sitting Bull, happened to be staying in their hotel in Chicago,

Emily couldn't resist meeting him. Just over six months after defeating General Custer at his mythical last stand at Little Big Horn, Sitting Bull was on his way to Washington from the Black Hills Reservation to have an audience with the president and ask for the white man to leave their country.

The Indian warriors were on the top floor of the hotel, in a suite of rooms entirely destitute of furniture. When we entered we saw thirty or forty mysterious-looking forms squatting on the floor enveloped in gay coloured blankets. Their long, straight, black hair, parted in the centre, hung to below their waists and, falling over the high cheek-bones, nearly concealed their faces. Through the dark greasy masses gleamed cold, uninquisitive, impassive, black eyes, and dabs of red and yellow ochre. Their sang froid was perfect. At our entrance they never moved, and scarcely seemed to see us. The interpreter spoke, and 'Sitting Bull' replied, with a not over-polite grunt, 'Ugh, Ugh.' 'Shake,' said the interpreter to me. 'Sitting Bull' put out his hand. I laid mine in it. And he closed with a grip, a slow, steady, unrelenting grip of steel. Presently a pain ran up my arm, I felt my bones would certainly crack. But with a desire to emulate the Indian calm, I stood it. And at last his grasp slowly relaxed. I was free. But I made up my mind that there should be no more shaking of hands with Indian chiefs for me.

Finally, Emily reached the destination she'd been dreaming of – the west coast of America, and San Francisco. This was a great opportunity – California had never seen a Soldene production before, and, feeling ambitious, they had booked a long six-week run in the largest venue on the west coast, the

California Theatre. At first it seemed their ambition was paying off. For the initial week the reviews were generally favourable, except a critic called Betsy B. As Emily says: 'I must say she went for me personally with a persistence worthy of a better cause, and asked "the Lord" continually what this earth had done that I should be placed on it.'

But Emily could laugh this off, because the important thing was the theatre was full. However, once again it seems it wasn't Emily that was the big draw.

> *Everybody (especially the men everybodies) came to the theatre, and there was a beauty boom, like unto that of our first visit to New York, Miss Vesey, Miss Rose Stella, and Miss Cissy Durant, being especial pets, while Miss Florence Slater, who danced the Priestess in 'Chilpéric,' nearly sent the boys crazy, as now and again, with vigorous kick, she sent her slipper up into the gallery. Strange to say, Mdlle. Sara, our prize kicker at 50l per week, did not meet with universal approbation. The men liked Slater best, and the ladies professed themselves 'real shocked.' Whether it was her short ballet skirts (Slater wore long ones, to her toes) or – well, there is no knowing what it was. A theatrical audience is so difficult. In one city something will be hailed with acclamation by excited crowds, which in another is left severely alone, unseen – a horror.*

Certain of these 'men everybodies' seemed happy to show the girls the sights, notably a Dr Cornelius Hertz. This serious man of science was very much a pancontinental citizen – he was the son of European immigrants but born in New York. Later Dr Hertz studied in Paris and was made a Knight of the French Legion of

Honour due to his service as a doctor in the Franco-Prussian War. But Dr Hertz's biggest moment was when he realised the potential of the new scientific discovery, electricity. He used it to treat his patients' nervous complaints and then turned his mind to thinking what else it could do. He struck a deal with Thomas Edison and set up the board of Californian Electrical Works. He later went back to Europe and was instrumental in promoting the spread of electricity across the continent. Unfortunately, he also became involved in the Panama scandal, lost large amounts of money and ended up retired in a Bournemouth hotel. However, when Emily met him, he was a man on the up.

He was profuse, extravagant, generous to a fault, and a regular godsend to the girls. Personally I liked him. He, in his official capacity and accompanied by some policeman very high up indeed in the city government, took us to Chinatown, where we saw everything – the opium dens, the tiny-toed demi-monde, the gambling, and the Fan Tan. We went into cellars, and cupboards, and down corridors, into which the nasty smells of centuries had strayed and never got out any more; to a Chinese restaurant, where gay young Chinese 'swells' were drinking tea and playing a game that looked like 'Thumbs up,' 'thumbs down'; to the Chinese Theatre, where a great Chinese star had just arrived. This was a striking entertainment, but appealed more particularly to the olfactory and auricular senses than to the artistic.

Dr. Hertz was the life and soul of everything, and when we left he immortalized himself by presenting one of the ladies with a beautiful plush bag, lined with wash-leather. On the outside was inscribed 'Souvenir of the Golden State,' inside was 1000 dols. in double eagles. This was not the only coup made by members of the 'Soldene' company.

A thousand dollars would be the equivalent of over $25,000 today. No wonder Dr Hertz was popular.

Despite all this extracurricular fun, when a new diva came into town the novelty of the Soldene girls wore off. A Miss Maggie Moore was playing *Struck Oil*, which for the prospector Californians proved to be unmissable, and the machinations of pastry cooks and bossy duchesses could not compete. Emily was moved into a smaller theatre down the road for her last couple of weeks, and Miss Moore moved into the California. *The Clipper* said of Emily's tour that 'the engagement had not been successful'.

Having seemingly used up all her novelty value in California, Emily had to decide what to do next. Chizzola had planned for the company to work its way back across the States to finish the summer in the Union Theatre in New York. But, so far, they had already travelled one way and the pickings had not been rich – as Charles Morton had found, the cost of moving the company, putting it in hotels and feeding it, meant they weren't even breaking even. This was not the plan.

However, there was one destination left where Emily might strike theatrical gold. It would mean another, even longer, voyage, and would take her even further away from her children and home; it would mean she would not be back for years. Should she stay or should she go? As we know, Emily could never resist a gamble. In July 1877 the Soldene Opera Bouffe Company set sail for Australia on board the *Zealandia*.

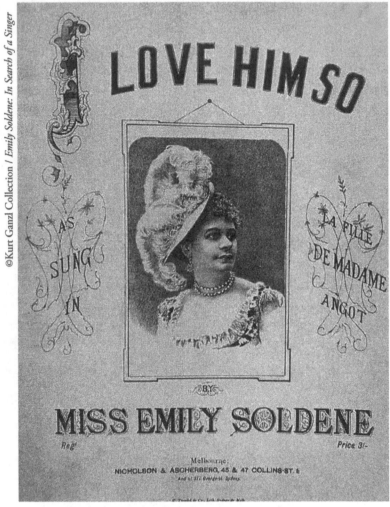

Emily sells her songs in Australia

Chapter Nine

THE CURSE

'God Save thee, ancient mariner!
From the fiends, that plague thee thus!—
Why look'st thou so?'—With my cross-bow
I shot the Albatross
('The Rime of the Ancient Mariner', Samuel Taylor Coleridge)

The Soldene Opera Company's first voyage across the Pacific was a magical experience where the albatrosses were left well alone.

We saw the Southern Cross, the flying fish, the nautilus, a white squall, lots of albatross, the sun drop suddenly into the sea, and the big moon rise, and the big stars shine over the big ship that moved along in stately splendour – moved along in seas of silver, and ripples of faint rosy, phosphorescent flame.

When the boat stopped briefly to deliver the post in Auckland, New Zealand's leading impresario, Julius De Lias, walked up the gangplank and asked if they could delay going to Australia and play Auckland for a few weeks instead.

As a colony, New Zealand was still relatively in its infancy. Apart from the 50,000 native Maoris, most of the half a million residents had arrived only recently from the British Isles. This brand-new nation on the edge of the earth had never had the pleasure of a touring opera company before, and not just any old company – but one that had successfully played in London's West End and New York's Broadway. Moreover, like most frontier societies, New Zealand was full of young men: adventurers, lured by the promise of gold or, at the very least, cheap land to farm sheep; and there was also a shortage of women, to the extent that the fledgling New Zealand government had schemes to lure young ladies to come to their shores. How could the Soldene Opera Bouffe Company with its rousing tunes, comic turns and risky, seductive dancing girls not be a hit? Chizzola and De Lias quickly came up with a deal, and suddenly there was chaos as the Soldene Company dashed to get together their luggage, props and costumes off the boat before it set out to sea again. Such was the stampede that one man fell down the steps onto his head and was seriously injured in the rush.

The impromptu stop immediately paid sightseeing dividends. Emily once again had an opportunity to put on her anthropological hat, although it isn't clear who was looking at whom:

We wanted to see the Maoris, and we did not have to want [sic] long. There they were, waiting for us on the wharf. Fancy us comic opera cockneys finding ourselves really in New Zealand, face to face with a crowd of coffee-coloured, ox-eyed, tattooed natives! The ladies carried their babies on their backs, and their husbands' pipes in their ears, where other people carry their earrings. The

Maori babies run the little vulgar boy at Margate very close
indeed in the way of requiring a pocket-handkerchief, and the
entire absence of anything resembling that necessary article.

Emily was entranced with this new world:

Auckland was charming, with Mount Eden towering up
into the sky, with tall Calla lilies growing in every crevice of
the volcanic rocks, and watercress (for nothing) waiting to
be gathered in the city gutters. Auckland, where they called
pheasants 'spring chicken,' where the hens roosted up in the
trees, like blackbirds; where, on getting up in the morning,
and taking a penny roll, a strong-bladed knife, and a walk
along the shore, one got one's fill of fat fresh oysters . . . Well,
I fell in love with New Zealand.

The feeling was mutual. This from the local newspaper's critic:

Three things may be affirmed of this company, – (1) That
everything is done by them with a taste and on a scale
worthy of the most critical audiences, (2) the organisation of
the company is almost perfect, (3) and that the balance and
selection of the voices display the nicest skill, to which may
be added great power. No performances could reflect higher
credit upon a management than these.

This must have provided some welcome relief for Emily after
the harsh critics in the States.

Eventually, though, it was time to complete their journey to
Australia. The Tasman Sea was characteristically choppy:

My sister, like some of Mr. W.S. Gilbert's people, was always
'very, very sick at sea,' and the only thing that pulled her
together was a game of cards. Clara was and is a born gambler,
and with nothing in her hand will go 5l. better, and rake in
the 'pot,'without turning a hair. Of course, coming up Sydney
Harbour for the first time in one's life is an event. The scenery
had to be (for future reference) looked at. Clara was on deck,
packed up with pillows, playing 'poker.' 'Do look,' said I, 'isn't
it beautiful?' But she was absorbed. Afterwards I said, 'Why
didn't you look at those lovely places?' 'How could I?' said she,
'I had a full hand.' 'Well,' said I, 'It's something disgusting,
you missed all the fine points.' 'Oh did I?' said she, 'Look here,'
and, lifting up her handkerchief, in her lap lay a little pile of
shining sovereigns.

Emily appears to be making a joke about Clara's non-compliance,
but something was shifting in the power balance between the sisters.

In September 1877 they finally landed in Sydney. Australia
was an altogether more settled prospect than New Zealand.
Most of its two million inhabitants had been born there and it
had a relatively urban population. Sydney at the time was one
of the largest cities in the world. Rich from mining, it already
had palatial municipal buildings (and brothels) everywhere.
The Soldene Opera Bouffe Company was playing at its largest
theatre, the Theatre Royal. An Englishman by the name of
William Sandover had paid a visit the year before and described
it as being so crowded that it was full of 'women tumbling
down, screaming and being runover and trampled'. He said it
would be 'a disgrace to an English country town'.

Of course, Emily and Clara, used to playing in the music

halls and pantomimes of Whitechapel, could handle this crowd. Particularly popular with the Sydney audience was *Barbe-bleue*, with Emily for the first time playing the part of the evil psychopathic seducer Bluebeard himself; a part which, interestingly, suited her:

> *The Soldene Opera-Bouffe company have made a hit in the Theatre Royal, and each succeeding opera but increases the attendance and the satisfaction of the playgoing public. Miss Soldene is certainly the best exponent of Offenbach we have heard in Sydney. Clara Vesey, pretty and piquant, has won the hearts of the Sydney gentlemen.*

Once again it was the deliciousness of the Soldene girls which proved the greatest magnet.

> *Our ladies made the same old sensation. All the boys lost their heads over them, and Miss Clara Vesey, Miss Stella, Miss Slater, Miss Durant, and Mdlle. Sara had great times. There were many husbands in the company, but they were kept in the background.*

Emily took full advantage of the opportunity to explore; she went to Botany Bay and marvelled at the flowers, she went to Coogee Bay and collected shells, she went to the races and made some money, and Chizzola brought her back a baby wallaby after shooting its mother during a kangaroo hunt. For their last night in Sydney Emily took a benefit which was patronised by the governor himself and his wife. She was presented with a jewel casket made out of an emu's egg. The *Western*

Independent of 13th November reported:

> *In speaking of Miss Soldene as an artist of the highest order it would be impossible to magnify or exaggerate her varied powers . . . The spark of nature's fire that animates and illuminates her whole nature is far above any art – it is the direct gift of Heaven, and can never be acquired. The gift is what we call genius . . . we fearlessly assert what we believe to be the truth in reference to a lady whose high accomplishments have delighted thousands in Sydney, and whose advent to this country is an era in its history.*

It was the start of a love affair between Emily, the city and its citizens, that was to last for the rest of her life. But for now, they were off to Melbourne and Emily was apprehensive: 'People said, "What went in Sydney was a dead frost in Melbourne," and we had been so successful in New South Wales that we felt we should be an utter failure in Victoria.'

Despite this, Emily decided to up the jeopardy by refusing to travel by steamship like everyone else, instead making the 550-mile journey overland in a Cobb & Co. stagecoach coach pulled by six horses. Why she did this is a mystery. There were no proper roads – just rough tracks through thick bush; it was territory only inhabited by wild animals and Cobb & Co. coaches were notorious for their colourful drivers. These iconic stagecoaches had flourished with the Australian gold boom, connecting the gold-mining towns to civilisation, and had an aura of the pioneering, wild spirit about them. As carriers of mail and gold as well as passengers, they were also targets for the Australian equivalent of the highwayman or the cowboy outlaw, the bushranger. Men with names like Blue Cap, Captain Thunderbolt and Captain Moonlite roamed the lawless remote tracks, fully armed, looking for easy pickings. Perhaps Emily hoped to encounter one of these notorious outlaws – it would have made excellent copy. A midlife crisis moment? Or perhaps she was just sick of choppy sea trips.

On a 'Cobbs' coach, drawn by six young horses, who galloped up mountains and flew down them, driven by coachmen more or less under the influence of the weather. One told us he had been out on a 'burst to a wedding, not slept for three nights,' but should be all right when he had had a 'nobbler.' We looked forward with much pleasurable anticipation to the 'nobbler,' but were horrified when we saw it – 'half a tumbler of whiskey.' Our driver tossed it off. He had not overstated its merits. It pulled him together splendidly, not that it made any difference to his driving, which was dare-devil and perfect, as was that of all the other boys.

It was a hair-raising, stomach-turning, roller coaster of a journey with not a steady moment, or a break from the constant adrenalin, like being on stage for three days straight.

Fancy a track of soft sand, cut into deep ruts, piled up high in banks, winding in and out huge trees, sharp corners, unexpected fallen trunks, monster upturned roots, every kind of obstacle, six horses always galloping, the coach banging, creaking, swaying from side to side! then suddenly down we go, down over a mountain as steep as the side of a house, down into and through a rushing, roaring, tumbling, bumping yellow river! Splash, dash. Then with a 'Houp!'

'Hi!' and a big lurch, out again and up the opposite side,
galloping, always galloping, breathless: the driver shouting,
cracking his whip, and the horses shaking the water from
their sides, tossing their heads, and jingling their harness.

Emily found it 'all lovely' except for the jolting. Fancying herself
as a bit of a Wild West Calamity Jane, she left Jack and Clara
inside and insisted on sitting on top of the box with the driver,
taking turns holding the reins. Out in the Australian outback,
with no one to watch and judge her, Emily felt a rare taste of
true freedom: 'it made one sick, not with fright exactly but with
excitement and the anticipation of some possible calamity.'

They arrived a few days later all in one piece. Fortunately,
Emily's premonitions had been wrong, and the Soldene Opera
Bouffe Company was almost as great a hit in Melbourne as it
had been in Sydney, and there were almost as many offstage
amusements. Emily's ego was boosted by the attentions of the
young son of a theatre critic who 'took quite a fancy' to her, and
according to Emily they 'went out driving together'.

In fact, the Melbourne leg of the trip was almost too
successful; the fame of its star performers had spread perhaps
a bit too far. The company had been due to go home after
Melbourne via India. But Julius De Lias persuaded them to go
back to New Zealand for Christmas. With three performances
left in Melbourne, Emily arrived at the theatre to find her two
star supporting sopranos, Miss Rose Stella and Miss Cissy
Durant, missing, and two local girls getting changed in the
dressing room instead. They said they had been hired to stand
in because Miss Stella and Miss Durant had suddenly been
taken ill. In reality they were making a dash to the harbour to

get the steamboat back to Sydney, having been poached. Rose Stella had been lured by an impresario called Mr Sam Lazaar and the promise that she would be the lead soprano in a new big pantomime. The bait for Cissy Durant was different but equally enticing – she had found herself a rich husband.

In later years Emily was to forgive Cissy. Emily understood that when it came to the matter of a wealthy husband, one had to take these opportunities when they came along, even if it meant letting a few friends down. On 1st April 1878 Cissy married Harry McQuade, a young, wealthy Sydney landowner. She never returned to the stage but had three children and became a prominent member of Sydney society. After Harry's death in 1893 she inherited his whole estate including Her Majesty's Theatre in central Sydney. Not bad for a chorus girl. Emily and Cissy remained firm friends, corresponded regularly, and met up for long, convivial reminiscing lunches whenever they happened to be in the same city. However, Emily never fully trusted Rose Stella again. Emily hired her when she needed to, but it was an uneasy truce and Chizzola later took Rose Stella to court, suing for breach of contract and the financial losses of the tour. It was a court case he lost.

Rose Stella was not the sole cause of Chizzola's financial headaches. What he hadn't known until he arrived was the fact that audiences in the Southern Hemisphere were not as wealthy as their American counterparts:

The theatre was crowded every night, but the receipts seemed small after the States, where, in the class of house we played in the lowest price was fifty cents. Coming to Australia, we found that people thought of a shilling as the Americans thought of a dollar.

Even when playing to full theatres it had been difficult to make money, but now without Rose Stella and Cissy Durant, the cast was weakened, perhaps fatally. The selling point of Emily's production had been that it was clearly a cut above anything that was home-grown. Now she had to fill in the soprano gaps with the best talent that she could find locally, and they just weren't good enough. They had also lost Sara the kicker who had decided to stay in Australia. It seems Chizzola didn't contract her for long enough, probably because he never thought they were going to stay that long, and now Wiry Sal had had a better offer.

Theatre folk are notoriously superstitious. They never say the name of the Scottish play; whistling is banned in the theatre; the last line is never spoken before the actual performance; peacock feathers, real money and jewellery are not allowed on stage; and the phrase 'put your best foot forwards' comes from a theatrical superstition that one should always put one's left foot out of the dressing-room door first. Emily was always to blame what happened next on the albatross being shot.

On Thursday 20th December they left Australia.

We had a very good crossing, but on the way an albatross was caught and killed; this rather alarmed me, for I remembered the fate of the 'Ancient mariner.' The bird measured sixteen feet from tip to tip of his wings, and weighed goodness knows how much. He ultimately absorbed all the alum there was on the ship.

Emily was horrified. She knew her Victorian classics and the message of *The Rime of the Ancient Mariner* was quite clear – don't kill an albatross, it doesn't end well. In the Mariner's case, it led to forty days and forty nights becalmed, with water, water all around and not a drop to drink and his fellow crew and passengers dying around him, the mariner condemned to survive and suffer: 'Instead of the cross, the Albatross, About my neck was hung'. Of course, Emily hadn't shot the albatross herself, and she would never have done so, but, knowing Coleridge's cautionary tale by heart, she was aware that bad things happened to the witnesses too – they all died for a start.

And bad things did happen. The new sopranos couldn't cope with the vocal demands of Offenbach. They kept falling sick and disappearing, which meant that Emily had to give up her preferred male roles and put on the costumes of swooning high-soprano heroines; no more Bluebeard. This was not an improvement. The rest of the cast kept having to swap roles too and were forced to play parts to which they were not best suited either. A vicar became enraged in Christchurch. Here is the letter the Rev. Robert S. Jackson sent to the papers:

> *There is a limit beyond which a sense of propriety forbids me to countenance as a Christian clergyman, and the limit was transgressed last night by the Soldene Opera Company. The piece had an immoral plot, the dresses, though handsome, were – some of them – very indecent; and the performance of one of the dancers at the end of the second act was, in this respect, as shameless as anything I have ever seen . . . I feel it my duty to warn my friends to keep their daughters away.*

It's not clear how many daughters were kept away from the Soldene Company, but bad luck struck again when they reached

Wellington. The newspaper reported:

> *Yesterday evening two ladies connected with the Soldene*
> *company drove out to Johnsonville, accompanied by two*
> *gentlemen. When descending a hill, one of the horses became*
> *frightened and kicked and reared until it had cut itself in*
> *several places in a very severe manner. The passengers escaped*
> *with nothing more than a fright.*

It's also not clear which two ladies were taking evening drives with local gentlemen, but it may well have been the two sopranos, who left the company at this point, deciding to stay in New Zealand. The company was now running dangerously low on ladies.

The sea crossing back to Australia was horrendous. Emily blamed the albatross again:

> *There were storms, the hatches were battened down, and*
> *everybody was saying their prayers in the saloon, kneeling in a*
> *foot or two of water. I performed my devotions in my cabin (still*
> *pursued by the albatross). I made sure it was our last voyage.*

Emily must have known that their boat, the *Arawata*, had recently collided and almost been run over by an enormous ship in Hobsons Bay; and, worse, fellow actress and manager Bessie Edwards and her company, on their way to an engagement at the Melbourne Theatre, were drowned when the boat sank in a storm just off Perth with the loss of all on board. But Emily and her company made it to Adelaide in time to launch its new opera house. The fledgling city was very proud of its latest addition and the opening night was an occasion to match the excitement. Emily swept onto the stage and made an opening speech which consisted of a self-written poem, packed with high Victorian hyperbole:

> *Let me then speak some sorry words of mine*
> *As a poor tribute at this Temple's shrine*
> *The Muses Temple we unveil tonight*
> *For ours, for yours, for all our friends' delight*
> *Time was Melpomene was doomed to hold*
> *Her mimic court within a poorer fold,*
> *And the great artistes of a bygone age*
> *Fretted their hours upon a ruder stage.*
> *Shakespeare first freed Drama from its thralls*
> *And housed its patrons within fairer halls,*
> *The tree he planted still bears fruit, and we*
> *Must own that fact exultingly!*

Emily went on in this manner, in her element; but to be fair, Emily knew her audience and they apparently loved it. Victorians were different.

The Soldene Opera Company did well in Adelaide despite the gaps in the cast. But now Chizzola was getting restless – they still couldn't make money. The Soldene Opera Company went back to Melbourne, but here they were tangled up in a scandal. Emily omits this in her memoirs, but it was reported in the local newspapers that a former mayor by the name of Ebeneezer Neil had become fond of one of the ladies of the company. He booked into the hotel where they were staying and went to see her in the opera house, after which he was supposed to join a friend for dinner. However, he never made it – and was found drowned in the river. It was suspected that he had committed suicide after being rejected by the chorus girl. Melbourne hummed with gossip and the company had to leave.

Now they were not only short of money but running out of places to play before their scheduled return to England. They were forced to go to some of the more prosperous mining towns for their last four weeks and Chizzola put all the staff on half wages. When the company went to Geelong, and torrential rain meant they played to a nearly empty Mechanics Institute, Chizzola had had enough. One day the cast woke up to find he had left the hotel early and taken all the company funds with him, leaving them stranded with no money to pay for their food and rooms, not to mention their passage home. They threw themselves on the mercy of the miners of Geelong and played extra performances. The local newspaper reported:

> *From what we could learn, it would appear that Mr Chizzola the manager left Geelong suddenly at the termination of the season which expired on Saturday evening for Adelaide, taking with him, according to the statements of the company, whatever funds were in their treasury. In this dilemma, it was found necessary to extend the season, in order to raise sufficient money to pay all hotel bills and provide for the return of several members of the company to England, and an energetic canvass of the town was subsequently made, the result being that the difficulty was successfully tidied over.*

It wasn't quite tidied over though, and the company straggled back to Melbourne where Emily sung a benefit to try and raise the remaining money for their return tickets. Luckily, she did manage to buy herself, husband Jack and Clara passage on a steamship bound for home, as well as tickets for a few of her old-timers including her wardrobe lady. The rest of the cast were left to fend for themselves, playing sympathy engagements over the next few months. Most of them made it back eventually.

Chizzola had behaved badly, but a manager deserting when money was no longer being made was not unusual – just as cast members would disappear if they had a better offer. That was the nature of the business: easy come, easy go, a gamble. But it was a shabby end to what had started out as a glorious tour. They had worked hard and delighted many people. Emily had made a name for herself, and the Soldene Opera Bouffe Company had been a critical success; she had had a great adventure the like of which many of us, even in the twenty-first century, can only dream of. But for Emily the problem still remained of how to keep making a living and supporting her family in her later years, and now she was two years older. Even Clara was thirty years old. Emily put a brave face on this embarrassment, but Clara may not have been so sanguine.

None of these things stopped Emily from having a good time on the journey home, her joie de vivre irrepressible:

I remember when I smoked my first cigarette. It was in the Red Sea, going home from Australia (the first time). Good gracious, when one comes to think of it, what a lot (in addition to astronomy) one learns at sea. Well, the cigarette – I liked it too. Still, I think a good deal depends on who rolls it for one. Don't you? . . .

Emily as Carmen, felled by her very own Don José, Durward Lely

Chapter Ten

Two Weddings, Two Funerals and Some Bad Management

I'm a lady not unknown to fame
Critics call me by my Christian name
And you see my photograph on show
Just wherever you may care to go!

...

Ah dear boys you won't be very glad,
When I'm married to a noble lad.
I shall turn most singularly prim,
And I reckon I'll look after him!
Oh, I'll be a very proper sort,
Quite propriety itself in short.
('Miss Plantagenet' in the musical, *The Shop Girl*)

On 9th December 1880, a tiny bride walked down the aisle of a church in Putney. Waists were smaller in those days thanks to the eye-watering constrictions of boned corsets – twenty-two inches on average – but Miss Clara Vesey was famed throughout London for her particular petiteness. As this was her wedding day, she would have been laced up particularly tight. Following the fashion set by Queen Victoria, her dress was probably white, and wonderfully chaste, with a straight long skirt, a high neck and long tight sleeves, with just a hint of lace at the wrists and collar, and a pointed bodice with tiny pearl buttons down the front, giving the impression that Miss Clara Vesey was all wrapped up like a tiny package of virtue. However, the view from the back would have been an extravagant riot of bustle, bows, pearls, lace and train which would serve to draw attention to her gently swaying, distinctly unchaste posterior as she sashayed down the aisle on the arm of someone who could not have been her father (Edward Soldene having died ten years earlier in the home of his other wife). You can take the girl out of the theatre, but you can't take the theatre out of the girl.

The groom waiting at the altar was young, six years younger than Clara as it happens, Clara being thirty years old and her groom just twenty-four. Not that she admitted this on the marriage certificate, giving herself the same age as him – a woman marrying a younger man raised eyebrows, although Clara was not unique in the theatre world in this respect. As in so many other areas, the normal social conventions did not apply.

So, who was this lucky young man? After all those years turning down offers from eligible young lords, Clara had accepted the hand of a German businessman, a corn merchant from Hamburg, Friedrich Carl Hoffmeister, who may not have been titled, but was already very wealthy. Clara was now moving with her husband to a smart mansion block in Victoria Street, Westminster. From here she would begin a life of conventional upper-middle-class respectability – no more flashing her tightly clad legs in breech roles, posing for saucy photographs, receiving gifts from wealthy admirers, or trips across the oceans to appear in foreign opera houses and mining towns. Instead Clara was to become a mother; her first child was born a year later and called Katie Emily Hoffmeister after the long-gone but not forgotten matriarch Katie Swain, and of course her sister. Katie was followed eighteen months later by a son, Charles Edward. It was an extraordinary change in lifestyle for Clara who, for the whole of her adult life, had been working relentlessly on the stage. Gone was her public life and independence. With a few short vows Clara Vesey disappeared from the world, transformed into Mrs Friedrich Hoffmeister, so simply done. The feted and adored Clara Vesey was gone for ever.

At the reception there would have been plenty of whispered speculation about the match. Throughout the 1870s Clara had been one of the most admired actresses for her beauty and vivacity, if not her talent. It was well known that she had turned down offers, seemingly unable to give up her theatrical career. The guests probably wondered what had led her to take this step now, with this unknown (if obviously wealthy) young German businessman. Of course, people would have realised that age might be a factor. Many people understood that actresses rarely admitted to their true age and that time was undoubtedly working against Clara. But the more theatrically aware guests may well have guessed at another reason. Clara had deserted the ship just as things were getting difficult.

However, Clara had not been the first person to desert. Sat in the church would probably have been Emily's eldest daughter, Katie, pregnant with her second child, and Katie's husband. On 18th May 1878, while Emily was trying to earn her passage home playing in Australian mining towns, Katie Soldene Powell had run off and married. She was only eighteen. Neither of her parents had ever met the groom and Katie had managed to deprive Emily of the chance of playing the mother of the bride, although to be fair Emily had deprived her own mother of this same pleasure. Priscilla had to wait until she was a widow and a great-grandmother before she could finally appear as the mother of the bride at Clara's wedding. In fact, Priscilla was the first mother to attend a daughter's wedding in five generations of Swain women. They seemed to make a habit of not inviting them.

The man Katie Soldene Powell had chosen was Robinson Henry Simpson, a twenty-five-year-old son of a judge's clerk. As a very successful stockbroker, he was to prove a more financially prudent choice than her mother's. But it wasn't just the wedding that the young Katie Soldene Powell had deprived her mother of. Daughters of actresses often followed their mothers onto the stage, and Emily might have been hoping that her children would eventually join her and Clara. Years later in an interview Emily declared:

'Let a girl of mine go on the stage?' she said, and this time there was no smiling lip. 'Why I'd give my soul before a daughter of mine should be an actress. My dear, I've been through it. My mother believed it was an ante-room to Hell and I know it is. And think of the thousands who fail and beat their hearts out. I was one in a thousand who succeeds. No, indeed!'

And yet it seems this might be another example of Emily protesting too much. Years later Emily's enthusiastic support of her youngest daughter Nellie, her eldest son Edward, and Clara's own daughter, Katie Vesey, in their acting careers, suggests that she felt otherwise, or at least conflicted. With her four children Emily had the potential to create a whole new theatrical dynasty and become one of the families like the Kembles, who were renowned and had the history of the British theatre running in their veins. To come from one of these thespian dynasties was the closest to becoming respectable. It was also a means to keep her opera company young and fashionable. Just as Emily had used Clara when her own youth was fading, Katie could have potentially taken Clara's place.

But now Katie Soldene Powell was never to go on the stage or work at all – she had gone straight from childhood to life as a wife and mother in comfortable upper-middle-class prosperity, a life similar to the one her Aunt Clara was about to begin. Katie had made a different choice to her mother; she always conformed to the Victorian ideal of what a woman should be, and her respectability was never compromised. But however Emily felt privately, outwardly she supported her daughter and was to grow very fond of this new son-in-law. At a time when her own future felt so precarious, Emily must have felt some relief that her own daughter appeared to have found a way to security and would not have to go through the unrelenting struggle that she still had to face. Bittersweet.

Weddings are one of those events that can be as much about who isn't there, as who is. Clara must have been acutely aware of the absences at her wedding, even if everyone was making a point of not mentioning them. One of the missing guests was Emily's husband, Jack Powell.

At the very beginning of the year, on 4th January 1880, a notice had appeared in *The Era*:

We regret to learn that Miss Emily Soldene was taken seriously ill the other night while playing in the pantomime of The Forty Thieves at the Gaiety in Glasgow. Miss Clara Vesey at a few moments' notice took the part of Ganem and acquitted herself in a highly satisfactory manner.

A week later it was followed by another notice:

Crowded and fashionable audiences nightly testify to the excellence of Mr. Bernard's sixth Gaiety annual. We are glad to be able to state that Miss Soldene has recovered from her indisposition and is again delighting Glaswegians with her brilliant vocal powers.

However, Emily had been in perfectly good health all the time; it was her husband, Jack, who had been taken seriously ill. While Emily was busy performing as the principal boy in *The Forty Thieves*, or *Striking Oil in Family Jars*, Jack had a major stroke. He was forty-five years old. He survived but was left disabled and Emily was left with a pressing problem – he needed full-time nursing care, but more than ever, money was needed, and Emily had to work. So Emily had to bring Jack south to the seaside and take a lease on a house in Bognor, the Victorians being great believers in the efficacy of sea air. She installed a live-in nurse brought down from one of the Swain ancestral villages in Hertfordshire. Emily then went back to Glasgow and proceeded to work to pay for it all, giving three performances a night through the dreary, dark months of January, February and March. There was no time to grieve or process the shock, and instead she kept going, the bright smile on her face – for Emily the show really did go on. She was also left without a manager, for the moment hiring agents in London to handle her affairs.

Jack's illness must have made Clara's decision to quit even more devastating for Emily. Just when she needed the emotional support, not to mention her understudy, Clara married up and out. It meant that in less than a year Emily had lost her two constant travelling companions.

But it wasn't only her personal life that appeared to be collapsing. Emily was also facing one of the biggest challenges of her career. Sometimes fashions change gradually and organically, and then sometimes there's a revolution. Within just a few months Emily's French opéras bouffes seemed so last year, and now it was all Gilbert and Sullivan. It's unclear how long it took Emily to realise that this revolution was taking place and that she was on the wrong side of it. In her memoir she writes:

> When I arrived from Australia, August 12th 1878, Mrs Langtry was a reigning beauty; Shiel Barry was a sensation at the Charing Cross Theatre, as Gaspard the Miser, in 'Les Cloches de Corneville;' the Alhambra was playing to empty benches, and 'HMS Pinafore' at the Opera Comique to half salaries.

And yet by the end of 1878 audiences were flocking to *HMS Pinafore*, and when *The Pirates of Penzance* came out in 1879 and was even more popular, and their promoter Richard D'Oyly Carte built the Savoy Theatre for them in 1881, Gilbert and Sullivan were firmly established as creators of the popular operas to go and see. No one was interested in opéra bouffe; Offenbach was about as popular as animals in circuses.

Emily was quick to recognise the appeal of the first major collaboration between the librettist William Gilbert and composer Arthur Sullivan, *Trial by Jury*. Together with Charles Morton, she was the second person to stage it in London, the version in which

Clara had starred so successfully. But Emily seems to have failed to grasp exactly why this was such a disproportionate hit – the fact that every time they performed it, it had been more popular than the Offenbach operas that it was supposed to be supporting. This was not a coincidence, and neither was it about (or just about) Clara's amazing charms. The fact is that *Trial by Jury* was a style of comic opera that appealed more to the British, and subsequently American, audiences than the adapted imports from continental Europe.

Opéra bouffe in the Victorian mind meant French productions with racy plots and revealing costumes. Gilbert and Sullivan decided to create something that felt different. They were to be absolutely respectable, with no swapping of gender roles or ladies in tights, absolutely no high-kicking, no adultery except by the odd caricature fool. Women did not have sexual desire. Lovers did not lose their heads, lust was absent, pragmatism ruled. Gilbert and Sullivan operas felt very British, and they were supposed to. The triumphant values were those of the conservative middle class. The wit was cerebral, the respectability of the troupe was publicised and decorum reigned backstage. Emily could never have got a job with D'Oyly Carte.

As the music critic, William Archer, wrote in 1883:

The general public seems, for the moment at any rate, to have turned its back upon the fleshpots of Egypt owing to powerful native competition in the shape of the most popular entertainments of the day, the Gilbert-Sullivan operettas. The victory of Gilbertian extravaganza over opera-bouffe as adapted for the London market is the victory of literary and musical grace and humour over rampant vulgarity and meretricious jingle.

Since Emily had come back from Australia, she had gone round the country touring the same old favourites, but the ticket receipts were telling Emily (and Clara) that the home-grown stardust was wearing off. Emily's Continental burlesques suddenly seemed terribly last decade. How many times did audiences want to see the ageing and enlarging Emily Soldene dressed in tights as a saucy pastry cook, making filthy suggestions? Audiences and reviews were generally lacklustre. Emily knew she needed to add something new to her repertoire.

Back in March 1875, while Emily was busy making her debut in the United States, in Paris another formidable lady was being premiered. Georges Bizet had finally finished writing *Carmen*. The first-night audience included Offenbach, Massenet, Delibes and Gounod, who was furious afterwards claiming that Bizet had stolen one of his tunes. They had been lured in by the gossip surrounding this Bizet offering. The rehearsals had overrun and it was rumoured to be sensational in all senses of the word: pushing the boundaries, something new.

The audience was certainly impressed, but not necessarily in a good way. Carmen was an unscrupulous, wild Spanish gypsy, a dangerously sexual woman on the margins of society who prized her liberty above everything else. The opera is the story of her battle to the death with a man who is sexually obsessed by her. In the first act Carmen stabs another woman, gets herself arrested and escapes by seducing the soldier guarding her, leading him to be thrown into jail instead. There are outlaws, an erotic dance in a smuggler's tavern and a magnificent toreador. Carmen comes to a sticky end when her former soldier lover stabs her to death. One can see why a Victorian audience might have problems with this new work – it was all rather brutal and sexual. By the time they had got to the third act the audience could barely clap; most of them sat in stunned silence. Bizet seethed afterwards: 'Don't you see that all these bourgeois have not understood a wretched word of the work I have written for them?'

It played to half-full houses, the theatre forced to give away free tickets to fill up seats, and Bizet died after the thirty-third performance at the age of only thirty-six, thinking his last and favourite opera was a flop. It was not staged again in Paris until 1883. However, there were a few people who saw *Carmen*'s merits and it was performed in other European capitals with much more success. In June 1878 it premiered at Her Majesty's Theatre and it was profitable enough that in February 1879 the first English-language version was put on at her Majesty's, starring Emily's old rival Selina 'Dolly' Dolaro.

One of the first things Emily would have done when she got back from Australia was to go and see this new controversial offering. Emily probably watched, riveted, fully immersed in the story, the occasional prickle at the back of her neck, perhaps tears springing when the toreador entered. Never would she have come across a part she wanted to play so badly, never would she have seen two leading men she wanted to wrestle with so urgently. Carmen, the wild, totally unscrupulous mezzo-soprano gypsy woman, who stabs a rival, seduces a soldier and dances erotically in a smuggler's den, is the object of a toreador's desire, and, even better, dies a tragic violent death. What was not to like? There was a lot Emily could identify with. Emily must have been furious that she'd missed out on buying the rights for London, but there were still the provincial rights – she dashed over to Paris as soon as she could and managed to buy them. She also hired a young tenor called Durward Lely to play her obsessive soldier lover. Years later in the Sydney Evening News she wrote:

Lely is my particular tenor, and was in my company for two or three years. He was the best Don Jose in Carmen ever seen on stage, or in any language. Ideal in appearance, long and lean and thin in the flanks, dark – so dark – a black Scotsman, with straight black brows, straight black hair, and hazel eyes. He and I were dreadfully in earnest in Carmen – flew at each other's throats when on the stage, and would not look at each other when off for fear of losing 'the atmosphere'. 'Art thou the devil, Carmen?' said he, fingering his dagger. 'Yes,' said I, fingering mine, and I meant it too.

In another column Emily was to admit just how much she meant it.

When I played Carmen, I always carried a bright, sharp, handy, business-like, wicked-looking little dagger. To do so was a particular and peculiar satisfaction to me, and gave reality and power to the situation and scene. A real weapon wakes up the blood. In the portrayal of great and violent emotion a wooden dagger would bring me off the heights at once.

The feeling was mutual. Lely is reported to have said to Emily:

'Never was such a Carmen as you. I've played the opera over and over again, with heaps of prima donnas, but it never went like it did with us.'

Emily smiled at him and said:

'Two devils'
'Yes' said he.

Leading ladies and leading men have always been prone to falling in love with one another. For a start there is the power of proximity. It's scientifically proven that as long as you start with either a neutral or positive attitude to the person you are to be spending time with, then generally your liking will increase. Then most actors work from the 'inside out' – that is, they rearrange their emotions to play their characters and they generally start to feel some of the same feelings. If an actor is supposed to be locked in a passionate relationship relentlessly night after night, it's not surprising if they develop an intense attachment.

In May 1879 Emily opened the first production of *Carmen* in Britain outside the capital, at the Old Theatre Royal in Leicester. People queued for hours to get tickets.

> *It was generally conceded that my 'Carmen' was a good one. I had a natural turn for the tragic, and my acquired taste and experience in comic opera enabled me to give many little touches which had not been thought of before. It was a very difficult opera to produce; and there was no end of bother with the orchestra. Fancy, three trombones all wanting 6l. per week each! The work was extremely exhausting for the principal singers. But at the Prince of Wales's Theatre, Liverpool, Mr. Lely and I made a record, which is still unbroken, singing 'Carmen' every night for three consecutive weeks to crammed houses.*

The reviewers agreed, *The Era* included: 'Miss Soldene as the cruel and faithless Carmen, sang and acted with appropriate dash, spirit and recklessness, and elicited repeatedly the heartiest applause especially in the more powerful and intensely dramatic scenes.'

Emily must have been quite captivating. Years later she was at a party and was introduced to a gentleman whom she didn't recognise, but he certainly remembered her:

'The last time I spoke to you was in your dressing room at the Grand Theatre Leeds in 1880. You were playing Carmen. I made a little picture of you and brought it to the theatre. Have a cigarette? You smoked so many in Carmen. You used to roll them yourself, you know.' 'Yes,' I nodded. I couldn't speak for wonderment at these revelations.
The cigarette was nice and we resolved ourselves into a smoke concert. 'Yes' said Mr. Phil, 'I was a poor fellow then, precious hard up, and would have done anything to keep in the theatre. I recollect everything you did in Carmen. Do you know, you were the first woman I fell in love with?' 'Good gracious,' said I, putting the wrong end of the cigarette in my mouth.

He tried to get a job as her luggage handler, but wasn't very strong, and then he followed her to Bradford and around the country until his money ran out. Today this might be seen as stalking and warrant a call to the police, but Emily was only too delighted.

This was all very nice indeed, and I wonder if you don't call that a romance of the stage, I don't know what is. 'I wonder what came to the little picture,' said I. 'Probably you put it in the fire,' said he. 'You received it, but did not seem paralysed by its excellence. I worked from a photo I bought of you, and my mother has that photo hanging in her room now, and would not take any money for it.'

Perhaps Emily had reached an age and stage in her life where her male fans suddenly seemed a lot more precious.

When your brand has become tired, the answer is to reinvent yourself. A relaunch. It was no easy task for a forty-two-year-old woman in the nineteenth century. But, by trying Carmen, Emily was attempting something different. It was the most operatic, vocally demanding part she had ever played. The production was sensual, but had a darker tone than her romping burlesque Offenbach offerings. Many felt she was stepping out of her league.

At first it seemed as if Emily was making a success of it. But as the tour progressed from Leicester in May and moved each week to Birmingham, Manchester, Sheffield, Hull, Leeds, Liverpool, Dublin, Belfast, Hanley, Southport, Blackpool, Edinburgh, Newcastle, Glasgow, Bradford and Brighton, finally ending up in Portsmouth in November, the reviews of *Carmen* began to get less enthusiastic. In Manchester the critic was dubious, stating that the company, though strong enough for comic opera, was hardly adequate to the performance of more ambitious works: 'only a powerful organisation can hope to do justice to a work of such magnitude'. And of Emily, 'the role is hardly suited for her, and her success cannot have corresponded with the importance of the task she had set herself'.

It was tiring work and it seems as though Emily and the rest of the cast started to flag. Emily reduced her performances of *Carmen*, and put on the old favourites like *Geneviève de Brabant* and *La Grande-Duchesse*, and she couldn't perform *Carmen* at all when she came back to London because she didn't have the rights. Her foray into more serious opera ended when they went to Liverpool and a pretty young lady, a merchant's daughter called Miss Alice Frances Harndall, sat in the front row and was as entranced as Emily by this long, dark Scotsman who glowered with sexual tension and fingered his dagger. Miss Harndall's repeated appearances did not go unnoticed by Lely, who started to sing his arias less to Emily and more to the young lady. Emily found herself having to work harder to keep his attention. It must have been particularly galling, after Lely had begun by being so passionately entranced by her Carmen.

With Gilbert and Sullivan now all everyone was talking about, and Emily's *Carmen* receiving lukewarm reviews, Emily decided that the market was too crowded at home, and she needed to go back to the States and take *Carmen* with her. However, Durward Lely refused to leave Britain and, despite Emily's best efforts and entreaties, went off and married Miss Harndall instead. A cruel blow. This left Emily without a leading man and again despite scouring the country she could find no one with the vocal ability, not to mention the sex appeal, that could take Lely's place. Emily decided she should still go to America even though she would be three and a half thousand miles away from a dangerously frail husband in Bognor, who might not be there when she got back. Such was the need to earn money; the show must go on.

But Clara didn't agree. She had had enough, and announced that instead of going to America again she was staying behind and getting married.

For Emily it meant she had to take this trip without the two people she relied upon the most. The famous Chinese proverb advises us to be careful what we wish for. It must have often felt as if Jack was in the way, holding her back, but sometimes we don't realise how much we rely upon someone until they are no longer there. Jack had always been portrayed as a shadowy figure, an afterthought in Emily's life, but now he was no longer around Emily might have wondered whether she was going to be able to manage without him. And without Clara too. It was a test to see how she could manage on her own.

This may explain why Emily hired Messers Jarvis and Froom as her promoters for this tour. She might have been drawn to the familiar. They had been on the Australian tour as companions to their wives who were cast members in Emily's troupe. In fact, Jarvis was the husband of the legendary high-kicking Wiry Sal, and Harry Froom was the husband of her lead singer, the absconding and no longer trusted Rose Stella. Again, perhaps this is a sign of how desperate Emily was – emotion seems to have overcome her judgement. Jarvis and Froom were actors, not professional managers, and Emily was filled with a sense of doom when she realised Jarvis had booked her first engagement in Brooklyn – a place Emily avoided at all costs. The reviews of her opening night did not help her mood – the whole company was accused of being under-rehearsed, and her replacement for Lely, Charles Campbell, of having forgotten his lines so completely that the show nearly came to a halt. The reviewer found Emily's voice 'harsh and uneven', her acting 'not up to standard', 'Time has not dealt gently with her and she is no longer fitted for the assumption of such parts as Chilpéric.'

Worse was to come. Among the most important responsibilities of managers is to book venues and plan the tour. This is the most basic requirement. It seems Jarvis and Froom were making errors from the start, booking two theatres on the same night that were often hundreds of miles apart, with the result that Emily, as the head of the company, kept being sued for broken contracts and arrested. As Emily said, 'This was all very worrying.'

In St Louis the sheriff walked in with a claim against Emily for $2,000 for breach of contract. He arrested her and then was planning to go to the theatre and confiscate the company's wardrobe until payment was made: '"Well," I said, "I thought it would be better if he would stay with me, while I sent a messenger for the manager to come right along." He didn't mind'.

Of course he didn't mind – Emily made sure she gave him a few hours he could dine out on for the rest of his life. Meanwhile she wrote a note to the trusted husband of her wardrobe mistress, Mr Quinton, telling him to hurry and register a deed at the town hall transferring the costumes to his property so the sheriff could have no legal claim on them.

I rang the bell for some whisky and cigars . . . The bell-boy came, I passed the note over the table to my friend. He was too much of a gentleman to look at the direction and passed it to the boy. My arrest was not very painful. My arrestor sat and talked, drank his whisky, and smoked his cigars. Quinton made no reply to my note. Time was getting on, and I was getting in agony. Conversation flagged a bit, and I brought out some albums of celebrities.

Like Scheherazade, Emily kept spinning tales to keep her jailor distracted, but even the winning Emily could not detain the sheriff for ever:

He went, but before going put me on my parole not to leave the hotel. I broke it and rushed off to the Barnum House where Quinton lived. Mrs. Quinton was in a dreadful state. 'Oh madame, we've been out; William only just got your note and has gone to the City Hall now.' I fled back to the

Planter's House, and threw off my things. Close behind me
arrived Quinton, breathless. 'Just in time, madame,' panted
he, 'I filed the deed five minutes before the office closed.'

Emily and her wardrobe escaped jail this time, but double bookings were just one of the appalling mismanagements. The popularity of a production is crucial to the success or failure of a tour, but in terms of profit, the terms made with the venues are just as important. No matter how full the house, if the relationship between the price of the tickets, the money owed to the theatre and the total costs of production aren't advantageous, you can still make a calamitous loss. A key component of these costs was the money given to the theatre in rent.

Jarvis and Froom had drawn up contracts with theatres that meant they had to pay large rental fees up front and in return could take all proceeds of the ticket sales, instead of the less risky option of paying less up front and giving up a percentage of the takings. This might have worked if Jarvis and Froom had had capital in the bank, but they didn't – Jarvis and Froom had gambled on using the early profits from the tour to pay for the theatres as they went along. Which was all very well, except there weren't any early profits. The American public weren't that enthusiastic about seeing Emily again. As in England, her comic operas were out of fashion, and something seemed to have happened to the company, as if there had been a collective loss of nerve. The critics were savage:

'The performance would have disgraced a concert hall'

'The Company can boast a few pretty faces, but there is a pitiable lack of both dramatic and vocal talent.'

'It was the most wretched performance of that opera ever given in Syracuse, even by amateurs. Soldene, fat and forty – or more – is not an ideal Serpolette in figure, while her voice is broken and unmusical . . .'

'The rare spectacle of an audience expressing its disgust and disapproval of a performance was witnessed . . . The troupe has not a singer amongst it, save Rose Stella, a little French girl who has some chic and is about all there is good of the organisation. Miss Soldene is homelier than she was before and can now sing only fairly well. Her Serpolette bordered on the ridiculous. No such embonpoint as is hers could satisfy the popular idea of the Tom-boy of Corneville. The opera dragged from the start, and at times was positively stupid. The sickly attempts to make the dialogue sparkle with puns fell flat and deserved the mock applause and hisses bestowed on it. The company seemed to glory in roundness of limb rather than fullness of voice.'

'The company has been reduced to almost nothing. The female chorus is weak and the male chorus is a nonentity. Rose Stella is the best in the company and she is only fair.'

And so they go on. The only person who was making any positive impression was the young, pretty, disloyal Rose Stella, who had taken Clara's place as understudy and Plaintiff, and second soprano.

Takings were so bad that the company were on half salaries almost immediately. Jarvis and Froom tried to renegotiate the contracts with the theatres as they couldn't pay the agreed rents, offering a percentage of ticket sales in return for reduced upfront investment. But the theatres had seen the reviews and were not convinced that these ticket sales would materialise. It was now up to Jarvis and Froom to put up the money out of their own pockets. Harry Froom had none and Emily sacked him, which can't have helped her relationship with Rose Stella. Jarvis agreed he would carry on as the company's manager for no pay until the artists had been paid, and he brought in his wife, the legendary high-kicking Sara, to join the company. Later Jarvis was to claim in a newspaper interview that 'he'd lost the savings of fifteen years as an actor in a few weeks in an enterprise which should really only be the pastime of a Vanderbilt' and that all he'd received in return was 'covered with vituperation and abuse'.

This shortage of takings meant that they couldn't go to the theatres that they'd planned, but had to take one-night stands at random small-town places, often making only just enough money to pay their train tickets to the next town:

During this tour we visited 'Eureka', a mining town, the only one I ever saw in the States without a church. The theatre was built of weather-boards, sawdusted, and lit with petroleum lamps. The lime-light was the head-light of an engine, lent by the railway company and placed in the wings. The dressing-rooms were calico screens. The lowest admission was five dollars, and the air was so full of sulphur you had to walk about with a pocket handkerchief to your mouth. Eureka was a dreadful desert of dry, sandy mountains; on each side of the narrow road were gambling saloons, and down it ran little streams bordered with green. The little streams came from the reducing works, and the green was a mineral deposit from the same source. One of the gambling saloons captured a chorus girl of ours. She could play the piano well; she got eight dollars per day, and a percentage on the drinks.

...

We left Eureka at 4am, and, as we walked past the saloon, heard through the thick and poison-laden air the tinkle of the piano played by Alice C. I saw her afterwards in San Francisco in 1891. She brought me as a present, a lovely canary in a lovely cage, and was in great form; had married the proprietor of the

Eureka Saloon, with whom she was now keeping one in 'Frisco.
'Oh, Alice,' said I, 'I was so sorry when you stopped in that
dreadful place.' 'Well you see, madame,' said she apologetically,
'I had my child to keep.' Alice was the widow of poor Tom
Melling, the Oxford harmonium player, who was drowned in
the river at York, leaving a young wife and baby.

It was a hard life and no wonder the chorus girl would rather work in a saloon bar on tours like these. It was hardly the stellar Broadway moment of Emily's first tour, or even the moderate success of the last. In the end the cast went on strike. As the local newspaper reported: 'The Soldene party declared war against their manager, JH Jarvis, after their performance on account of salaries not being paid, and refused to go any further: Promises finally settled it.'

Probably the biggest promise was the prospect of their first decent venue in a month and a half, in Philadelphia where Emily had had so much success in the past. However, when they turned up the weather was abysmal and the cast got terrible colds; one of the tenors' was so bad that they left him behind. Emily struggled through the first week, but had to retire to bed in the second and her understudy, Minnie Marshall, went on instead. Unfortunately, she seems to have done rather well: 'It is perhaps an ungracious thing to say, but the hearty applause showered on Miss Marshall seemed to indicate that the substitute gave better satisfaction than the principal.'

Being upstaged by the understudy must be every principal's nightmare and is definitely not good for one's confidence or self-esteem. Years later Emily was to brush it off:

Do you know the great thing in the theatre when the prima
donna assoluta falls ill and the understudy 'goes on'? Why, all the

company dresses, and everybody dodges the stage manager, and stands in the wings and hangs over the flies, to gaze upon and criticise the performance. As a rule the understudy is found to be highly superior to the original .

...

'Ho! Hain't she bewtiful. Look hat 'er, Smithy 'An' there's happlause for yer!' 'Ho! She's got 'er bokay!' 'An 'er encore!' 'er nice smack in ther face fer Miss Stuck-Hup, has don't think this hurth's good enuf fer 'er to walk hon', sniffs the second lady's dresser (who has also to look after half a dozen ladies of the ballet). 'Don't be so unfeeling, Jonesy, Miss Montefiore de Vere is very ill'. 'Hill! Temper – that's wots ther matter – temper! You'll see, she'll be hon again tomorrer night, Look at the little 'un. Why, Monte can't touch 'er.' 'Well, wun thing', says Miss de Vere's personal attendant, who is boiling with rage. 'The c'orus girl won't wear hour dresses. I won't hallow wunt ter go hout hof hour room . . .'

I imagine Miss de Vere's personal attendant may have been Emily's real-life wardrobe mistress Mrs Quinton. She's making a joke of it, but underneath I have a feeling Emily wasn't laughing. Minnie Marshall disappeared from the company soon after.

After they did tolerably well in Pike's Opera House, Emily did manage to get herself a new pair of agents, Bob Miles and Louis Ballenberg, both theatre owners in Cincinnati. They negotiated six weeks in San Francisco and promised a new comic opera, *Billee Taylor*, which was eagerly anticipated by the locals and press, as it was the latest hit on Broadway. The San Francisco critic Betsy B was back again, her attitude uncharacteristically soft.

Soldene, having put a girdle round the earth, comes this way once more. You may know her lithographs by the hat, an article of gear in which she always affected a particularly rakish style. The big prima donna was rather shone down on the occasion of her first engagement here, by the erratic Sara, the small Saxon-looking minx dressed like a Japanese property-man, whose kick was the town talk for at least one moon. There is no Sara this time, but the prudent Soldene – who, off the stage, looks essentially the business woman her prosperous career would indicate her to be – knows well the charm of accessories and includes a ballet in the list of attractions. Forty artists! Think of this number grouped on the little Standard stage in Chilpéric, say, which was a pretty spectacle, and one of the successes of the first engagement. No less than three or four new operas are announced for this season, and with the idea that there is something in a name, people are looking forward with more than usual interest to Billee Taylor.

Except that *Billee Taylor* never appeared. The premiere kept being postponed and the press kept wondering. The managers fell out with the theatre and had to transfer to the less prestigious California. The reason for the delay was that they were waiting for a stage manager to arrive from the east coast to produce it. But when he finally landed in San Francisco, he'd left the script on the train. The one and only script. While they were waiting for a replacement to arrive, another theatre put on their own version of *Billee Taylor*, written by their manager. It was a hit. No one came to see the old Soldene company. Why would they?

The Soldene engagement is one of the most ruinous that could have been made for San Francisco at the present time. It was next to insanity to suppose that an opera company with the ancient Soldene as the leading attraction could do anything for a management.

Note that Emily took the blame rather than Miles and Ballenberg. How much was there a bias against women of a certain age and independent businesswomen? But worse was to come.

Sara the kicker had left with her husband, Jarvis the manager. Her replacement was a dancer called Maggie Duggan whom Emily had worked with many times, and who was proving a popular enough replacement. Unfortunately, she had brought with her a comedian husband called Clive Hersee and all was not well between them. Maggie was rather too enthusiastic in her kicking and when Hersee got combative with her he was arrested and fined $20. When he got back from his night in the cells he tried to assault Duggan, but she hit him over the head with a beer bottle and he ended up needing stitches for a horrible gash. After this Duggan continued to dance the cancan every night while Hersee got terrible reviews for his comedy routine: 'for some unknown reason [he] was permitted to violate all rules of stage etiquette and intensely disgust the audience by his mal apropos buffoonery.'

A few weeks later the Soldene Company was travelling east to Denver, and waiting to pick up a train at a junction. According to later newspaper reports, Clive Hersee enjoyed a convivial lunch at the café drinking beer with the proprietor. Afterwards he walked out onto the bridge, made a greeting to one of the chorus girls and then as she walked off, he climbed over the railing, stood on the ledge for a brief second, and jumped into the tumbling current twenty feet below. Emily says in her memoir: 'I can see his blue eyes now, looking straight out of the water up to the sky. Then his head went "bash" on a big rock and we saw him no more.'

Everyone saw the jump, and there was uproar. Hersee was not killed but resurfaced. He managed to get free of his coat and struggled desperately to reach the shore, but the current quickly swept him downstream. A crowd from the depot ran along the riverbank following him, expecting to see him gain a footing, but Hersee seemed unable to extricate himself from the river. The bystanders discussed whether to try and rescue him, but decided it was too dangerous. After about half a mile Hersee appeared to stop struggling, as if he'd run out of strength. The newspaper reported: 'His features which were plainly visible to those on the bank, were as fixed as marble, but showed frightful agony.'

Then there came the moment where he didn't surface any more.

The consensus from the witnesses was that he didn't really mean to kill himself, only to shock his errant wife, Maggie Duggan, whom the newspapers suggested was planning to divorce him when they reached Denver. Other papers were more specific in their blame:

Clive Hersee, the member of the Soldene troupe who lately committed suicide, is said to have been at one time an officer in the British army, and was driven to commission of his rash act by domestic infelicity. It is said his wife Marie [sic] Duggan, treated him as though he was a boy, and never allowed him to be away from his apron strings.

In reality, Maggie was distraught and refused to accept that he was dead, believing he had made it to the shore upriver. She offered a reward of $30 for anyone who had a sighting of him. But six weeks later it was reported: 'his remains were found at a place called "Beaver Brook," twenty-two miles west of Denver; his body was ground by the rocks to a pulp, and his clothes had disappeared'.

Hersee's death seemed to sap what remaining enthusiasm there was in the troupe. They arrived for their summer engagement in Cincinnati, demoralised and bickering. Maggie Duggan was said to be on the verge of insanity. Without Clara or Jack to vent her frustrations to, Emily seems to have let her tongue run rather freely. It's never good news when a star falls out with their manager. Emily made the mistake of calling Ballenberg a 'petty flute-player' within the hearing of a girl whom she knew would tell everyone. The local paper reported the spat: 'The upshot is that Miss Soldene is in Cincinnati, languishing for back salary, and other members of her troupe are as impecunious as she. Moral – if a man is a petty flute-player, let the fact die with him.'

The result of this indiscretion was that Miles went east and Ballenberg not only refused to pay her, but their venue in Cincinnati fell through and the 'petty flute-player' refused to fix another one. But Emily continued her indiscretions:

A reporter of the Post Dispatch interviewed Soldene and she spoke freely about her facial peculiarities, the prudery of audiences and the Clive Hersee suicide, together with a very free criticism of her late company who have arrived in town and are very wroth over the 'interview', particularly Miss Duggan (Mrs Hersee) whom Miss Soldene designated as 'Liverpool Irish'. Developments may ensue.

212

Unfortunately, developments did ensue. There was a mutiny. The whole company disbanded. With the latest flattering reviews spinning in her head, Rose Stella decided she'd be better off at the head of her own company and, together with Maggie Duggan and most of the rest of the cast, set up the 'Rose Stella Combination'. With Ballenberg's help, they took over the Cincinnati theatre that was supposed to be the home of the Emily Soldene Opera Bouffe Company for the whole of the summer. Emily had been ejected from her theatrical ship like Captain Bligh from HMS *Bounty*. With no cast, no theatre and no manager, Emily had no choice but to quietly make her way back east to New York, and slip on a boat for home.

One thing that must have preoccupied Emily on the return trip was whether Jack would still be alive when she got back. As it happened, she was just in time. Emily went straight down to Bognor and paid one last visit to Jack. He died a few nights later while Emily was singing at Crystal Palace, playing her old role of Drogan in *Geneviève de Brabant*. The day after his death she starred in *La fille de Madame Angot*. She had taken even less of a break than when she'd had her children. It was her mother, Priscilla, who on the night of 14th September 1881 was by Jack's bedside when he died, which was slightly ironic considering how much she had opposed Jack and Emily's marriage. For Emily of course the show always went on.

At many points during this Wild West roller coaster of a trip Emily's thoughts might have turned to the alternative lifestyle of her little sister. As Emily fought with cast, managers, sheriffs and the press, Clara would have been living a life which looked (from the outside at least) like one of ease and luxury, filled with evenings at the opera in a box rather than on a stage, trips to see friends, parties and suppers. There was the odd confinement, but no childcare duties, only bed rest, as opposed to being back on the stage the next week, as if nothing had happened. The nearest Clara got to performing was entertaining guests with an appropriate song from her old repertoire at the end of a supper party. Likewise, there might have been comparisons between Emily's daughter's life at the age of twenty-one and her own back in the day – a mother of three, being frightened to death by Howard Glover in singing lessons, lunchtimes battling nerves at concerts and nights in the stalls at the opera gazing enviously at divas. Emily might have been wondering where on earth she had gone wrong. She'd done all the work, but her sister and daughter seemed to be reaping all the rewards.

But was she? Emily's writing suggests otherwise:

I have had two offers of marriage on the cars, the would-be bridegroom in one case, offering to find a parson on board the train, and have the thing settled 'right away.' I have been as nearly as possible 'side tracked' by the handsomest cowboy in Arizona, Colonel Charles Spencer. I have been 'snowed in' at Truckee, and 'washed out' on the Plains. I have lunched on the Summit of the Rockies, and mailed a postcard (which was safely delivered) to London from the summit of the Sierras. I have been down a silver mine in Virginia City, where the temperature was so high you had to take a hot bath before returning to the surface, and I have been up a mountain in the same locality an hour later, gathering ice to eat with the strawberries just arrived from 'Frisco. I have eaten bear's pad in St. Louis, and been introduced to native and growling lions at Green River . . .

Would Emily Soldene have swapped places with Clara Hoffmeister or Katie Simpson? Perhaps, despite everything, the alternative of being married and staying at home seemed rather dull. As Emily says at the end of her memoir:

Let me take this opportunity of saying that my art has been, and still is, the one great delight of my life; and in whatever direction engaged, or whatever the grade of the audience, I have been always the same. I gave them the best of my ability and all my heart and soul, and could do no more.

Emily's nemesis, the singer and fellow impresario, Kate Santley

Chapter Eleven

The Duchess di Begonia and the Very Incarnation of Vice

Although there are nice people on the stage, there are some who would make your hair stand on end (Charles Dickens)

Emily's first official retirement came on 5th December 1883 at the Globe Theatre, with a grand 'Farewell to London' concert. All the usual suspects turned up to perform except for Clara who was now playing at being Mrs Hoffmeister in the audience. Instead, Emily's younger daughter, Nellie, had been brought in to play those cute, character page parts. Also absent was the dreadful Kate Santley who, despite saying she would turn up right up until the last minute – her name was even in the programme – was a no-show. However, the main star was Emily, who allowed herself to sing all of her greatest hits.

The familiar music was once more warmly welcomed and the spirit and humour infused into the part gained general appreciation, and at the close of the opera Miss Soldene was again called for, and a parting cheer bestowed, showing that her old friends and admirers have not lost their former regard for her.

Which is all very well, but what was an ageing Victorian actress to do next?

Emily decided it was time to stop performing and run her own theatre. She bought a seven-year lease to the Gaiety Theatre in Hastings. This little seaside gem had an obvious appeal – the theatre was small but perfectly formed. It had been a vanity project for a local entrepreneur called George Gaze, who felt that it was high time that his hometown had a proper theatrical venue, one that would attract the very best touring companies from London. He had spared no expense in building a grand, ornate building just back from the seafront. Inside he had decorated it with all the best velvet swag trimmings and golden gilt, purchased from the capital. It even had the new electric lighting installed. Emily fell in love with the Gaiety; it could be her very own doll's house of a theatre where she could play in her more mature years, as she had done with sheets and puppets as a child when her mother wasn't looking. Hastings itself also suited Emily. It was relatively close to London, just a couple of hours direct into Charing Cross. It was pretty, its winding hilly streets lined with brightly coloured Georgian houses and shops. It reminded her of one of her favourite places in the world – Brighton, except it was smaller, one could say more exclusive, and a smaller stage would allow Emily to shine more brightly. She could be the queen of this fashionable resort.

In the new year of 1883, Emily moved what was left of her family – the children Edward, Nellie and John Arthur, her mother Priscilla, as well as a few Hertfordshire servants – to Hastings. For her first season as proprietor she put together a programme that included Gilbert and Sullivan's latest hit, *Iolanthe*, *Much Ado About Nothing* and *She Stoops to Conquer*, although the first production under her tenure was *The Two Orphans*, the very musical which Kate Claxton had been starring in on the night of the Brooklyn fire.

That first summer Emily had a great time, not least because managing the Gaiety allowed her to play host to the celebrities of the moment:

Oscar Wilde came to give a morning lecture at Hastings Theatre which I was at that time running. So unconventional, not to say impertinent. Kept the audience (all ladies) waiting for ever so long, made a delightful apology. They forgave him. The lecture was on 'Beauty' and the lecturer looked very handsome, debonair, thrown-back wavy hair and the blue eyes; he wore a brown velvet Norfolk jacket, loose knee breeches of the same, knitted stockings, shoes with buckles, and a large sunflower as a boutonniere. Those were the sunflower days, you know . . .

In the autumn she reserved three weeks for herself to take over the stage and play a few of her favourite parts with some of her old friends, and to give a platform to her youngest daughter Nellie, who was trying to launch her stage career. It must have been fun down by the seaside with friends coming to stay, plenty of good seafood, pier entertainment, watering holes and bracing walks along the promenade. But as the days drew in and it got nippy in the early mornings, I imagine a feeling of dread started to creep in. The audiences were simply drying up; by the end of October the theatre was empty. It now became apparent why no one had built a proper theatre there before. Without the summer holidaymakers, there simply weren't enough theatre-going folks in Hastings to fill it. And yet not only the rent, but also the fixed costs of the theatre still had to be paid. Emily realised if she didn't act quickly she would soon go bankrupt.

Fifteen years after Miss FitzHenry had retired, Emily left her son Edward in charge of the Gaiety, got on the train to London and went back to the music hall. This time she couldn't disguise herself under a pseudonym – she needed the money too much not to use her real name. So Emily Soldene went onto the stages of music halls like the Trocadero in Haymarket, and the Cambridge in Bishopsgate, singing the old tragic ballads that the more downmarket audiences had fallen in love with twenty years before. Once again Emily was beloved by the crowd, and found herself dashing backwards and forwards across London to play several different venues in an evening. Then she went off and did the same in Birmingham and Liverpool. It can't have held the same thrill as it had when she was a young woman. It must have been exhausting for a portly grandmother of fifty-four years old. There must have been times when she felt humiliated – no one in the business was under any illusion why Emily was doing this. The Australian paper *The Lorgnette* commented:

> *Emily Soldene's farewell benefit merely signified a descent from the operatic to the music-hall stage. The dear old lady now appears nightly at the Trocadero where she opens her large mouth to warble 'Dream Faces', 'Golden Love' and other amorous ditties.*

In 2017, Andrew Lloyd Webber revealed that the cost of running one of his theatres was £38,000 a week. However much one might earn as the star turn, the cost of running a theatre was in a different league. In anything other than the very short term the sums just didn't add up. So the finances in Hastings continued to be wobbly and got worse. Emily dashed back in May and tried to boost the takings by putting on *Trial by Jury*, even persuading Clara, briefly, to put away Mrs Hoffmeister and her role as the mother of two small children, and come back as the plaintiff Clara Vesey, in order to support her sister. The relief was only temporary.

Early on the Monday of 28th July 1884, Emily's nemesis, Kate Santley, turned up at the theatre with her production company, ready to start rehearsals. She was 'trying it out on the dog': the new practice of putting on a production in the provinces before deciding whether to take it to the West End. Kate had put aside her differences with Emily to play *La cosaque* for a week. However, when the cast arrived at the Gaiety, the doors were locked. After much banging, the doors were finally opened by the bailiffs. Emily hadn't paid the rent and George Gaze wasn't going to put up with it. It was also claimed they had not obtained a licence for the play from the authorities – which Edward Soldene Powell, as the acting manager, should have done. Kate Santley immediately took to print, making sure the following handbills were distributed among the citizens of Hastings (and also sent to the national theatre press):

To the public of Hastings – Monday afternoon – I have just arrived with my company to fulfil an engagement made some time since with Miss Soldene. Without any warning whatever from that lady or her acting-manager, I find the bailiffs in possession. Under these circumstances I am obliged for the first time in my life to break faith with the public I have the pleasure to serve. There can be no performance tonight, but the same programme will be carried out tomorrow (Tuesday) and the remainder of the week at the Public Hall. Your obedient servant, Kate Santley.

The Era, sensing the makings of a jolly good diva spat, printed this and then a series of letters from the grand dames to the paper's editor. The first blow was dealt by Santley:

Sir, an event so unprecedented has happened to me that I cannot help writing to ask you to give it publicity . . . When I arrived with my company at 2.30 the first intimation of the state of affairs was from my acting manager. Neither Miss Soldene nor her representative has taken the slightest notice up to this – ten o'clock Monday evening. Had Miss Soldene informed me of the state of things I might have made other arrangements.

It then got personal. Santley went on to quote the last letter Emily had sent to her, which was thanking Santley for her help in singing in a benefit in Hastings:

'You did me a great service, and a friend in need is a friend indeed. EMILY SOLDENE'

It is a cruel return for showing my kindness when I could ill spare the time. I may say none of my company would have played for her, as they informed me they played for Miss Soldene's benefit to oblige me.

It was a very personal blow which Emily could not let go of without defending herself. She wrote her own letter to *The Era*.

> *The theatre was ready for Miss Santley, the license arranged for, and everything prepared for the performance, but Miss Santley at the instigation of a local idiot refused to appear. I can refer you to Miss Santley's acting manager for the correctness of my statement as regards the licence. As to any difference I may have with the landlord it did not affect Miss Santley's obligation to appear, and that matter will be fully ventilated in a court of law.*

There was then a letter printed from Santley's acting manager, William Harrison: 'Allow me to say that most emphatically this statement is utterly false . . . Perhaps Madame Soldene who can have no personal knowledge of the case, was misled by some "local idiot" in her own employ.'

This was obviously a dig at Emily's frequent absences from the theatre and the management by her son Edward. There then waded in another 'representative' of Santley's by the name of Henry Ashley:

> *The only answer I have to make to Miss Soldene's ladylike epistle is to say that if, as she threatens, the affair is ever to be ventilated in a court of law (which I very much doubt) I shall be prepared to repeat on oath every statement I have made. The letter of Miss Santley's acting manager is a complete answer to her assertions, and I may supplement it by stating that Mr. Gaze, in my presence and that of other witnesses, distinctly stated that he objected to any performance without a licence, and that it would be at Miss Soldene's own risk.*

Mr. Gaze, whom Miss Soldene, with that exquisite taste she displays in all her actions, described as a local idiot, is the proprietor of the Gaiety Theatre, and the gentleman who put the bailiffs in for a very large sum of money owing to him for the rent.

Was it just an unfortunate coincidence that George Gaze decided to close the theatre just as Emily's greatest rival was booked to go in? From the angry epistles it looks as if Santley's company could have performed, but she was taken aside by George Gaze and persuaded otherwise. Gaze was a powerful man in Hastings and Emily had not delivered what he had expected – a West End leading-lady manager and all the stardust that should follow with her. Instead his precious theatre had been left in charge of her inexperienced twenty-one-year-old son and they were seriously behind in the rent. He wanted Emily gone, and Kate Santley helped him with his plan. A friend in need is a friend indeed.

As predicted, Emily didn't have her day in court, not least because she simply didn't have the money for serious legal manoeuvrings. Instead, she packed up the family and left Hastings silently and quickly, just as the summer season was really getting underway. With debts still to pay Emily did what she knew best: got together a company, and went touring the provinces yet again with the old opéras bouffes.

At this point the professional choices of Emily's youngest daughter, Nellie, are quite telling.

Nellie didn't seem to suffer from the debacle at Hastings; in fact her own career started to flourish. She had taken the name of Nellie Vesey, which is interesting. Why not use her own surname,

Soldene, the name that had been made so famous by her mother, a much more renowned name than her aunt's stage name, Vesey? Unless, by this time, the Soldene name had become not so much famous as infamous. Nellie had progressed from pageboys to touring with a successful company called The Babes, playing a model dairymaid with a couple of solos all of her own, and then she was promoted to a starring breech role. The critics found her 'fresh, crisp and charming', and she appeared to be on a path to success. But less than five months into this promising career, while playing in Bath, Nellie slipped away and married a Scotsman called William Chalmers Lee who called himself an 'engineer', although this was one of those professions that was bandied about on Victorian marriage certificates as a euphemism for anything. Following family tradition, Emily wasn't there to see her daughter wed, but was herself in Scotland, treading the boards in Glasgow. Nellie's brother, Edward, gave her away. Nellie immediately retired from the stage and started the full-time job of being Mrs Chalmers Lee, and very soon afterwards emigrated to California with her new husband, never to be heard of again. In fact the last record that can be found of Mr and Mrs W. Chalmers Lee is in a San Francisco directory in 1891, listing them as living in rented accommodation.

Nellie was twenty-four years old when she married, just reaching her prime potential earning years as an actress, and seemed to have a good career ahead of her; and yet she walked away from the stage to marry a man from a meagre background with little earning potential. Either Nellie was very much in love with Mr W. Chalmers Lee, or she really wasn't that excited about a career on the stage. Perhaps Nellie had seen too much. After Nellie had seemed to be following in her mother's footsteps, her exit might have felt like a vote of no confidence for Emily; she never mentioned this youngest daughter again. It's as if Nellie had never existed.

Another of Emily's attempts to build a new career included taking the role of the 'character' actress. Complaints about actresses over forty years old being confined to the parts of mother, grandmother, the nun, the headmistress, anything that doesn't involve an element of desire and sexuality, were even more applicable in the nineteenth century. In 1883 *The Stage* magazine defined a character actor as one who 'portrays individualities and eccentricities'. Emily, with her formidable figure, forceful presence, and gift for comic innuendo, was perfectly placed to carry off the grande dame parts. In 1886 she was offered the part of the Duchess di Begonia in a Hervé opéra bouffe creation called *Frivoli*, opening at Drury Lane. The opera was as frivolous as the name suggested, but it gave Emily the chance to play a role that was thoroughly comic, and although she had only one solo, it was a meaty one and a favourite of the audience. It earnt her an encore every night. Potentially this move to character roles, while not making Emily a fortune, could keep her financially afloat for at least another decade. Immediately the Duchess di Begonia started receiving interesting offers. One night in the audience there was a New York producer called Colonel McCaull, on the hunt for good prizes to take home. Emily caught his attention:

She was simply magnificent. I was thunderstruck. Her acting and her stage appearance were perfect. As I sat in the theatre I said to myself, if she don't want the earth I'm going to have her, dead certain for America.

Emily had done well. Colonel McCaull was a former lawyer and Confederate general, and now one of the most successful Broadway producers. He had a kind face, plenty of enthusiasm, and a droopy moustache. Emily booked herself on a liner back to New York immediately. As soon as she arrived stateside she was interviewed by the *New York Dramatic Mirror*:

> *It was a small part at first, and I did not think I could make anything of it; but it turned out to be a great success for me. It's a woman just about my age – but you mustn't think I'm going to say how old that is. It's five years since I left America, but I have not played here for a good twelve years. I was with a lot of nice young girls. I don't believe such a collection has been gotten together since.*

Emily sounds here like some top-class madam boasting about her team of fresh-faced charges for sale, but then, to the nineteenth-century ear that probably sounded quite all right.

> *'My engagement with McCaull's Opera Company is for nine months', she said, 'and that is a long way to look ahead; so you must really excuse me from telling you what I'm going to do after that. I have only just now had my part in Josephine Sold by Her Sisters given me, and I haven't even had a chance to look at it . . . Though as a rule I don't blow my own trumpet, I will say that I am singing as well as ever. My voice is a good stayer. I am feeling better now than I have for some time. In fact I always improve in health in America. I shall go back quite a sylph.'*

The colonel had bought a new comic opera from France, a variation on the story of Joseph and his technicolour dreamcoat that swapped gender, and in Emily he had spotted the perfect Mother Jacob to them all. It was an excellent part that made use of all her comic tragedy and knowingness. The *New York Press* approved, though commenting on her last visit said that while her musical abilities were appreciated:

> *Her massive figure, however, rather interfered with her posing at that time as the interesting heroine of her opera, and militated somewhat against her in spite of her talents as an actress and a singer. This, however, will be a distinct advantage to her in comic opera, and her debut is anticipated with lively interest.*

Unfortunately, *Josephine Sold by Her Sisters* did not meet the high expectations of the critics and was deemed a slight disappointment. It finished in New York and went to Philadelphia, and was still a slight disappointment. As they carried on across the States to lukewarm reviews, Emily had a bit of a 'moment' when the leading lady decided to have an impromptu wedding with the leading man. Emily shared a dressing room with the leading lady and was taken into her confidence and asked if she would give her away in a secret ceremony straight after that night's performance. Emily loved this moment of high romance and described herself in her memoir as 'electrified'.

> *The bride was married in the stage costume she had been playing in. It was all very sudden and delightful and I, like an idiot, cried my eyes out. You see I had no experience,*

had never been a bridesmaid, and only once a bride. The only wedding I had ever attended was my own (a runaway one).

How much must this spontaneous wedding have made Emily feel her many losses – not just reminding her that the need to work had kept her away from the weddings of her sister and two daughters, but also inspiring memories of her own runaway wedding to a man who was now dead? It might have been the moment when Emily realised what she had missed. She probably felt quite homesick. When they went to Chicago the next week, she drank whisky punch until 'all was blue'. It would have been better if the career had been going well. It might have seemed worth it.

The colonel, being a ruthless businessman, scrapped Josephine and all her sisters and tried out another new comic opera called *Lorraine* instead. This fared no better. Emily faced reviews like this in Boston:

Emily Soldene – the gods preserve us! I remember years and years ago in my boyhood, I thought she was rather clever in a coarse way, in coarse burlesque, but today in refined comic opera – oh no! Please remove the corpse . . .

At the end of New York, instead of going to Pittsburgh with the rest of the company, Emily was sacked. Emily was furious and served a writ on the colonel for breach of contract. So ended the new career which had started off so promisingly.

Emily's next attempt was to go the other way into full burlesque. She set up the Emily Soldene Burlesque and Novelty Company and set off around America, once more donning her apron and being a saucy pastry cook in a potted, even more suggestive *Geneviève de Brabant* and including in the cast the ever bendy high-kicking Mdlle. Sara. One review condemned her as 'the very incarnation of vice'. At the end of the season Emily packed up and came home. It was her last venture into burlesque.

Before Emily left though, she paid a visit to one of her greatest rivals, Selina 'Dolly' Dolaro, who had settled permanently in New York:

> *She was living in 24th Street – had some millinery parlours there. She was looking delicate and fragile; but not badly off, having recently had a benefit, got up at the 'Lambs' Club' of New York, at which something like 4000 dols. was cleared. The idea was to send her to Florida to recuperate, but she would not go. 'Rather die in New York,' said she, 'than live in Florida.' She was gay and bright, and walked down Broadway a bit with us. The next day I sailed for England, and three weeks after poor Dolly was dead.*

Dolly had died of cancer. The average life expectancy for a woman born in 1838 was forty-four years. Emily was now fifty-two. She may well have been feeling her mortality.

In London she made her final attempt at opéra bouffe, performing *La fille de Madame Angot* at a matinee in the new Terry's Theatre in the Strand.

> *We deeply regret that Madame Soldene should have been so ill-advised as to expose herself, in a part now entirely unsuited to her, to the jeers of a pit and a gallery whose conduct, although reprehensible, was not without extenuation. We hardly know*

how to convey to Madame Soldene with sufficient delicacy
that there is a period at which it is wise for an artist to rest
on her laurels, and not to court comparison between her past
and present powers and appearance . . . But the spectacle of
an elderly lady indulging in the slightly suggestive business
of the part of Mdlle Lange, and twitching her petticoats in
the regular opera-bouffe manner, was so unutterably sad and
ghastly to behold that a number of persons rose from their seats
in shocked silence, and quietly left the theatre.

It seems that this was the final humiliation; it was to be Emily's last performance on a London stage, a sad end to a fine career. Emily hadn't been able to quit while she was ahead. She just didn't have enough money. But the public were unbearably cruel. Would they have said the same about a middle-aged man?

She now decided to take the role of elderly relative fallen on hard times, seeking refuge with her more fortunate close relations. In this Emily was treading a well-worn path and stereotype where women, still being legally the responsibility of their nearest male relative, often ended up taking up residence in comfortable places, but in return were forced to play the role of being professionally grateful, helpful and nice. Of course, Emily was also following the example of her mother who had now taken up permanent residence with Clara.

Emily seems to have divided her time between her eldest daughter Katie, who was at Oaks Lodge in Croydon, and Clara, now living at 'The Cottage', Mill Hill, Barnes Common. It was a very different life to the one Emily was used to.

We had little fancy ducks at Barnes, and I would take them out for a little walk on the common, and they would waddle along 'quack, quack,' appreciative little quacks and in between nibble, not to say gobble any old thing at hand, and presently laying little heads on one side they would look heavenwards with one eye and thank the giver of good for the green juicy grass.

The cottage is still there, but it seems to have been named ironically because it's a large Victorian Gothic, castle-like mansion, painted white with turrets and battlements.

Eventually Emily seems to have tired of taking the ducks for a walk, because in August 1891 it was reported in *The Era* that 'Emily Soldene is to make her home at San Francisco where she will teach music hereafter'. Emily again went across to America and this time made straight for the west coast where her youngest daughter was living with her husband. Her youngest son, John Arthur, may also have been in San Francisco. However, Emily didn't teach music. She went back onto the stage at the Orpheus opera house, performing Gilbert and Sullivan, but within months the theatre had gone bankrupt. Her ventures seemed to be failing ever more quickly. Since the age of twenty Emily had been a wife, mother, sister and performer. Now she was a widow, her sister had a family of her own, her children were gone, her career seemingly over. Emily was facing a very empty nest; in fact she didn't even have a nest. With no home even to call her own any more, she seems like a nineteenth-century wandering minstrel, condemned to go backwards and forwards across the world, relying on the kindness of others and the odd performing opportunity that never seemed to quite work out.

There was one place left to try. A place that was a bit behind, where there wasn't so much competition, which had taken her to their hearts. Emily was reported to be going to New York to catch the boat back to London, but at the last minute she changed her mind and jumped on a liner heading the other way, to Australia. She arrived on 19th July 1892 and the papers reported, 'Miss Emily Soldene now in Sydney states her intention of forming a company for the production of operas old and new in this part of the world'.

For one last time Emily dusted off her apron and sailed onto the stage as the pastry cook in *Geneviève de Brabant*. It did not fare well:

The famous singer and opera bouffe actress was received with great enthusiasm and in every respect the attitude of the audience towards the prima donna was of sustaining sympathy. Miss Soldene stood in need of moral support, for the attempt to resuscitate Geneviève de Brabant taxed her severely. Conscious that the libretto of the opera had become musty and timeworn, Madame Soldene and her managers wrote it up to date with ruthless hand, and such light as the opera may have possessed spluttered fitfully and feebly beneath the depressing weight of commonplace gags and political allusions.

The fatal blow though came from Emily's friend and former colleague, Cissy Durant, or rather as she now was, Mrs Cicely McQuade. Cissy had of course become a very wealthy widow after running away from Emily's 1875 Australian tour and marrying a Sydney property developer, whose portfolio included Her Majesty's Theatre. It was unfortunate that just as Emily opened with her decades-old favourites, Cissy had brought in London's Gaiety Theatre Company, with its world-famous duo Fred Leslie and Nellie Farren, and a brand-new burlesque opera.

When the season finished Emily's financial partners disappeared and she was left penniless.

Emily was stranded on the other side of the world again with no money to buy her passage home; but this time she was on her own, with no husband or sister by her side, no home to go back to, and little prospect of earning the passage home anyway. If Emily couldn't theatrically make it in Sydney it was unlikely she could make it anywhere else. This had been her last chance.

It's at this lowest of all points that the universe seems to have sent Emily an angel, in the unlikely guise of the deaf investigative journalist John Plummer. The man who had written to Emily so encouragingly after her opéra bouffe debut as the Grand Duchess decades before, just happened to be in Sydney too. He'd gone for a short visit, discovered lots of things that needing investigating and stayed. Now he paid a visit to Emily, and, distressed by her circumstances, determined to organise a benefit for her. He enlisted an impressive array of Sydney's top menfolk to be on the committee. The mayor was chairman and generously donated the town hall as the venue for a grand New Year's Eve benefit 'to recoup Madame Soldene for some of her recent losses'. Apparently letters of sympathy poured in and the news spread. This even appeared in the London theatrical press:

I imagine that the talented lady whom I once knew as Miss FitzHenry, and who afterwards did great things as Drogan in Geneviève de Brabant, is not in greatly affluent circumstances. Things have changed since 1872. Miss Soldene was an excellent artist, and where, in comic opera or opera bouffe, can we find such a conjunction of talent

*as was forthcoming at the Philharmonic in 1872, when
Soldene and Dolaro were in their prime?*

A big New Year's Eve party culminating in Emily singing a couple
of her ballads, followed by 'Auld Lang Syne' at the stroke of
midnight, Emily's benefit was deemed a great success. It must have
made enough money to tide her over, but it didn't solve the basic
problem that Emily needed a new career. But what could she do?
Or rather what talents did she have, other than singing or acting?

John Plummer had an answer. Emily was good with people,
good at parties and fabulous at gaining confidences; she was also
witty. If she could just translate the wit she used in conversation
onto the page, John Plummer sensed a great opportunity for
her. It seems likely that he made introductions for Emily with
the two Australian papers he was associated with, and for the
next three years she worked as a theatre critic and reviewer for
the *Evening News* in Sydney and Australia's largest national
newspaper, the *Town and Country Journal*.

*From July, 1892, to July, 1895 I resided in Sydney, New South
Wales, whither I had been enticed by a business ignis fatuus,
a Will-o'-the- wisp..... not of the most brilliant kind either.
But no matter. When my futile Will-o'-th'-wisp disappeared
in a spluttering and splenetic incapacity, out of the darkness
rose a gleam of light, which, gradually brightening, disclosed
to my interrogative eyes a bottle of ink and a pen, a pen
"pointing t'wards me." I seized the chance, also the pen, and
for three years pursued the congenial occupation of pulling
the beam from my cosmopolitan neighbour's eye, oblivious of
the mote in my own . . .*

Emily became what was termed in those days as 'a lady journalist' and once she had started writing, she didn't stop; she carried on writing until the week she died. As she said in 1897: 'So many people have asked me, What made you think of writing? Self preservation was my first incentive, and when I got a chance of writing, I wrote.'

Emily was successful, too. A Melbourne paper reported that 'rumour credits her with writing some excellent theatrical and musical notes for one of its papers'. The paper uses the word 'rumour', because unfortunately we don't have any examples of Emily's allegedly prolific copy during the three years she worked as a journalist in Sydney, because she never had a byline. She wrote anonymously, which seems unlike her. It was also a rather strange thing for the newspaper's managers to omit – why hire such a famous and experienced theatrical celebrity, if not to make use of their name? This is almost certainly a reflection of the prevailing attitude towards women journalists. By choosing to segue into journalism, Emily was making yet another controversial career choice. 'Lady journalists' were almost as scandalous as actresses.

Working in a profession that was seen as 'male', surrounded by men, travelling around unchaperoned, having and expressing opinions on matters outside the domestic sphere, sometimes controversial opinions – all these were deemed suspect and not the kind of thing a respectable lady would do. That's if they *could* do them at all. There was a widespread belief that a lady's health was too delicate, and they did not have the staying power to be journalists. The esteemed Victorian journalist Lady Blessington had a male biographer who considered her professional ambitions 'the intellectual species of coquetry' and saw her pursuit of them as precluding her from 'all that is calculated to make a woman happy', the 'wear and tear of literary life' being ultimately destructive. A woman's opinions did not have the authority of a man's and would not be deemed so credible. Up until the 1890s, with the exception of a few women like Harriet Martineau and Geraldine Jewsbury, the majority of women journalists remained anonymous or took on a male persona.

The women who were brave enough to put their names to their articles often went to great lengths to emphasise their home-making skills and propriety; just as leading actresses of the time went to great lengths to portray an image of respectability and domesticity off the stage, even when the reality was often more interesting. Mary Billington, having defended Rachel Beer's record as editor of a Sunday newspaper, ends her article portraying Mrs Beer as a society hostess opening her drawing rooms to charitable societies. Mrs Frederika Macdonald managed her charming house, including three well-brought-up and educated children, without a housekeeper and while still doing a great deal of press work. Mary Cowden Clarke, reflecting on a long life in which writing and editing had been continuous, deliberately included evidence of her skill at broiling a mutton chop and making her husband's dress waistcoats to demonstrate that 'a woman who adopts literary work as her profession need not either neglect or be deficient in the more usually feminine accomplishments of cookery and needlework'. They too were making every effort to make it seem like they could do it all. It sounds exhausting.

But, generally, women just remained anonymous. As journalist Bessie Parkes wrote in the 1880s, 'If editors were ever known to disclose the dread secrets of their dens', the public would learn of the women 'whose unsigned names are Legion; of their rolls of manuscripts, which are as the sands of the sea'.

It's difficult to know just how many women journalists there were in the nineteenth century; what is almost certainly true is their numbers increased as the century went on because, as in so many areas of British life, the press underwent both a technical and cultural revolution.

Firstly, the cost of newspapers and periodicals fell. During the 1830s the government reduced the advertising and stamp taxes, and then printing technology improved, so that the press became much more profitable. The penny paper appeared with many more pages and the market was flooded with cheap periodicals with serialised fiction. At the same time the middle classes had more leisure time and the working classes became more literate. All these things meant that there was a need for more journalists and opportunities for women to fill the gaps, and they did. In 1894, the year after Emily started her career as a columnist, the Society of Women Journalists was founded in London by newspaper proprietor Joseph Snell Wood with initially 300 members. One women's magazine reader wrote complaining that lady journalists were to blame for the lack of good dressmakers: 'Our girls will rush into journalism, teaching or the stage, three professions already overstocked, and neglect really useful branches of employment by which they might earn a steady if not luxurious livelihood.'

However, there was a final revolution which was to have a profound effect on Emily's career. In 1894 the journalist Matthew Arnold coined the phrase 'the New Journalism', which referred to a new popularism in reporting, an appeal to the emotions of readers, a commercialism or, as some saw it, democratisation. This New Journalism was loathed by many people as brash, full of mawkish serial stories, gossip columns and invasions of privacy. But it was a lighter, more popular style of writing, which would play to Emily's strengths. It also saw the end of anonymous writing for all but the most factual news. It was the beginning of the cult of the celebrity journalist where the name and reputation of the journalist became attached to their articles. People now expected to know who was saying what.

In 1895 it was announced that Miss Emily Soldene was returning to England to pursue her new post as the London correspondent for the *Sydney Evening News*. She would be writing a weekly newsletter, 'London, Week by Week', and this would very definitely be under her own name. Emily had finally found her new career and her home.

Emily in later years after retiring from the stage and becoming a writer

Chapter Twelve

Young Mrs Staples and Some Recollections

I am under the imputation of having written a book that is nearly as is
possible unique and more than naughty. In vain I protest my innocence
(Emily, 1898)

When Emily travelled to England in 1895, she was coming back
to start her career as a lady journalist, but she also had another
secret ambition: to become a novelist and a writer of books. Emily
had a story she wanted to tell, a truth she needed to speak to the
wider world and, hidden in her cabin, two manuscripts written
in her flowery longhand. As well as writing columns, Emily had
spent the last three years in Australia busily working on a novel
and her memoir; now she was looking for a publisher. In the end
it was Downey and Co. Ltd in York Street, Covent Garden, who
agreed to publish both books, bringing out the novel first. *Young
Mrs Staples* was published early in 1896. It's still in print today.

*I had nearly all my life been associated with writing people
. . . Charles Dickens and my father-in-law were very old*

friends, and had been in 'the gallery' together . . . and my
subsequent connection with the Powell family explains how I
crept into a sort of association with a literary circle.

Emily might have been name-dropping here – Dickens had been dead for over twenty-five years and actresses regularly turned to writing to boost their incomes, especially when the parts were drying up, especially if they used their theatrical background as material. Actresses held an infinite fascination for the Victorian public. Novels based around the lives of fictional actresses, of a more or less salacious nature (including plenty that were erotic), were published throughout the century and were very commercial. Victorian actresses had a unique opportunity to be women who moved through the world with a bohemian artistic freedom. They appeared to have exciting lives and people wanted to read about them. And a novel was also a good way to make a point and tell a cautionary tale without giving oneself away. The guise of fiction could give a certain amount of protection.

In its style *Young Mrs Staples* is of its time, more so than Emily's other writing. Emily's non-fiction scribblings are intimate and effortless, as if she is gossiping over a bottle of fizz with you. However, Emily's fiction is more mannered and self-conscious – she doesn't spare the adjectives. It feels like she is trying a little too hard, but then, reading Dickens isn't easy either. Authors often write about what they know, especially for their first book. Sometimes there is just one story they really need to tell, which is why the theme of Emily's one novel is so telling. The basic storyline is ridiculous, relying heavily on absurd coincidences, but Emily had spent all her life in the world of opéra bouffe, which has similarly unfeasible plots. It's dark, with a touch of Edgar

Allan Poe, and an unhappy ending which borrows from *Romeo and Juliet* – doomed lovers commit suicide and the evil seducer lives happily ever after. The heroine, Nannie, is annoyingly daft. A simpering, spoilt, too beautiful teenager who keeps fainting, and likes to be dominated and looked after by rich men. She is typical of the literary heroines of the era, but perhaps something different might have been expected from Emily, who herself never seemed to lack agency or be a victim. Except that the submissive Nannie and her hypocritical husband come to a sticky end. In this way Emily's heroine shows very much how not to be a heroine and perhaps gives a clue as to the whole raison d'être of the book.

Nannie is the granddaughter of a Creole exotic dancer who has been left in the care of a wicked stepmother in a stately home in the English countryside. At sixteen, by virtue of being such an exotic beauty, Nannie is engaged to the local landowner, John Staples, but runs away with a painter to France presuming they are to be married – but when she presses the point, he tells her he is already married. Nannie pushes him off a pier, and he is lost in the stormy seas, presumed drowned. She is able to get back to England before anyone notices, and marries the landowner as planned. She then falls in love with him and finds out via a newspaper that the painter didn't die but was rescued by a boat. She has a few weeks of happiness where Mr Staples showers her with expensive gifts, and takes her for drives in his handsome carriage and to the theatre where she observes wicked ladies. Then Nannie realises she is pregnant with the painter's child. She gets an abortion, nearly dies, and confesses all to Mr Staples, who, disgusted, runs off to the Continent where he lingers with French actresses and courtesans. A heartbroken Nannie goes travelling with a wise old widow, Mrs Winslow, and ends up in America. Mr Staples sees the error of his ways. They meet by chance in a boarding house in San Francisco, are reconciled, and have one night together before Nannie sees a picture in a London paper: a portrait of her pushing the painter off the pier (done by the still-alive painter). She thinks everyone will know it's her and Mr Staples will never recover from the shame, so takes some poison. He is back later than he promised and, finding her dead, kills himself. The painter, now a widower, marries an heiress, is the most famous portrait painter of his generation and lives happily ever after.

It's a tale that contains a fair amount of Emily's experience – theatre and rich gentlemen behaving badly with all too willing actresses, chorus girls and courtesans and men who are already married pretending they are not. She draws heavily on her travels – Paris, New York, New Orleans, San Francisco, a train journey across the States where Nannie bumps into cowboys. Even Nannie's childhood home is set in the Hertfordshire countryside where Emily grew up, and the grand manor is modelled on Clara's white turreted house on Barnes Common. But the point about *Young Mrs Staples* is it gave Emily an opportunity to say things that she might not have dared if they were officially her own views. For example, Emily has the opportunity to have a dig at the most famous actress of her generation, Sarah Bernhardt, when she has John Staples take Nannie to the theatre:

Frightful bore for John, who having no feeling for art, thought the divine Sarah a 'bit bluff, don't you know,' cut all her teeth, etc . . . he did not care for these accomplished steppers, he liked a yearling that did not know, and that consequently one had to break in, and teach all its paces.

Which also tells you all you need to know about the hero's attitude to women.

Despite the occasional twinkle in Nannie's eye, she is terribly submissive. Her favourite pastime is being driven around by her husband through the streets of Kensington:

John sat up very high in the cart and Nannie's head came somewhere between his elbow and shoulder, and as he turned and looked down at her in a patronizing sort of way, she really enjoyed her own inferiority, and felt it was good to be protected by such a magnificent reality as 'your affectionate husband, John.'

Emily ensures that no good comes of Nannie's submissiveness and John Staples' chauvinism. It's a cautionary tale of where such attitudes might lead – in the case of Mr and Mrs Staples, death.

However, it is with the opinions of the worldly-wise widow, Mrs Winslow, that Emily openly speaks her truth to a wider public. Under Mrs Winslow's protective cloak, Emily is able to put forward a radical opinion and agenda regarding one of the defining characteristics of the Victorian era – sexual conservatism. Via Mrs Winslow, she calls society out, in a polemic which lasts for more than ten pages. It is prompted by news of a young girl who, having got pregnant out of wedlock, has drowned herself and the baby in the village pond. Nannie asks Mrs Winslow what she thinks, and she shocks the ladies present:

'I believe in the equality of the sexes,' repeated Mrs. Winslow, with crushing severity, 'and in such a case as you mention,

Nannie, of course the woman is always blamed. But I think
there is just six of one and half-a-dozen of the other'

Mrs Winslow asks why a woman should be blamed rather than
the man, and expected to naturally resist temptation: 'As a matter
of fact, woman naturally is not more chaste than man'. The idea
that women could experience as much sexual desire as men was a
highly unusual and controversial view in the nineteenth century.
Mrs Winslow then declares that men are so wicked because
society doesn't make them suffer the consequences of their
actions: 'Why should the man be promoted to high places and
honour and respect, while his fellow sinner, the woman, passes
her life in darkness and dies in despair?'

Mrs Winslow says that an unmarried woman who has a child
out of wedlock should not be shamed, ostracised or held up as a
shocking example. Instead, the fallen woman should be helped to
gain her self-respect, the illegitimate child should bear the name
of its father 'as a means of identification, like earmarking stock',
and it should be known whom the mother is mistress to.

'Let him own up, before his wife (married men are always the
worst), his mother-in-law' (much excitement purrs of delight)
'or his fiancée, his club, his minister, his stockbroker, his
banker, his Sunday-school committee, and all the rich friends
that are his. That would soon stop it.'

Mrs Winslow then puts forward a plea that the baby not be
considered a vile thing and in fact the mother's suffering should
sanctify it. With gasps from her audience Mrs W points out
that some of the greatest names on earth have been illegitimate,

like Abraham Lincoln, George Sand, Leonardo da Vinci, Alexander Hamilton, d'Alembert, Erasmus, Émile de Girardin and Alexandre Dumas. 'In the blaze of glory surrounding these names, the accident of birth is forgotten.' Of course, the name of Emily Soldene could also have been added to this list. She points out that an illegitimate child has no rights, cannot inherit and in the eyes of the law does not even exist: 'I say that it's an everlasting and burning shame, that hearts should be broken and lives blasted by such cruel and unequal laws.'

Of course, the young Emily Lambert-Soldene hadn't legally existed either. How much is Mrs Winslow voicing an early profound wound around the circumstances of her illegitimate birth that Emily had carried all her life – how her father had seemingly walked away with no consequences, her mother had been shamed and Emily had been brought up condemned to live a lie, in perpetual fear of being found out as illegitimate? In *Young Mrs Staples* Nannie envies those nice, comfortable English county families:

> *Respected, stupid fathers, good, slow mothers, surrounded with virtuous daughters, and blessed with irreproachable grandmothers (probably on account of their antecedents not having been fully enquired into). To be sure their daughters were lanky and bony, angular and vapid, uninteresting and straw-coloured. But – they were good.*

As if Emily too might have given up the glamour and excitement of her life, and taken being plain, in return for being legitimate, her ancestry clear and respectable.

Mrs Winslow then goes even further, saying that women live

in fear of many different kinds – fear of disgrace, social ostracism, unemployment, a mother's judgement, a lover who will leave her when she becomes a nuisance. Society and its hypocrisy are to blame for women seeking abortions. And then Mrs Winslow, having lectured the ladies for ten pages, finally delivers her killer blow and comes to her triumphant conclusion – asserting that once ladies start having abortions they acquire a strange fascination for them, and carry on until they end up in a wheelchair or a lunatic asylum or moving between the two, making prolific use of morphia. In Mrs Winslow's view women have been driven by society to commit murder.

In the last decade of the nineteenth century a new phenomenon was taking up column inches in the media, not to mention becoming the topic of debates in the clubs and parlours of the people who mattered, and this was the emergence of the 'New Woman'.

'The New Woman' was a phrase first used by the novelist Sarah Grand in her 1894 article 'The New Aspect of the Woman Question' where she insisted women were 'awaking from their long apathy' to realise their potential. It was thereafter adopted by the British press as a catch-all reference to anything or anyone 'feminist' and the debates that were raging about suffrage and women's roles. Typically the New Woman had attended one of the women's Oxbridge colleges, probably Girton, rode a bicycle and wore bloomers. She did not marry or have children, but pursued financial independence as a novelist, playwright, poet or journalist. She was probably sporty and muscular. She campaigned on women's matters. This symbolic New Woman divided opinion. For some she was a heroine and the future; for many others, men and women alike, she was a 'modern mannish maiden' degenerate, unnatural, and she threatened the whole fabric of society. Typical are the fulminations in the popular journal, *The Cornhill*: 'She proves nothing. She has tried to prove that woman's mission is something higher than the bearing of children and the bringing them up. But she has failed.'

The New Woman was probably more imagined than real, punching above her weight in terms of coverage in the press. But the important thing was that she existed at all, a harbinger of things to come. This was the debate that was raging when Emily wrote her novel. Emily was not a New Woman, although she had pursued a life with aspects that many of the young feminist activists were advocating. She was literally an old woman – her morals and world view had been set in a different time, and her later columns often expressed bewilderment and contempt of the New Women and their agendas.

However, in her novel, Emily is making some controversial arguments that the New Women would have agreed with. Firstly there is the whole moral of *Young Mrs Staples* – that society is hypocritical, that women are discriminated against sometimes with tragic consequences, that there is a collusion (with both men and women as perpetuators) that gives men a free pass. That illegitimate children should not be discriminated against, that such a thing is wrong, unchristian even. That women have the same sexual desires as men, but live under a cloud of fear. Many feminists of the era were also opposed to abortion, seeing it as forced upon women by thoughtless men who would not accept a woman's right to say no, resulting in marital rape and the seduction of unmarried women. This was the problem, not the abortions themselves.

For working-class women in the nineteenth century abortions were the most common form of contraception, and as the century progressed there was an impression that greater numbers of married women were having them. There were many different methods, ranging from hot baths with gin and falling down stairs, to surgical procedures performed by midwives and doctors, an estimated thirty per cent of which resulted in the mother's death. The most common method was herbal abortifacients or purgatives, often advertised obliquely in the press as 'women's pills to aid menstruation'. However, while abortions were increasingly common, attitudes against them were harshening especially among the middle classes, where it was largely regarded as murder. As the nineteenth century progressed there were more prosecutions and harsher penalties. The fertility rate was declining and there was much debate about the causes. *Young Mrs Staples* was centred around a topic that was currently live. Emily was brave being as specific as she was about abortions in her book. They were seen as culturally unmentionable and therefore rarely directly discussed in fiction. Mary Wollstonecraft in *Maria and the Wrongs of Women* has one of her characters, Jemima, openly talking about her abortion, but then Wollstonecraft dared to state all sorts of opinions about the female experience that were culturally shocking – an exception that proves the rule.

Emily was deeply exercised by the everyday hypocrisy around women's sexuality and the issues surrounding it in Victorian society. Fiction enabled Emily to say the difficult thing; it provided a platform to say the unsayable. Mrs Winslow was her mouthpiece to finally speak of something that had shadowed her whole existence – not just her career as an actress and singer, but from the moment of her birth, and indeed her mother's whole adult life. The questions of judgement, reputation, respectability and morality from those who had often behaved no better, but were just in a better position to get away with it, had defined her life and Emily was going to have her say. Writing can give a unique agency. I didn't understand why Emily had written *Young Mrs Staples*, until I came to Mrs Winslow's moment of expression. In this context *Young Mrs Staples* makes perfect sense.

We can't know what Emily's readers made of *Young Mrs Staples* and whether they heard Mrs Winslow's message. There are two reviews of the book (written by men of course), and neither mentions the controversial subject matter, being more concerned with grammar and gossip. The first complains:

> *Many pages suggest that the author is hardly aware that she herself, as well as her characters, is talking slang. Such expressions as 'fetching', 'pins' for legs, 'evoluted', 'beastly' and so forth used seriously, have a queer effect. Neither in her taste nor in her grammar is she quite irreproachable.*

The second, meanwhile, merely digresses:

> *Miss Soldene has lately written a work entitled Young Mrs Staples, (published by Downey&Co), in which there is a lot of racy writing... Miss Emily Soldene is not only alive, but alive and kicking... if any person, after calmly taking stock of our comic opera performances will be kind enough to inform me where I can hear duets sung as they were once sung by Soldene and Dolaro, I shall be infinitely obliged to him.*
> *While I am on the subject, let me say now and again I see Miss Clara Vesey at the theatre and our halls of dazzling light.*

She looks, perhaps, a little more matronly than she did at the time when she was want to titivate her sister, Mme Lange, in Angot period, a good and pleasant-looking woman.

It seems the moral of Emily's story may have been lost here. By contrast, Emily's *Theatrical and Musical Recollections*, published two years later in 1898, caught everyone's attention in exactly the way she intended. It caused the biggest fuss of any such memoir to date, and while *Young Mrs Staples* may have provided Emily with a way to make a point, the *Recollections* provided her with a vital means not just to boost her flagging bank balance, but practise what she had preached in her novel – by outing those rich and famous men who lived lives of respectability while risking the reputations of the actresses they had dallied with. Emily had been collecting her experiences in diaries for years, sensing a potentially rich seam of gold which could be mined when the time was right. What Emily hadn't known was whether she could write; her columns had shown that she could.

True stories about actresses were even more popular than novels about them. People wanted to know more about the private lives of celebrities, how their public personas matched their domestic selves. There is something about the public intimacy of the star, the ability to make the reader believe they are in the room alone with them close up, and yet they know nothing about them – the combination of widespread visibility with an actual remoteness, that is very compelling and leaves the public longing to know more. Celebrities have been compared to the equivalent of tigers and cats in the animal world – fascinating, mysterious and quite unbiddable.

Actresses were frequently the subject of interviews, biographies and memoirs, some of which were intentionally salacious, some of which were intentionally the opposite. Just like today, there was a need for the successful actress to manufacture a private persona for public consumption, and the written word offered an opportunity to boost their profile, control their brand and paint a picture of respectability. Ellen Terry, Mrs Patrick Campbell, Lillie Langtry and Marie Bancroft were among the famous actresses who wrote their memoirs, all of them leaving out the more exciting details of their complicated private lives, which almost certainly would have made for better books. Typically, these authorised writings emphasised the actresses' private lives as daughters and happily married wives, driven to the stage by the need to earn a living. They portrayed a life where hard work, talent and beauty could triumph over social class. They were offering an early blueprint for how a woman might have it all.

In some ways Emily's *Recollections* ran along similar lines. Mother, Priscilla, is portrayed as a thoroughly respectable middle-class matron who believed in the Bible and beatings. Mr Soldene the solicitor is her father, except he wasn't – either her father, or a solicitor. Emily speaks of a London childhood with nurses and maids, but she was almost certainly largely brought up in the Hertfordshire countryside in a pub by her landlady granny. She is creative with dates so that it looks as if she rises to fame on a quick, straight-upward trajectory, ignoring the hard graft in dodgy East End music halls and spells of unemployment. And her children are invisible; husband Jack is mentioned only twice in passing. Emily does confess to the odd bit of financial bother and brush with the authorities, with joking snippets from the odd bad review. She owns the public's obsession with her weight and uses it to her own advantage. But successes and good reviews vastly outnumber the mention of struggles, which is your prerogative, of course, when you write a memoir.

What's different about her book is that Emily is happy to reveal all when it comes to certain other people, like the noblemen of the realm who in their youth used to hang around backstage with the ballet girls. Following through from Mrs Winslow's manifesto in her novel, Emily now practises what Mrs Winslow had preached and outs them in long lists:

The Marquis of Blandford, Lord Rosebury, Lord Macduff, the Marquis of Angelsea, Mr. (now Sir) Douglas Straight, Lord Alfred Paget, Lord Dudley, Lord Londesborough, Sir George Wombell, Sir James Farquharson, and the Posnos.

Hector Tennant, Mr. (now 'Lord') Gerard, Lord Gifford, Lord Rodney, Lord Mayo, just home from India, Lord St. Leonards, 'Johnny' Woodhouse, diplomat, Ralph Milbanke, ditto

These names are unlikely to mean much today, but when the book was published these men were the most public of public figures – the great and the good who were running the country. Emily seemed determined to undermine them with her little asides: Lord John Hay was a 'frequent and delightful visitor so fond of sitting in a box and criticizing the girls skirts', Sir James Farquharson (Piccadilly Jim) 'a little peculiar', Sir George Armitage a 'dear old man, like poverty, he was always with us'. On the Dukes of Sutherland and Newcastle: 'one of her principle ladies could not eat her dinner unless her particular duke cut it up.' She made fun of the judge 'Handsome' Huddlestone QC, saying he was known as a 'toady': 'He had an immense reverence and weakness for the aristocracy'. One of their constant visitors was Lord Wallscourt, whom she described as charming and debonair with perfectly cut waistcoats which he bought at 'Kino's for 10s 6d'. She wrote of backstage appearances by the famous and 'pale' spiritualist Mr Holmes, who was supposed to have been in the confidence of the late Emperor Napoleon and still with the 'Czar of all the Russias' (which suggests he wasn't a very effective psychic); and of the famous explorer Captain Burton. Tall, dark, masterful and tanned, he was 'much addicted' to 'long conversations' with the ladies of the ballet and the pages (which must have included Clara): 'Still I could not get away from the fact that he was artistically made up, the cheeks rouged a little and the eyes Indian-inked a lot, just as if he were going on the stage.' A man wearing make-up, especially a macho, brave pioneer, would have completely dumbfounded the Victorian general public.

One of Emily's greatest indiscretions was her tale of Queen Victoria's favourite maharajah:

> *He wore some wonderful diamond rings, and would often insist upon my wearing them for the stage. I was always glad to get them off, and return them. One Sunday he gave a swell dinner at Vevey's, and, in introducing to my notice some very fine caviare, said he always sent his own man to Russia, who brought it right through – no intermediate parties. In the Alhambra chorus was one very tall, elegant girl. She filled the ideal bill, got twenty-five shillings a week, wore sealskin, sable, and magnificent diamonds, came in her carriage and pair, and her footman waited at the stage-door with her cloak. She could go into the directors' room at any time without knocking at the door, and sometimes gave His Highness the Maharajah a lift.*

Duleep Singh was the last maharajah of the Sikh Empire who having inherited his throne at the age of five, was deposed by the British and sent out of harm's way to exile in London, where he lived the life of a British aristocrat. For a while his home was Claridge's. He was very handsome and Queen Victoria liked to have him around. 'Those eyes and those teeth are too beautiful,' she said. The chorus obviously felt the same way.

But it was Emily's revelations about the late Lord Alfred Paget that were among the most salacious. Lord Paget was a great friend of Queen Victoria, her Chief Equerry, a top-ranking military man and former Member of Parliament. He was married to Cecilia Wyndham and father of sixteen children. Emily says that some thought him 'rather awful', and he was not allowed behind the scenes in some theatres: 'He was always busy, and invariably shabby, wearing a frock coat that had seen no end of better days, and round his neck a large silk and rather greasy handkerchief (generally a "birdseye") tied like an old fashioned stock.'

She tells of bumping into him in the Strand after one of her American tours:

> *'Dear Emily,' said he, 'dear old friend; where can I buy some long black silk gloves? There's a girl can't go on to-night till I get them for her' . . . Everybody was very surprised when they heard he had left £100,000. 'Fancy!' said the ballet, rattling their bangles, 'with that coat too.'*

Even royalty did not escape. Emily tells of the time when they were rehearsing and suddenly there was a big fuss, a baby show in the green room with sixpence admission to be used by the stagehands to drink the baby's health.

'What baby?' said I, 'and why sixpence?' 'Oh my, Miss Soldene; what, don't you know? Why, it's a Royal baby.' 'Royal rubbish,' said I. 'It's true,' said little Miss Brown, 'I know all about it, Lardy told me. Why it's the Duke of—' 'Miss Brown called,' shouted call boy. Miss Brown flew, and the secret is still unrevealed, at least, unrevealed by Miss Brown.

The father of the baby was Prince Alfred, Duke of Edinburgh, second son of Queen Victoria, and the mother, chorus girl Lardy Wilson, an old friend of Emily's from the Oxford Music Hall days. A few months later the Duke was put out of the way of mischief by being married off to the Grand Duchess Maria Alexandrovna and Lardy disappeared from public view.

Emily even claimed to have had a brush with Jack the Ripper. While performing in *Frivoli* at Drury Lane in 1886, she alleged that she had received a threatening postcard from him:

That deadly persuasive person not only expressed himself in very definite and distinct terms, but endorsed his views by impressing upon the document a bloody thumb and finger . . . how we crowded round and gloated over the horrid thing, and the fascination of the bloody sign was irresistible.

The notorious Whitechapel Murderer was drawn to fallen ladies who appeared to live lives of dubious morality. Of course, for many people actresses were no better, or even worse, publicly flaunting themselves, behaving suggestively, promoting bad behaviour. Why wouldn't the Ripper try and slit the throat of a few of these Jezebels while he was at it? It's no wonder Emily was a bit spooked, but worse was to come.

Emily was leaving the theatre late one night and walking back to her lodgings in Charlotte Street, Bedford Square, where, as she pointed out, she lived next door to Elizabeth Bellwood and Lord Mandeville. The streets were empty; all was quiet. As she walked down Russell Street and then onto Bow Street she was surprised to see a broad white arrow drawn on the pavement in chalk. It was pointing north. A hundred yards further on there was another, and then another at Merryweather's corner pointing slightly to the left. She crossed over to the west side of Endell Street and hadn't gone far when she saw yet another pointing ahead: 'By this time I felt creepy and seemed to understand the arrows were a direction, also that I must follow that direction.'

She walked to the end of Endell Street and there the arrows stopped. But then she saw them again across the road, pointing north to Bellew's Chapel.

At this moment of my midnight walk, to have had my head suddenly pulled back and the gleam of a razor flashed across my eyes would not have surprised me. 'Jack the Ripper' was in the air. I stood still and looked round with apprehension, nobody, not a footstep, only the sound of a distant cab. I walked quietly across Oxford Street. There was the confounded thing, against the doll shop, bright, shining, pointing straight ahead. I crossed over into Charlotte Street. There it was again, at the side of the house of Forbes Robertson. I felt a temptation, a dreadful curiosity, I must follow it, and went on opposite and past the house where I lived, on till I came to the Square, crossed over to the enclosure, and then, close to the railings, there it was again, palpable, commanding. 'Come,' it said, 'Follow.' Then, suddenly I got a panic and ran back, fancying a step behind

me, ran back as fast as my legs would carry me, to No. —, and
standing on the doorstep, breathless, shaking and trembling, had
the unspeakable happiness of hearing the mellifluous voice of the
celebrated Bessie, making the equally celebrated inquiry, 'Wot
cheer,' Ria?' What could the arrow have meant? Somehow, I felt
that night I had been very close to a rat-trap.

Whether Emily really had a close shave with the Ripper or had
just been drinking too much brandy and soda we shall never
know. It was a good story though, and Emily, always with an eye
to the salacious, managed in the telling to allude to the infamous
affair between Lady Elizabeth Bellwood and Lord Mandeville.

In her *Recollections* Emily even managed to squeeze in the
prime minister, Gladstone, although he was no fan of the theatre,
it embodying all the vices he thought akin to the devil. She was
touring near his country home in Chester, and decided to take an
invitation personally to come and see *Carmen*. Characteristically
she manages to turn the visit into an adventure, noticing men
everywhere in the country lanes:

Every now and then a face would appear above the hedge,
another would be regarding with much interest the bursting
blooms of the already blossoming May; another with vacant
eye stood stock still while we passed him. Somehow these people
aroused and irritated my theatrical instincts – they were out of
the picture – they did not agree with the situation, and they had
no local colour, and were out of tone with their environment.

It was a time of trouble in Ireland and the countryside was
infested with bodyguards. Emily was not allowed in to see the

prime minister because of the security crisis, but he sent his apologies and promised to write.

> Mr. Gladstone did not visit the theatre, but that evening I got a letter from him, not written by a secretary, but by himself. The letter was as follows:-
> 'Hawarden Castle, Chester
> 'Mr. Gladstone presents his compliments to Madame Soldene, and is sincerely sorry, as is Mrs. Gladstone, that they are not able to come into Chester for the purpose of attending at the Royalty Theatre. They wish well to Madame Soldene's enterprise, and she is at liberty to make use of their name this week, if she thinks fit. May 17th, 1883.'

Somehow Emily managed to get herself mentioned in Gladstone's obituary when he died the same year that the *Recollections* came out, a fact Emily mentioned with pride in her column:

> In the London Daily Telegraph of May 21 is an article 'Mr Gladstone and the Stage'. In that article there is exactly thirty lines about a certain person named Emily Soldene . . . If you think Emily Soldene is not nearly off her head with joy and pride at being so associated with the memories of this greatest of great men, you are mistaken, because she is . . . Poor old Gladstone. Everybody is so sorry about his death they forget his mistakes. I expect the funeral will be a tremendous function. We shall have to get up at 6am on Saturday morning.

Emily had an excellent nose for publicity. Once word got out that she had named and defamed all sorts of worthies, her *Recollections* began selling fast and were serialised in all sorts of papers. In the end it was one of the bestselling books of 1898. The reviewers loved her juicy theatrical offerings:

> *Miss Soldene writes vivaciously and, in the main, accurately, and the task of reading her revelations to those who know the personages and things with which she deals is not unpleasant . . . At the time she knew them, they belonged to the jeunesse doree. Now not a few of them are statesmen, judges, peers, what not. Relentlessly she reveals to the world what she knows of their lives. If they loved not 'some bright particular star', but some actress more endowed with symmetry than with talent, the fact is set down. If the conditions or the results might justify proceedings in the courts, divorce or other, all is told. Nobody is spared, not even those in highest position, and were the succession in doubt it is possible that claimants might refer in vindication of their pretensions in this book. Nothing is sacred to a sapper, says a song which Miss Soldene should have an acquaintance. She is not a sapper, but shows a sapper-like contempt for social prejudices.*

The London correspondent of the *Washington Post* wrote:

> *It has remained to Miss Emily Soldene to write the most interesting and certainly the most sensational book of the season . . . since its frank revelations about the gilded youth of statesmen and fathers of family men like Lord Rosebery and Lord Dunraven began to be known there has been a great rush for the book. Most of the men who twenty-five years ago were 'going the pace' in London have read its pages with fear and trembling, while the rest of the 'upper ten' are chuckling over Miss Soldene's revelations.*

Emily knew exactly what a fuss her *Recollections* would cause. A few weeks before publication, she hopped on a boat to Australia, thus ensuring she was on the other side of the world when it came out. There was talk of legal proceedings and defamation actions, but in the end nothing happened; probably because the publicity around a trial would have made things worse – and also, of course, Emily's revelations were true (well, at least about other people), and actually she could have revealed a lot more. This was a fact she was to allude to occasionally in her columns in later years; that she was thinking of writing a sequel, she was being harassed by her publishers to produce another volume, that she had plenty of good material, and it would be even more scandalous. She never did write that sequel and I don't think she was ever going to, but it was good to keep certain people on their toes. In a way she did exactly what Mrs Winslow had been advocating in *Young Mrs Staples* – Emily named some of the eminent men who were behind the damage to actresses' reputations, who had previously managed to behave how they liked, without censure. It is as if her novel laid out the moral ground for the memoir that was to come. I think Emily knew the meaning of the saying 'revenge is a dish best served cold'.

However, just as Emily was in the midst of one of her greatest moments of triumph, she suffered a terrible loss. On 4th April 1898 while Emily was enjoying the Sydney races, her youngest child, John Arthur Powell, died in San Francisco at the age of thirty. It is not known how he died and Emily only mentions it once in 1906, when she writes about the fires in San Francisco in the wake of the latest earthquake: 'I have a dear son sleeping at Cypress Law,' which is the big cemetery on the outskirts of the city.

Nine years after the publication of her *Recollections*, Emily was off to report on the last public performance of the lady who had inadvertently started her career by making her so jealous that she marched off to get singing lessons. Adelina Patti was to perform in front of 10,000 people in the Albert Hall; but in the end it wasn't the great soprano Emily wrote about, but rather what happened to her on the way to the concert:

> *Nice, tall slender girl got in the 'bus, opposite corner to me. Very busy. Lots of papers. Bulky book. Spectacles. Sort of Girton get-up. She packed herself away as closely as possible, and by holding her elbows closely to her side managed to open her book. What do you think it was? My book! My Recollections! My portrait. By some psychological process she lifted her eyes – looked straight at me. I nodded 'yes'. She gasped and leant forward. 'I was at the matinee' said she. We had a little talk – delightful. She, as became a Girton-looking girl, carried a fountain pen. I autographed the book. Admiration on the part of the packed 'bus. (Push my new edition, 3s 6d). She bound for Victoria Station, I bound for Albert Hall, and so at St. George's Hospital we parted.*

Emily's encounter with a New Woman must have thrilled her. After all, Adelina Patti may have been singing a farewell concert to 10,000 people in the Albert Hall, but she had never had a book published and never had the experience of being asked to autograph her book by one of that most modern of phenomena, a New Woman. Again, revenge truly is a dish best served cold . . .

A relaxed Pip Powell and Katie Vesey on the boat to Australia

Chapter Thirteen

THE GREAT UNDEFEATED

'Do you know what we call you?' said he.
'No' said I.
'The Great Undefeated' said he
(John Hollingshead to Emily, 1902)

How do you want to grow old? If you are fortunate enough to have a third age, what do you want it to look like? Growing old disgracefully with a twinkle in your wrinkles has always seemed preferable to the alternative. That old woman wearing purple and a silly hat – which is how Emily seemed to have negotiated her way through ageing – not going gentle into the night but skipping through it, mischievously. Although to be fair, Emily was hardly making up 'for the sobriety of her youth', as Jenny Joseph suggested in her famous poem.

The other day a prominent gentleman of the city, high up in her councils, and most people's regards was introduced to me. 'I am so glad to meet you, Madame Soldene', said he, 'for I hear you are so delightfully wicked.' This was dreadful – I,

who have been striving for – and trusting by strict attention
to business to arrive at – a reputation for unremitting and
much goodness . . .

But she wasn't fooling anyone. No retirement homes for Miss Soldene, or minding the grandchildren, knitting by the fire, sitting in a rocking chair, having tea with the vicar, wearing black, playing the odd hand of solitaire, and annoying her children. For the rest of her life Emily filed a report almost every week for the *Sydney Evening News*, written in Emily's longhand with one of the relatively new ink fountain pens. Emily would have strolled to the post office every week and posted them off to newspaper headquarters on the other side of the world, from where they would be printed five weeks later. Indomitable, and yes, undefeated.

Emily could write about whatever she liked as long as it might be of interest – a rare, if not unheard of opportunity for someone from her background and class. By 1895 there were a handful of women journalists who had their own columns, but they were either bluestocking activists writing earnest articles about war, workers' conditions or women's rights, or aristocratic writers delivering features on culture and lifestyle – i.e. they were either from the privileged end of the middle class or truly upper class. This means when we read Emily's reports, we are seeing the Victorian and Edwardian worlds from the rare perspective of a late-middle-aged, uneducated working-class woman.

Her topics ranged from gossip to politics, general goings-on in the capital, especially royal and society events, technological progress (a particular favourite), strikes, riots and Christmas – her every festive season described in great detail, as were her many bacchanalian lunches and dinners. And then there was the reminiscing, often with a casually slipped in nugget of scandal from back in the day. In fact, titillation was sneaked in wherever possible. Emily couldn't help herself, the Music Hall indelibly marked through her core; or perhaps she just knew her audience. She wrote about her everyday life, and her family too. Her columns were a personal, approachable, intimate affair.

To facilitate this new incarnation, Emily declined to make her home with either her daughter Katie, now the lady of Shirley Manor, or with Clara living conveniently central in Southampton Row, Holborn. Instead, Emily decided to take a room in a boarding house just around the corner from Clara in Bloomsbury Square. A lady living on her own in lodgings was a controversial affair. However, as a renowned fifty-two-year-old widow, Emily could live independently without raising too many eyebrows. This central location allowed her to come and go at all times, to easily reach theatres and parties and the events that might provide good copy.

Emily's new career came with invitations. As well as first nights and parties, she was regularly given tickets to sporting events, parades, weddings and funerals. However, she was not always welcomed by the other (male) journalists, as happened when she turned up at the Imperial Institute to report on a presentation from the Agent-General of New South Wales to General Baden-Powell:

My ticket said 'Press'. The press table, a long one, in front of the platform, full of gentlemen of the fourth estate. 'Any room?', said I cheerfully. They simply glared at me, spread themselves out, drilled their elbows into the table, and glued their noses into their blotters. No other feminine

scribe present. But a little thing like that doesn't worry me.
Only one chair available. I put my hand on interrogatively.
'Engaged', growled a nearest and chivalrous one. No matter.
I got another, sat down, put my bag, my ticket, my gloves,
my notebooks, my pencils, my bunch of violets etc. on the
sacred table. They all looked up speechless. I had paralysed
the press of London with my impertinence.

As a journalist, Emily did not adhere to any one political party but took a more pragmatic attitude, claiming that the only thing she really cared about was taxes not going up – 'the sight of the tax collector is as disagreeable to me under the reign of Sir George This as it is under the regime of Sir George That'. She might have seen too many politicians close up to retain much respect. Only occasionally does Emily break out into a frothy opinion. One of these exceptions was the subject of suffrage. Despite Mrs Winslow boldly stating that women and men should be equal, Emily did not support women getting the vote: 'The women pull the strings anyway. Let them do it gracefully and quietly, and let the strings be silken ones.'

Emily was now part of an older generation: a Victorian in an Edwardian era. To us the differences might seem subtle, but at the time the world of 1838, the year in which Emily was born, and 1908 when she was writing, must have seemed like different universes – now there were trains, electricity, photographs, telephones and even cars. Women were going to university and riding bicycles and having jobs in offices, learning typing and shorthand, and working in department stores and wearing bloomers. Unions had formed, women had movements. Ladies were not bonneted in crinolines and whalebone corsets, but wrote books and articles, openly, under their own names. They had loose, flowing dresses, and sometimes showed their ankles. When does the baton pass from one generation to another? Perhaps it's almost inevitable that at some point Emily would feel left behind as the generation below sped past with their new ideas and technology.

Saturday morning great crowd at Bow-street. The magistrates called on the (suffragette) ladies to say why they should not be bound over . . . Up spoke Christabel (Pankhurst) – made a manlike and moving speech. But in the midst of it broke down, convulsed with sobs and tears (Still, for all that, she spoke for 66 minutes). Why did she cry? That's when she upset the cart . . .

Good gracious! If we got a lady Prime Minister, and she got heckled by some horrid Opposition man as to her conduct of the Treasury, and her capability for ordering Dreadnoughts and that sort of thing, what refuge would she have? Why, a flood of tears! And the Leader of the Opposition would snub his inquiring supporter, take the lady out to dinner, and wind up at Hunt and Roskell's (the Bond St jeweller) . . .

Was Emily a feminist? Not if it meant being a suffragette. But it might be that her ideas for the best way forwards for women were framed in a different, earlier, context. Equality for the sexes means different things to different women. But if feminism is the fight to make the world a better place for women, then Emily was a feminist. Social hypocrisy and stigma were what bothered Emily, not votes.

In 1908 a group of eminent actresses including Lillie Langtry and Ellen Terry formed their own branch of the suffragette movement, called the Actresses' Franchise League. Emily was invited to their first 'At Home' which was held at the Criterion Restaurant in Piccadilly. She couldn't resist looking in:

Great Hall very full indeed. Every nobody there. President and most of the vice-presidents conspicuous by their absence . . . Mr Forbes Robertson in the chair. Mr Forbes Robertson most funereal, called us 'women of my calling', and 'dear sisters'. Asked us in a solemn way had we read John Stuart Mill on 'The Subjection of Women'. Of course we hadn't, but didn't say so. If we hadn't, the precious thing (paper covered) was there within our reach, price sixpence. I didn't get one, not built that way. I like to be subjected . . .

A lady spoke of the degradation of woman, who was not allowed to pay her own bills, her husband being sued for her derelict debts. Other ladies did not seem to catch on to the idea of personally settling their sartorial obligations with entire rapture and much shaking of heads took place over the suggestion . . .

A dull business. I don't care a hang about the "franchise for women," and I consider my cab money, my shilling (yes I put a shilling in the plate, had to you know) and my two hours in my busiest day as being utterly thrown away.

Colonial matters and the Boer War took up many of Emily's column inches, reflecting the preoccupations of late Victorian Britain – the morality and existence of the Empire never questioned and greatly celebrated. Two public figures in particular caught Emily's attention – Winston Churchill and Cecil Rhodes. She was equally repelled and fascinated by Churchill. Early on in his career, decades before he had become the national hero, she spotted something unusual about him. Freud's paper on narcissism came out in 1914, too late for Emily, but I think that's what she might have labelled him. She became slightly obsessed. This on the Boer War:

> Isn't it a pity Winston Churchill has got a swelled head, and sends home patronising and superior and damning with faint praise dispatches worthy of the Kaiser himself? The latest story about him is that half a dozen of his former brother officers sent him a telegram, 'Don't make an ass of yourself', to which he promptly wired back 'Impossible, for I have left your regiment'. Smart, isn't he . . .

Emily was not even above repeating damning gossip:

> Winston Churchill is on the warpath, the envy of the young, the hope of the old. But I hear strange and ghastly things about him. He showed his arm the other day to a friend of mine. It was covered with punctures, injections of morphine. Bad Winston. Better pull up. Better take a peg or two.

By contrast Emily is decidedly taken with the great coloniser of southern Africa, Cecil Rhodes, who managed to have a whole country named after him. Rhodes was an imperialist who believed that the more of the world was ruled by the British, the better. Emily had no moral qualms about this famous man and went to see him off on his last trip to Africa. At Waterloo station she pushed her way through:

> 'Where is Mr. Rhodes?' said I to the nearest magnate (The crowd was made up of men whose faces one is familiar

with from pictures.). 'Mr. Rhodes is not here just now. Wait a minute. You can't miss him. He's got a billycock on'. 'I must see him', said I 'I've come all the way from Australia for the purpose'. 'Oh, by Jove! Get out of the way, Beit. Where's Rhodes?'. Here he comes, and out of the refreshment room walked the Empire-builder, smiling, and surrounded by regular court. 'I say, Rhodes, here's a lady come all the way from Australia to see you'. The smiling brown eyes looked down upon me – the swayer of South African destinies lifted the billycock. 'Is that a fact?' said he 'Then we shake hands'. So we did. 'People think a great deal about you in Australia' said I. 'I'm glad of that' said he. 'How long shall you be gone?' said I. 'About a year' said he. 'Ah – we go and come back, and go again' said I. 'That's about it' said he. Not a brilliant conversation – miles behind a dolly dialogue, but it did . . . 'Would you like to get close to his carriage?' said a gentleman. 'I would', said I. 'All right stand back', said he to the millionaire mob. The carriage moved a trifle. The gentleman held my arm. 'Goodbye Mr. Rhodes' said I, holding up my hand. 'Goodbye!' said he, putting his out, and I was absolutely the last one to shake hands with him . . .

Which in a way was true, because Cecil Rhodes never did come back to Britain. He died in South Africa later that year at the age of forty-two.

Emily's enthusiasm for warrior colonisers like Cecil Rhodes may well have been influenced by her young grandson's distinguished service in the Boer War. Katie's son, Henry, went to South Africa in 1899. Emily keeps her readers informed of his progress in some particularly personal missives. She goes to a patriotic poetry reading which is raising funds for the families of the soldiers killed in the campaign:

> *Someone sang a patriotic song 'Victory! Victory! It must be Victory!'. But the British public sat tight and never said a word. Coming out, a cyclone of news bills flourished in one's face. Loud hoarse shouts from newsboys – 'Great British Loss!' 'Awful Slaughter.' I felt I should faint.*
> *'Buck up, Auntie Emily', said my Brighton College boy escort (Christmas holidaying). 'Of course, where there's a war, men are bound to be killed'*

It was Clara's son, Charlie, who was her unempathetic escort. Two years later on a quiet Sunday afternoon, Emily was alone and feeling slightly miserable, trying to pass the time reading *Barnaby Rudge*, when she heard the sound of voices getting nearer.

> *The bells rang out loudly. Our cook rushed in. 'Peace, Madame, peace. 'Ere's the paper. Fourpence. Peace.' The sorrows of Mrs Rudge had worked me up. I could do nothing but kneel by the window and cry my eyes out.*

Emily's agony was over, and her grandson came home, along with some medals – he was awarded the Queen's Medal and three clasps.

When Queen Victoria died, it affected Emily profoundly: *Personally this thing has haunted me – no proper sleep for nights. The anticipation of an event, the preparation for which has no parallel in history – the extreme gloom pervading everything and everybody – indicated a sense of nervous excitation. Dreadful disease, like the portents of old, destroyed what are conventionally known as the hours of rest.*

I felt ashamed of a feeling that felt to a certain extent artificial. The Queen is dead – the Queen is to be buried. Well, the Queen is the visible representative of our national life and liberties. Well, the Queen being dead the King reigns, and the national life goes on. All the same the sense of desolation, of personal loss, the absolute prostration, continued.

The death of Queen Victoria, a constant, steady presence throughout her sixty-three years of reign, seems to have brought on a crisis for Emily, a tremor to her foundation that was common to the rest of the nation. It might have been more shocking knowing the new King Edward VII so personally; perhaps it was difficult to conjure up the same degree of respect and reverence for a man she had witnessed amusing himself with her former colleagues. Only a few weeks before, she had been making comments about his bald patch at the theatre.

This existential crisis might also have been because Emily had only just lost another seemingly immortal matriarch, and that was her mother Priscilla. She had died a few months earlier at Clara's house, of 'senile decay', at the magnificent age of eighty-eight. Emily never mentions the loss in her writing, but one apparent consequence is that Emily felt able to be even more candid about her own life:

This 'limited marriage' business is not an original or new idea. Twenty-five, or perhaps thirty years ago, I knew a man who propounded the same doctrine. He was, of course, married. His wife was 'not congenial'. He considered congeniality the wine (with a large W) of life, thought marriage should be modified (in its duration, I mean). But, with the daring of the pioneer, mentioned three months as a reasonable time in which to demonstrate each other's uncongeniality. Needless to say, he preached his gospel to a lady whose congeniality to himself he found irresistible. 'Wouldn't she try it?'. The lady, who had been brought up in close proximity to a Baptist chapel, was horrified at such advanced views, and thought — ah, but that's another story . . .

Often Emily took on the role of roving reporter at large, giving eyewitness accounts of major events. When London hosted the Olympics in 1908 Emily had to go, but for someone who had spent a life in comic opera, the Olympics felt a bit flat: 'Stadium a ghastly sight, pouring rain, shivering athletes, biking athletes, place so vast the athletes looked like flies'.

By contrast, after hearing reports of a gunfight between the police and Latvian revolutionaries, Emily's foray down to the East End to get a look at the siege of Sidney Street was a bit too exciting. She jumped on a bus to Stepney but was increasingly alarmed by the state of the mean houses and 'dirty foreigners'. She jumped off the bus but found herself in the middle of a mob.

Crowded round by Yiddish children, pointing with gravity to various sights, I find myself shoulder to shoulder with the verminous, unwashed throng. They push this way, that way. Presently big, loaded drays, powerful horses, come right through the mass of people. We fall back, or are pushed back, or get pushed back. I find myself close to the stirrup of a mounted officer. To tell the truth a trifle frightened. 'Better get out of this m'm' says officer. 'There's nothing to see, only carpenters building a hoarding'. 'More bodies?' 'No, no more bodies.' Turns his horse. 'This way, I'll take you through'. And so I chucked my job, seen nothing, not the burnt house, not the bodies, seen nothin'. Policeman on point duty at Aldgate conveyed me through a mass of traffic. 'Busy time down here' said I. 'Yes' said he, 'I was in a warm corner, too; bullet went through my helmet knocked down another of our chaps about three yards off. We lifted him up, shook him, opened his tunic, out fell the bullet, no damage.

Emily was so shaken that she had to have a stiff brandy and soda when she got home, and made the surprising assertion that quiet people who did not care for an excess of excitement were now emigrating to Moscow or St Petersburg.

Emily was most excited about the technological innovations that were proliferating, not least the revolution in transport. She couldn't wait to try the new Central Line or, as it was generally known, the 'tuppeny toob'. Opened in July 1900, it ran from Shepherd's Bush to Bank and was very popular due to its cheap tickets – a two-pence flat rate. She went through the barriers amazed by the scrum, squeezed into a lift with sixty other people, and then arrived on the platform. She was confused by the wind blowing through but was told it was caused by the electricity, a forced draught. 'So cool, so refreshing, and my mind flew back to that inside cabin of the Ortana', she said, and impressed by the beautiful carriages, 'made in America, I'm sure. Long and light, such pretty inlaid wood.' But when they all took their seats, the train didn't move.

It's deadly quiet – no people, no porters – only the people in the carriage. Not a sound. The engine don't snort. We look round. How clean everything is – no dirt, no dust, no smoke, no cloudy atmosphere, no choking sensation. All beautiful.

Why don't we start? . . .

We all wonder why. Presently, we say so. Some daring spirit suggests trying to open the door. Shall we? We jump at the idea. General movement and – just then – a shrill whistle. At last, we are off.

The same thing, the same wait at every station . . . 'Twenty minutes' says a gentleman looking at his watch. 'Fifteen minutes lost since leaving Oxford Circus'. 'Oh, that's nothing' said a crumpled up old man. 'Er friend er mine was in this ere drain poipe er matter hof er hour th' other night.'

That's pleasant. Hearing these things, one looks round, in view of possibilities. After leaving each station, the train runs through a succession of tunnels, with no spare room on either side. Given an accident, how is one to get out? What's the good of thinking about accidents? Che sara, sara.

The tuppenny is not exactly everything that could have been wished. 'The vibration is dreadful'. Folks who work in cellars are falling victim to seismic disturbances, other folks who work in offices, feel the movement 'much', and a young lady typewriter has been dismissed for persistently dotting her i's twice. 'That nasty toob' says she with lacrimi di voce.

Another invention that Emily reported on, but which took much longer to reach the public, was the mobile phone. An American called Martin Cooper is supposed to have come up with the idea while working for Motorola in 1972; but just as Mark Twain once said, there is no such thing as an original idea. A demonstration of a prototype of 'the new pocket wireless telephone' was given at the Great Exhibition at Crystal Palace by a Mr Rossenburg. Emily spotted the downsides immediately.

That's all very well, but the question crops up, is this going to be a beneficent boon or a holy terror?

Suppose Mrs Jones insists on Mr Jones carrying a receiver from home. She can worry and scold him all day. The poor man cannot reply, only listen and make profane remarks . . . There is a difficulty. A receiver will not receive unless it is in tone with the sending instrument. Now, when a thousand or two of these are in circulation, the chances are that a number of tones will be identical, and if half a dozen dreadfully busy Mr Browns are rung up that 'Mr Robinson is waiting in the office', five Mr Browns are going to get very angry indeed. And if Mary Jane whispered 'Bertie, meet me at Redfern Station 2.40' and when she got there found four and twenty Berties waiting for her . . . why, where are you?

Emily was also initially sceptical about the car. She could see that it would be useful not to keep the horses standing out in the chilly rain when one went to the theatre in the evenings, but the lack of appropriate apparel exercised her greatly. The automobile attire question was finally solved for Emily by a visit to the Motor Show at Olympia, where there was a special salon set aside for the Ladies' Automobile Club:

A study in toilettes. Tea and transmissions, coffee and clutches, macaroons and magnetos, discussed with ardour and zest. When motoring for ladies first came up, people said it 'wouldn't do', 'wouldn't catch on'. Motors could not be repaired with a hairpin and motor coats and general get-ups were horrid. But we've changed all that. Ladies, it is told, can be taught to drive a car after ten-minutes tuition, and

can be put up to all repairing after twenty minutes' ditto.
And, as to toilettes, motor hats, veils, wraps, gloves, boots etc.
have been metamorphosed from ugliness to elegance.

By 1911 Emily is a full convert. Here an account of a jaunt while having a miserable time in Selsey Bill:

My granddaughter has a bungalow and a motor at East Wittering and my message says 'Come and take me out of this windy place'. In two hours buzz of motor, tall young lady in white chauffeur coat, white wool cap, wind-blown curls drives up. Drives motor herself. Lovely little grey racing car. She tucks me up in a fur coat, fur rug, veil &c. Off we go. 'Goodbye. Goodbye, Selsey Bill . . . Such a glorious drive! Now I am going to show you what 40 miles an hour is like', says the driver. 'No, don't,' say I. But she did. Immense! What a spin! Delightful! How the fascination of pace gets into one's blood. 'Fast', 'fast', 'fast', 'fast-er', say I. 'What?' says she. 'Well here goes'.

The other big transport revolution that Emily witnessed was aviation. She reported to her readers that the first aeroplane had arrived in London in November 1909 and was being kept at the Savoy Hotel until it was ready to fly in the London to Manchester race. She reports excitedly of the first airmail:

Immense crowd to Hendon. First post from Hendon to Windsor. The king gave permission for aerial postmen to land on Castle grounds. People went down to Hendon, wrote cards and letters on the spot, put cards in letter bags at the latest possible moment . . . great send-oo for M Gustave Hamel, the first aerial postman.

It took ten minutes to travel the twenty miles to Windsor at a speed of 121 miles an hour. It seems today as if the increase in our interconnectivity is unprecedented, but for Emily now approaching her seventies, the world must have seemed transformed out of all recognition. When she was born in 1838, the first railway in Britain had only been open for eight years.

A large proportion of Emily's columns were filled with gossip including tales of funerals. Emily loved a good funeral and when Arthur Sullivan died, as in Gilbert and Sullivan, she was determined to go. Sullivan had apparently arranged his funeral meticulously – he was to be buried next to his mother in Brompton cemetery. According to Emily he got the fatal chill while visiting her grave on the anniversary of her death.

The service was not sublime, for the Dean's glasses were out of order, and during his reading of the first lesson, when they were not falling off his nose on to the sacred book, he was picking them up, holding them tightly with his right hand, and turning over the pages uncomfortably with his left . . . Nothing has been said in the papers, but all the world and his wife are remarking on the extraordinary fact that no sign was made by Mr W S Gilbert, either by flowers, message or presence. In spite of their unfortunate differences, it was generally thought that WSG would be among the pallbearers . . .

Naturally theatre visits took up plenty of copy. She was often accompanied by Clara, the two of them enjoying the opportunity it gave for gossip. Emily wrote of the news that the widow of the actor and impresario Sir Augustus Harris was to remarry, saying she was not surprised after seeing them together at Her Majesty's Theatre:

'Clara', I said to my sister, 'they're going to make a match of it'. 'Ridiculous', said she. 'Why?' said I, 'and see he's had his hair cut'. 'What of that?' said she disrespectfully. 'You're always finding something out'. I was right, you see, consequently I'm not surprised.

Sometimes Emily used gossip to put across a point. Lillie Langtry's husband was found wandering on train lines, arrested, released and then found drunk in a field with eleven pence in his pocket mumbling about being strangled by a woman with her long hair. He was put in an asylum where he committed suicide. Emily wrote of the talk surrounding the affair, with people feeling sorry for Mr Langtry and condemning his wife for mistreating him, with comments like 'what can you expect from an actress' (which was bound to hit a nerve) and 'fancy the prince taking such a woman into the enclosure at Newmarket, of course the other women there ignored her'. Emily has her say: 'Well, there were only twelve women there, and perhaps you would find me a woman who would mind being cut by twelve other women because she was being entertained by HRH'.

She pointed out that Mr Langtry may have only had eleven pence in his pocket but he had always received a good allowance from his wife, and while his death may have been sad, a man who received a quarterly cheque from a famous wife wasn't so hard done by.

Emily even appeared to admit to taking drugs when she reported that mescal was the latest fad in London:

Nasty to take, nice after taking. An extract from a certain cactus of the southern plains of America. Is worshipped by the American Indians. Induces colour visions – violet shadows, glorious fields of glorious gleaming jewels, dancing, iridescent fireflies, gorgeous butterflies and that sort of rot; a drug habit but does no harm.

Wake up next morning know nothing about it, no headache.

And then there was fashion news – she informed Australian readers of the heated debate around the new empire line. Where should a gentleman place his arm when dancing – around the natural waist or the waistline indicated by the dress, which was inconveniently near the bust? As for the new craze of women wearing the 'hareem skirt' – what we would call trousers – Emily was all in favour, and predicted they would be normal attire by the next year:

> *Don't get tied up in one's skirts. No twisting around to get out of the clutches of entangling kilts. I feel I'm up-to-date and free from conventional prejudice when I see neat little figures, lithe, straight limbs, tiny tootsies, big bows of ribbons, Louis Quatorze heels, and a general fetching ensemble tied at the ankle, defying the wind and all its works.*

And then Emily sometimes wrote about the plain bizarre:

> *The weather is so fearfully hot, that people not only die of the heat, they go mad and walk about without their clothes, which is pleasant to them, but confusing to others. Yesterday a man undressed himself in a railway carriage full of ladies. They screamed, but the more they screamed the more nudy he got, and as he removed each garment he threw it out of the window. Language fails to describe the distress of these poor ladies by the time they reached Victoria Station, where waiting and expectant friends beheld to their horror travellers in close companionship with a capering, naked lunatic. Everybody went into hysterics. The man said he was not a*

lunatic but a reformer. But there are always two sides to this
sort of question, and they 'ran him in.'

What makes a good journalist? Emily seemed as comfortable scribbling missives as singing an Offenbach aria, as if it was another part she was born to play. She was able to use her wit and humour, her observation and general curiosity about the people and the world around her. She could sense a story and had the instinct for what would interest people, the ability to let her personality shine through and yet not overwhelm the story itself. Emily also had the sheer determination to get close enough to where the action was happening. All those years of hard work, travelling, meeting people – her worldly wisdom – were now bearing fruit and being put to good use. Reading her articles, it doesn't feel as if Emily was just ticking boxes to earn money. Her joie de vivre bubbles up in her prose, like the literary equivalent of Offenbach's champagne bounce.

When she wasn't writing, a large amount of Emily's time seems to have been spent on fine dining. My favourite Emily food story is her visit to the Olde Cheshire Cheese in Fleet Street. Walking down Fleet Street one afternoon she bumps into an old fan who insists on buying her lunch. Emily agrees on the condition it's at the ancient hostelry. She goes down the narrow, dusky passage, squeezing past the old leaning walls and through a small door into a black low-beamed room complete with sawdust on the floor. There she meets the landlord who is delighted – he remembers going to see Emily at the Phil when he was a boy. Emily says it's such a pity that the Olde Cheshire Cheese rump-steak pudding season is over, only to be told it was due to be served that day at 1 p.m.

Presently enters a waiter with piles of hot plates – willow pattern plates – then two waiters bearing gravy – willow pattern bowls – then smoking hot potatoes. Then a movement. I thought everyone was getting up to make obeisance to what? Why, the pudding. No use trying to describe the pudding – 'same pudding Dr. Johnson used to have' – it weighs over a hundred pounds, looks like a pantomime pudding, it is rumpsteak, marrow, oysters, mushrooms, larks and kidneys – a most delectable composition, the crust not fatty – flaky, light and boiled 10 to 20 hours. The recipe is a family secret, a trust. The proprietor locks himself away in a secret room while compounding it, and when the pudding is confided to a confidential cook, and the 'secret' is locked away in a safe of many combinations . . .

After the pudding, I held a reception. I think all the newspapermen in Fleet Street came to shake hands and say 'Howdy?' Absolutely delightful.

The building hasn't changed much, but they don't make pies like that any more, and journalists paying homage? Perhaps they weren't so chauvinistic after all, or perhaps by this time Emily had earnt enough respect to be allowed into the club, an honorary gentleman journalist.

As well as constant meals out, Emily's days are filled with shopping (food and clothes at the new department stores; White's was a favourite), gambling (days at the races frequent) and trips to the countryside surrounding London, boating on the Thames especially. Bank holiday weekends were spent at one of her favourite seaside resorts – usually Margate or Brighton (never Hastings!), the resorts that were convenient for London and so fashionable in the Victorian era. Sometimes she went on a longer summer holiday sailing in her son-in-law's yacht. She also managed two more trips to Australia to see her old friends where she was treated as royalty and indulged in serious gastronomy:

A progressive dinner party for 12 is on the tapis. I think it is going to be great fun. The proceedings will commence at 7 in the evening, and six carriages are to be in attendance. The party will meet and drink the ante-prandial cocktail at the 'Marble Bar', then taking the carriages, they will drive to the Trocadero for the hors d'oeuvres – to Chinnery's for oysters, to Paris House for soup, to Woodward's for fish, to Café Francais for entrée, to City Buffet for joint, to the Imperial for asparagus, to the Metropole for poultry and game, the Australia for sweets, to Petty's for cheese and salad, to the ABC Café for ices, the Grosvenor.

Then there were the parties. Emily was often invited for old times' sake, dining out on her past glories:

A great supper at the Savoy Hotel given by a certain Indian Maharajah who is rather 'in' with the Gaiety crowd. Delightful decorations, the table a perfect picture, covered with fresh violets laid loosely on the cloth, and here and there green leaves; the room scented with Roger and Gallet's very best 'extract'. A bodice boutonniere for each lady, and a gold safety pin with two hearts in pearl and turquoise to fasten them. It is little amenities like these that reconcile one to the exigencies of everyday, or, rather, everynight life.

Of course, if Emily had remarried after Jack's death, she never would have been able to go to these sorts of dinners.

But there was a disparity between the glamour of Emily's public life and her domestic existence in the boarding house in Bloomsbury, with its German manservant who slept in the communal bath. A contrast between the shiny public persona, and the cold dark moments that come from living alone when money is tight. There were moments when Emily couldn't be dashing about, when the isolation didn't seem so splendid, when she felt ill and old and vulnerable, when the only thing keeping her warm were memories and thoughts of far-off sunnier times and places. Occasionally she couldn't help herself and her sadness slipped into print:

My quarters are high up – a pale grey light creeps in very early. It is cold, and one shivers. I can see from Southampton Row – a long way – past Bloomsbury Square, past the British museum, well on to Tottenham Court Road, and that's what I do. Sit and think, and wonder what is going on in certain sunlit lands. Have eaten nothing solid for ten days. Am dreadfully hungry.

Perhaps partly to escape from these moments, Emily spent significant amounts of time with her family, most of all her eldest daughter, Katie, now settled down in a beautiful manor house in Shirley, Surrey. The times she liked best were the festive seasons spent at Katie's. Every Christmas is described in great detail, giving a biscuit-tin picture of extended family perfection that could rival Dickens himself. On reflection it's not surprising that Emily liked Christmas: eating, drinking and being merry – apart from gambling, her three favourite pastimes. This for Christmas 1901:

Such a Christmas – a wonderful Christmas for me . . . A real country house, with a large house party. Such decorations!

Lots of holly and mistletoe down 'them pairts'. Christmas eve delightful. All hands to decorate the floral screen for the village church. So lovely! Holly and ivy and big white chrysanthemums made on a lattice work and carried by four gardeners through the grounds to the church; received by the vicar, the curate and the girls, putting artistic and finishing touches.

Large dinner party. Lots of music. Christmas carols and church choir boys singing in the hall got port wine, new shillings and Christmas cake. No end of a time!

In this house old time English fashions reign. All the outdoor servants — stables, garden etc. get a joint of beef, plum pudding, Christmas cake, a bottle of whiskey and ditto of port.

Christmas day, presents all round. I had a lot — they came in mysteriously early with a cup of tea. To church to give thanks; then lunch, then a walk, then a rest. Thirty to dinner, and all sorts of coins in plum pudding.

Boxing Day, Christmas boxes all round — from a guinea each to the coachman and the butler, to 2s 6d for the bootboy. Quite a tray of money put up by the young daughters of the house, with the name of each man and maid on each packet. Not so cold, so we vote a long drive and the landau . . . such a popping of guns — here there and everywhere. Everyone's gone out to kill something or somebody.

More dinner party — lots of people from London — keep on dining until 9.30, then bridge, music, ecarte, cake walk, coon songs and carriages at 12.

Sunday, a little rest? No. Church, lunch afternoon tea, Christmas cake. Many callers, more dinner party, champagne and mince pies all the time.

Unfortunately, this was the last happy Christmas Emily was to have at her daughter's house.

A year later and Katie was seriously ill. Emily doesn't mention this in her dispatches. Instead she again paints a picture of a classic Dickensian Christmas with showers of holly and mistletoe, carols, cake, mince pies, blind man's buff, hunt the slipper, crackers, forfeits, bagpipes and a curate with a feeble tenor voice. But, despite all this bravado, Emily must have known that Katie was ill because at the beginning of November she had been booked to travel on the *Ophir* to Australia for Christmas, but she cancelled. For a woman who rarely let her children get in the way of her travels, Emily must have known that it was serious. But still for the first two weeks of the year Emily's dispatches are light pieces of gossip: 'A new cult has started – the cult of drinking at one's lunch and dinner only – no intermediate "nips". This is called "semi-teetotalism". To be "semi-teetotal" sounds so much better than "half seas over"'.

The columns for the next two weeks are missing. Emily's daughter died on 20th January 1903 at home in Shirley House, of cervical cancer. She left behind her husband and three children: Henry aged twenty-two, Helen aged twenty, and Elsie aged eighteen. She was buried three days later in the graveyard in Shirley Church. Her husband, Robinson, later erected a large tomb over her grave. One of the local newspapers commented, 'She endeared herself to all who came in contact with her.'

Emily's next report is simple:

The last day but one of January and spring, treading so closely on the heels of winter, is already with us. Violets, primroses in the hedges, birds singing in the trees. My spirit just now dwells in the past. A great sorry has fallen on me. If you find this screed more than common dull, extend your forgiveness and your sympathy.

Next week she is back in London and writing about the transformation of Holborn and the building of Kingsway. But this lack of emotion is deceptive. On a couple of occasions, Emily gives us a glimpse of the profound depth of her grief. It's Lord Kitchener that triggers her, or 'K of K' as she calls him:

When my daughter came near the Borderland, her one craving was to see her son, then on service in India. Went there with K of K. Won his step in South Africa. Did something smart in the way of 'intelligence' in India, and was noticed by K of K. So K of K was cabled for 'leave'. 'Impossible!'. Cabled again. 'More impossible'. After three weeks came cable. 'Leave sail tomorrow'. But our reply cable was, 'Too late!'

Seven years later Emily made a point of meeting Kitchener at a reception held by the High Commissioner for Australia at the Ritz:

Crush, crush . . . sensation . . . Lord Kitchener, K of K. I ran him down. 'I would like to shake hands with you', said I. 'Pleasure', said he with a smile. Firm, immovable, autocrat, he has a beautiful smile. Not a worn out smile. 'Cos why? He trots it out so seldom. He looked down at me graciously as Jove moved from a pinnacle . . .
K of K, warrior and woman hater . . . and looking at him and speaking to him on Monday it all came back. And I found in my heart my mourning was forever.

Grief can constellate around individual moments, things said, not said, done or not done, as if they capture or symbolise the deeper tragedy. Something about this piece of cruelty, that Katie's dying wish to see her son one last time had been denied to her, seemingly pointlessly, penetrated down to Emily's permanent layer of grief. She hid her sorrow well, and carried on (I presume she didn't like the alternative), but that didn't mean that she wasn't suffering – as we know, she was a great actress. But meeting Kitchener brought it all back to the surface. Note that she calls him a 'woman hater' – Emily here publicly highlighting his rumoured homosexuality, a little piece of revenge, perhaps, in the days when to practise homosexuality was a criminal offence.

Two years later, Shirley House had been sold and turned into a hotel and Emily's son-in-law, Robinson Henry Simpson, was also dead. His death certificate states that he died in an asylum in Virginia Water. More than that isn't known but there is something inherently tragic in just the simple fact of Henry, Elsie and Helen losing both parents so quickly, and then their family home.

Emily must have felt increasingly alone. She had been a widow now for many years, her mother was gone, her oldest and youngest children had passed away. Nellie was last seen in San Francisco and never heard from again, and may well have died too. John Arthur had, of course, died years before while Emily was at the races in Sydney.

Emily's eldest son, Edward, was still very much alive, but on the other side of the Atlantic making a precarious living as an actor. He had come to London in 1901 with his new wife and a successful production of *Sherlock Holmes* starring a certain William Gillette, who was quite a star on Broadway.

The idea of an American playing Sherlock Holmes had been controversial, but Gillette was generally hailed as a triumph in the part, certainly by Emily. Unfortunately, Edward only had a minor role in the hit production; but it meant Emily could meet this new wife – a glamorous, mildly successful New York actress called Harriet Aubrey – their first child, and, moreover, could be around for the birth of their second, Gillette Powell (obviously named after the leading man). She was born in December 1901 in Tennyson Mansions in Fulham. The family stayed until March 1902, during which time Emily went to see *Sherlock* several times, basking in its success: "'W.G." great as ever, perfectly delightful, tremendous house and distinguished company.'

There were many other visits to the theatre as Emily showed off London's West End to her new daughter-in-law, although they may not have been the best of friends. They seemed to have a different idea about what an older lady might want to do with her life. Here a disagreement about the then American president's wife, Mrs McKinley:

I've got a recently arrived American daughter-in-law. 'Well', said she, 'I consider it real mean for Mrs McKinley to go junketing around the country, out west and all that. Everybody knows what a sick woman she is. She ought ter be in a Bath chair all the time. She does not need the White House – a Bath chair in the garden. 'But suppose', said I, 'Mrs McKinley does not care for 'a bath chair all the time' and prefers taking on the White House now and then?' My new daughter shook her head . . .

At the end of March 1902, the visit came to an end when *Sherlock* started to tour the provinces, and Edward and his family went back to the States. It was the last time Emily ever saw them.

The Christmas after Katie's death, Emily stayed in Bloomsbury:

Did you ever lie awake a'nights? Horrid, isn't it? Well, that's what I've been busy at this week. Have counted the sheep jumping through the rails, have walked the floor to get cold, have crept back into bed to get warm, have had hot milk 'ast thing', and a glass of cold water in the middle of the night, have had the German 'cure everything', a cold compress. All in vain, no good. Have pulled up the blinds to see if anyone else was in trouble like me. No, all dark, dismal, pull them down again. Listen to all the noises of the night, the creak of the boards, the step on the stairs, the fall of a cinder, the joyous squeak of a mouse playing 'tag' with another mouse among my papers. I slither into my sitting room, switch on the light. For one awful moment mutual consternation. Mice flop on the floor, I make a beeline for the bed, tuck myself well up (very particular about the toes), and fall fast asleep in the blankets and a deadly fright. Next morning, shaken up, with difficulty wake up, with disgust. 'What's the time?' say I. 'Alf past 10, an' yer breakfast has cold has a stone' says the maid with severity. Good gracious, and I've an appointment at 11.

Well, these things the result of Christmas. Any amount of church services, attention to one's family ties, mince pies, dinners, lunches, receptions. New Year's Eve, everybody not entertaining being entertained . . . Home at 3pm. So tired. New Year's Day, terrible. Never had such a time in my life. Always been so careful. Somehow, now, so uncareful. Why? Goodness knows.

Ask me another. More 'so tired'. That's the reason I couldn't sleep.

Sometimes we drink to forget; it doesn't always work, though. In the end, it just makes us feel worse.

Of course, there was still Clara, and her two children, Charles and Katie Hoffmeister. Emily seemed to enjoy the company of her young nephew, taking him out to tea when he was a boarder at Brighton College, discussing politics and cricket, of which he seemed to have plenty of opinions that amused her greatly. But it was Katie who took up most of Emily's attention, as she followed her mother and her aunt and went onto the stage. Her choice of career is interesting. She had been brought up as a young lady on Southampton Row, with no need to earn a living and plenty of reasons not to risk her reputation. However, at the age of sixteen Katie Hoffmeister changed her name to Katie Vesey and took part in her first production, seemingly encouraged by both her aunt and her mother:

> *I wonder, do the outside young ladies who speak so glibly of 'going on the stage' ever think of the amount of work necessary for the preparation? My niece is engaged for the pantomime at the Adelphi, and Clement Scott – speaking of her – says 'Miss Katie Vesey is a daughter of Clara Vesey, the mention of whose name carries us back to the times of Genevieve de Brabant and other delightful works, whose like we cannot find nowadays . . . My sister writing, says 'Katie is to play a French girl' (Katie speaks French, German and English). 'This morning she had a lesson at 10 with D'Auban (dancing), after that a lesson in music, then a band rehearsal at the 'Palace' and an hour's practice. Then to Peter Robinson's to be fitted for a walking*

dress, then a singing lesson. She is a wreck and so am I'.
That's a good day's work, don't you think? Well that's the sort of
thing that goes on day after day. But Katie is a real artiste, and
tells 'Auntie Emily' that she loves it.

Emily seems a little bit proud of this niece. But also note how Clara is accompanying her daughter in this exhausting round. It is perhaps understandable that Clara, knowing what she knew, might want to chaperone her young daughter. However, this carries on for the rest of Katie Vesey's long theatrical career, well past the age when she must have been able to look after herself. Rehearsals, performances and tours, Clara is there, the uber-stage-mother. Clara married late and seemingly returned to theatrical life, as soon as she respectfully could. It might be a clue as to how much she enjoyed playing the role of the conventional upper-middle-class wife and mother.

By December 1900, Katie had become one of those celebrated Gaiety Girls – the girls that danced in the chorus of the musical comedies at the Gaiety Theatre. Famed for their beauty and stylish attire (they were given free outfits by London's top couture designers), they were considered more respectable and chaste than their earlier opera burlesque counterparts. They were also famous for marrying well – May Gates married a Norwegian, Baron Von Ditton; Sylvia Storey married William Poulett the 7th Earl Poulett; Gertie Millar became Countess of Dudley; and Olive May became first Lady Victor Paget and then the Countess of Drogheda. As Emily said:

How different are the massaged, manicured, frilled-
furbeloved, voluminously-flounced chiffon-clad houris of

the present to the simple sealskin brigade of the past. In those days of light and leading, the less one had on the better, and polished nails were an accident. Well here's to the Gaiety Girl of the present, and a rather 'orty and petted young person, long may she reign and have as good times as the Gaiety Girl of the past.

With her own Katie gone, Christmas 1904 saw Emily spending the festive season in Liverpool with Clara, who was chaperoning her Katie in pantomime, and then for Christmas 1905 Emily joined Clara to watch Katie play the principal boy in Cinderella: 'Naturally, we all went along to give a hand. Wouldn't you? Of course you would.'

But much as Emily enjoyed following her niece's theatrical career, it also took Clara away from her. In 1910 Katie went on tour to Australia. She had stopped being a glamorous chorus girl and was now part of a music hall song and dance double act with a man called Pip Powell (no relation to the other Powells). Katie had met him at the Gaiety where he was part of the chorus too, and Pip Powell seems to have popped up in the casts of the many varied productions that Katie had played in ever since. Pip was a married man with children. This didn't stop him leaving his family on the other side of the world and travelling with Katie. It is also interesting that Katie didn't get married at the usual age that a young woman might. She was a pretty chorus girl, she must have had admirers; they all did. Of course, it could be that Katie didn't make an advantageous match because she didn't have to. Having a rich father meant she would have had the luxury of being able to afford to have a long-running affair with an attractive man who wasn't particularly wealthy. There is a photo of them together, looking like they are 'together', on the boat over to

Australia. He does look handsome, in a slightly cocky, 'I've got the girl' kind of way. Or perhaps that may be reading too much into the photo. At any rate, it seems that Katie was not sticking to the stage for the love of performing. While in Australia Katie and Pip gave an interview to a magazine called *Table Talk*:

> *In a cheery drawing-room with chintz covered furniture Miss Katie Vesey comes forward to greet a morning visitor; a pretty, graceful girl, much younger than she appears over the footlights, with a very quiet manner. 'Mr Powell has not arrived yet, but he said he would come', is her first remark, and then she introduces her mother who is sitting on the other side of the room absorbed in a book, and tells how she was here thirty-three years ago. 'Thirty-three, wasn't it mother?' And mother assents, adding 'but I was only a girl and cannot remember much about Australia, for things did not make the impression on me that they would now.'*

Clara's reticence to talk about her past glories (and those of her sister, now a famous columnist for Australia's leading newspaper) is puzzling – unless she didn't want to steal the limelight from her daughter whose career was relatively modest. The interviewer (rather archly) goes on to say that Clara remains:

> *Smilingly listening, and occasionally nodding agreement, but says very little. She is unfortunately rather an invalid just now. She looks amused when her daughter says 'Everyone thinks we are married', with a look at Mr Powell. And he corroborates with a nod. 'Yes, they always give us one dressing room, taking it for granted, and we have to enter into explanations every time. I always say I spoilt Kitty's chances, and kept everyone away!'*

Clara seems to have come across as fragile, although she always did have those moments when she looked like she might depart the mortal world, especially after a long voyage.

At the end of the interview Katie and Pip both assert that, despite having come from theatrical families and grown up wanting to go on the stage, they 'emphatically declared they hate the life and the work now, and their idea of happiness is home life'. Pip said he would like to be a land agent and they both were in agreement 'condemning the stage as a profession, especially for women'. They claimed they had been pushed into variety work. 'They would not take no for an answer.' Pip bid farewell to the interviewer with, 'Be sure and tell them we are not married, please.'

Emily was supposed to be going out to Australia to join them, but her health was beginning to be a problem. She had a nasty bout of flu and then found herself uncharacteristically blue, in a dip that for once she couldn't shake.

Better? Yes, much, thanks. The bee in my bonnet not nearly so big, not nearly so buzzy. Still, not altogether out of the bush, as they say down in my country. Just waiting for the 'after effects', which of influenza are particularly ghastly. I did hear the coroners were putting in for extra fees in consequence of the alarming increase in their duties. All on account of – not Eliza – but of the 'after effects' of influenza, said effects (generally fatal) taking the form of ascertaining the depth of the domestic water butt, trying the strength of the domestic clothes line, inspecting the bottom of the nearest canal. Many variations on the theme of getting rid of oneself, one's relations and one's responsibilities – all put down to the same cause 'after effects of influenza.'

It seems that the effect of a nasty virus on one's mental health is not a new phenomenon.

But it was not just a bad case of the flu; something new creeps into Emily's writing after her daughter's death – nostalgia, less excitement, a weariness, a note of longing. Like many people as they approach their final years, Emily increasingly retreated to her childhood, the country childhood, running across the fields with her Swain cousins in the Hertfordshire villages; as if as the end comes speeding towards her, she retreats to the beginning.

Such a busy day Tuesday – Primrose Tuesday. Everybody wearing a bunch of primroses. Why? it's the sentiment of Spring, the anticipation of a good time at hand, the sentiment of youth, the sentiment of hope, the remembrance of long ago days when, as children, creeping on hands and knees amongst the soft moss and under the young trees of the home copse, we filled our hats and bonnets and pinafores with primroses and violets and wild hyacinths. How we laughed and listened to the 'cheep', cheep' of the baby birds, to the rustling of the squirrels, and lifted our faces to catch the glint of the pale sun . . .

Well in these hustling days it's good to have memories of old times, old ways, old people, at least not all, some old people dreadfully disagreeable. Used to make me sit on a three-legged stool and sew my seam when I wanted to be out in the meadow picking buttercups and daisies, or in the orchard, up a cherry tree, filling my best 'pinny' with black cherries. Somehow all the cherries lingering in my memory are black, perhaps because the black cherries soiled the white diaper 'pinny' and swift grandmotherly correction overtook the culprit. In those days, a little birch would hang from a convenient and easy-to-get-at nail. The admonishing 'hold-out-your-hand' was much in fashion. Grandma's slipper sometimes took an active part in the game.

Grandma Catherine ('Katie') must have been formidable, having had nine children in eleven years, with a disgraced husband who was away fighting in Canada for five years and then died of alcohol poisoning. This was a woman who ran her own inn, and whom countless daughters were named after, including my own great-aunt and my cousin.

In November 1911, a simple line appeared in the newspaper. Emily was not going to be writing next week's column because she was going to have an operation. She wrote: 'Au revoir . . . if all does not go well, it means "goodbye"'.

Five days later the paper reported on the top of its front page, 'EMILY SOLDENE RECOVERING. "LETTERS" WILL SOON BE RENEWED.' Two months later she is back:

'Have you missed me?' I am wondering – are you wondering what has come to me? Will tell you. Bad times – horrid times. Cruel times, narrow escapes, long journeys, travelling to the Beyond – to the Borderland. Standing on the brink, weak, misty, grey clouds, wavering, uncertain. Faces of the past flit by, they beckon. Voices, too, calling. I'm ready. No, not always the same. One day struggling for life, the next placid, quiet, resigned, waiting for the other thing. No regrets. Passing in peace. Then. Drawn back by skill, strong firm hands, strong as iron, delicate as butterflies' wings hovering over me. Science most profound, service most devoted. Drawn back softly, gently, once more in the world, trembling feet once more touch the uplifting earth.

Emily was treated by a famous young surgeon called Mr Ironside and a physician called Sir George Hastings who was obviously a little older – 'firm friend since we were both young and gay, free and frivolous, roses all along the line. (Both say I am a marvel. Two-year-old not in it)'.

All the nurses insisted she was only thirty-five: 'Splendid don't you think? Now I'm assured I'll be like a new woman. Wonder if you'll like me as a New Woman.'

It was a joke aimed at the bicycle-riding, mannish Girton ladies of course. Behind her hutzpah though, it sounds as if Emily had had a rough time – severe nurses in a boring nursing home in Clacton. She tells of the day that the ship left for Australia, the one she'd again hoped to be sailing on: 'I, by the sad sea waves at Clacton-on-the-Sea, sat asighin and acryin'. Dreadful. All the fault of anno domini.' The nursing home was expensive, and the nurses put her in mind of the bricklayer 'who, as the clock strikes, drops his hod'. Personal effects had a habit of going missing and 'patient, pretending to be asleep, listens to night and day nurse faking reports for morning visit of the doctor'.

By February she was back in London, spreading the usual gossip as if nothing had happened. Then on 4th April 1912 she posted this missive.

Invalids (I'm one you know) wake up early in the morning. Lovely morning – rejoice – basking in a blazing and unexpected sun. Whistle for the taxi, drive in the park; beautiful fresh air. Who knows the joys of fresh air who only fresh air knows? Big bunch of violets in the taxi, some fresh peaches from the Cape. How delightful. Will drive right away to Hampstead Heath. Perhaps call at Willow Cottage, and gracious! How dark.

Down it comes. Dreadful storm . . . better luck next time.

But there is no next time. The following are her last written words – in something of a death-row meal moment, it's her menu for Easter Day lunch:

Smoked Salmon a l'huile
Consomme printanier
Boiled turbot, Dutch sauce
Veal cutlets a la francaise
Fricassee of chicken
Roast leg of lamb, mint sauce
Asparagus with carrots
Baked new potatoes
Orange shape with cream
Maids of Honour

Only drawback no gooseberry pie

Perhaps it was this extraordinary lunch that proved her undoing, because it was later that night on Easter Sunday that Emily had a fatal heart attack. She died in her bed in Woburn Place. Her niece, Katie Vesey, was listed as present at the scene of death, and her great appetite was almost certainly the underlying cause of her death. On her death certificate it states the causes as 1) diabetes and 2) coma, cardiac failure.

Emily was buried with her daughter, Katie Simpson, in Shirley churchyard. It was a small, discreet funeral that seems out of step with the dramatic, high-octane, very public way Emily had lived her life; the only family present was her granddaughter, the smart motorist spinster Helen Simpson, whom she had appointed as her executor. No Katie Vesey or Charlie Hoffmeister, or her grandchildren Elsie and Henry. Of course, her surviving child, Edward, had a good excuse not to be there, as he was living on the other side of the Atlantic. Emily left him all her estate in her will – £893, the equivalent of £70,000 today. Not a fortune, but still, for the struggling actor it must have been very welcome. But not even Clara made an appearance. Perhaps she too had been unwell. I can't help but feel sad, at Emily going out with a whimper – after such a huge life filled with so many people. I'm sure Emily would have wanted some faces there, and a big wake, with plenty of food and booze and gossip and people behaving badly, so she could look down from the celestial stage and chuckle. Although she would not have wanted long faces. After a visit to a churchyard in Salem, Massachusetts, Emily once wrote: 'Why should people affect to be so sad as a "transition," which in its heavenly rewards is to make amends for every earthly bliss we have missed or been done out of? Why?'

Of course, the downside of living many years past the average life expectancy is so many of your friends and family are not there to mourn you. And at least there were the obituaries.

The Times wrote:

It is nearly thirty years since Mme Emily Soldene (whose death was announced in The Times of yesterday) retired from the stage, it is even a good many – half a dozen or more – since her unmistakeable personality ceased to be frequently seen at first nights. And it needs a longish theatrical memory to know at first hand what Emily Soldene meant to her generation – the generation which though nothing of going

*to Islington-green to hear Offenbach and Emily Soldene
in Offenbach. Mme Soldene was a fine and highly trained
singer. Exeter Hall loved her in oratorio no less than the
Canterbury, the Oxford, or the Alhambra in more worldly
work, but it was in opera-bouffe that her voice, her vivacity
and her magnetism first found their perfect material . . .
America was no less enthusiastic about her than England,
but in the later seventies her vogue in England had declined
to something like ordinary popularity. She toured much
in America and Australia where she settled for some years.
Unlucky investments compelled her to turn to journalism
and other writing, in which she showed no less vivacity than
in opera-bouffe.*

It seems appropriate to give the last word to one of the few old
friends who outlived her, John Plummer, the deaf journalist,
who had been such a huge supporter from the very start of
her career and had probably found Emily her second career as
a journalist. In an obituary for her newspaper, he wrote that
Emily was:

*Essentially an optimist who radiated joviality and
happiness . . . she was full of vigour and perennial youth
. . . warmhearted, full of optimism, and acquainted with
everyone in the world of music and theatre . . . it seemed as
though one who was so happy and always trying to make
others see the smiling side of life should have lived forever.*

The perfect pair, Emily Soldene and Clara Vesey

Epilogue

After Emily's death the next generation of the Soldene family moved very quickly away from its theatrical roots. Emily's son, Edward, had three children in the end, but they grew up in America, and were left as orphans a few years after Emily died. First Edward Soldene Powell's wife, Harriet, died of a sarcoma in 1908 (she never got to the stage of being pushed around in a bath chair) and then Edward died of a haemorrhaging stomach ulcer in 1915, three years after his mother. They were both buried in Emily's detested Brooklyn. Their children were brought up by the Actors' Guild and passed around theatrical friends. I have managed to find a few grandchildren of the baby born in Tennyson Mansions in Fulham, with that unusual name, Gillette. They knew nothing about their great-great-grandmother and had no photographs. None of Katie Simpson's children had theatrical careers. Henry went back to India and continued with his distinguished military career and then served in the Great

War as Colonel Simpson of the Royal Artillery. He was awarded the DSO, Croix de Guerre and Order of Danilo. At the end of the war he became Lieutenant-Colonel CMG, Commander of the 27th London Air Defence Brigade. Emily would have been so proud. But then if Emily had been born a man I think she would have loved soldiering too – all that travel, the drama and courage required. She probably possessed the right degree of recklessness. Henry married and had two daughters (one of whom was called Katie) and retired to Hove; there the trail has run cold. Elsie lived in Feltham, married a bank manager and had three sons, one of whom was a schoolteacher, and again, no more is known. Helen, the chic granddaughter with the motor car, never married but lived a life of fun upper-class pursuits, parties, hunting and trips. Perhaps she decided that, like her grandmother, independence was more important than doing the expected thing.

The Vesey theatrical dynasty ended with Clara's children. Her son, Charlie, after Cambridge, went back to Brighton College as a teacher and housemaster. He was known as 'Houghie' and was remembered for his sterling performances in staff theatrical productions. Katie Vesey Hoffmeister never had children either. She carried on with her theatrical act until in 1921, at the age of nearly forty, she married a widower, Thomas Forrest Garvin. It was rather a good match. He was a barrister, a colonial widower from Ceylon, who became a King's Counsel and was called to the bench in 1924. In 1930 he became Ceylon's senior judge and when he retired he was knighted. Katie Vesey achieved what no one else in the family had managed – she became a Lady, Lady Garvin. Emily would have been ecstatic, as would Clara of course.

There is one person who very quietly disappeared and that was Clara Vesey. After Clara's visit to Australia with Katie and the dubious Pip Powell, there is no mention. As we know, she wasn't at Emily's funeral. However, thanks to the wonders of Ancestry and an email conversation with a very distant relation, I have found another sighting of Clara. It seems she took one last voyage. In 1921 at the age of seventy-three, Clara set sail for Ceylon never to return. Presumably after Katie's smart central London wedding, she went with Katie and her new husband to live with them in their tropical home. I wonder how she managed her insomnia and seasickness on the trip without Emily. I hope she still played poker the whole way and had some winning hands.

In their later years Emily and Clara had very different lives. Of course, if Emily hadn't run away and married Jack Powell so young (perhaps in an attempt not to repeat her mother's precarious romantic arrangements), like Clara she too might have had her career on the stage, and then when it got difficult, married a rich man and had a retirement of luxury and respectability. In this Clara might seem to have had the best of both worlds. It looks as if her daughter, Katie, thought so, following her mother's example by becoming a glamorous Gaiety girl and travelling the world, before making a conventionally advantageous match with an upright judge. But actually Jack had died relatively young, and Emily had plenty of time to remarry. It's unlikely she wouldn't have had male admirers; in her memoir Emily tells of a marriage proposal on a train, with the gentleman so keen he wanted to run off and find someone to officiate. And for all the luxuries of marrying well, Clara wasted no time going back to living a vicarious theatrical life chaperoning her daughter. By contrast Emily's Katie wanted none of her mother's life and married a stockbroker when she was barely eighteen.

It seems that Emily made a conscious choice to remain single. She might appear to be ahead of her time in choosing to stay a widow with all the independence that brought, and to earn her own living rather than rely on someone else to provide for her. However, I wonder how much women are still grappling with a choice between the traditional path and something more unconventional. How much is there still pressure to conform to the historic trajectory and how much are we still being judged for the life choices we make? In the twenty-first century who would we rather be – Emily or Clara, Katie Simpson or Katie Vesey?

There are many other ways in which I have been struck by how much things have changed, and yet in some ways so little has changed too. Being an actress is no longer equated with being a sophisticated prostitute, and yet to what extent does the casting couch still exist? How many actresses are still objectified and sexualised? But then how many women are still using their sexuality to promote their careers? Emily's assertion (via Mrs. Winslow) that women can experience as much sexual desire as men was a very radical and shocking proposition in the 1890s, but now is widely accepted. However, to what extent is there still a double standard for women and men's sexuality?

The Empire is gone and colonisers like Cecil Rhodes are no longer celebrated, but we too have a long-reigning, elderly queen who is widely revered as a unifying symbol of stability and continuity. The cult of celebrity was alive and well in

Emily's time, long before Hollywood and gossip magazines and social media; it just has more outlets now. Opéra bouffe is no longer in fashion – although Bizet's *Carmen* is enduringly popular – but the direct descendants of Offenbach's light, yet sophisticated, operas thrive as West End musicals. Actresses are still struggling to get good parts in their later years. Some expand and extend their careers by going into production as producers or directors, or even owning their own production companies, although I can't think of any who have made the transition into journalism. In this Emily seems to be unique.

One thing that was very different in the nineteenth century was the role of motherhood. Emily was able to live the life that she did, not least go abroad for years at a time, because it was perfectly acceptable for a mother not to actually bring up her children herself. If the children were provided for and cared for, then you were free to roam with no judgements made. In this respect, Victorian women were freer than mothers today, although there were plenty of other barriers to prohibit ladies having adventures.

As Emily herself once said, 'Some moments are worth years of ordinary things.' A line that conjures up an image of Emily dressed as the wild gypsy Carmen, fingering her dagger and looking into her dark Scotsman's eyes. I felt metaphorically breathless writing this book; there was so much more that Emily had done that wouldn't fit within my word count. How is it possible to squeeze so much action into one single life? To work so hard and yet play so hard, to travel to so many places without planes? To have met so many people when just a bonnet maker's illegitimate daughter from Clerkenwell? To eat so much food and drink so many brandy and sodas and live so long? To receive such harsh public criticism and lose so many loved ones and yet keep getting back on the stage? In the end I think she just loved life with the same appetite that she possessed for food, and approached everything as she did a horse race.

I came across Emily by chance. But if I hadn't been writing that other book, if I hadn't in a moment of prevarication picked up the phone to a local historian and sent an email to Kurt Gänzl, I would never have known she existed. How many magnificent ancestors do we have without realising it? How careless that so many disappear, sinking into the quicksands of the passing years; lost usually, for ever. How many stories of women who have lived extraordinary lives have vanished not just to their families but to the wider public, partly because history up until the late twentieth century has largely been written by men?

Emily's life turns the Dickensian stereotype of the Victorian woman, as either a fragile, simpering flower or a grotesque, caricatured evil hag, on its head. In real life women were indeed constricted by legal inequality and conservative social rules, but within those it was still sometimes possible to have agency – in Emily's case to run a business, to travel, to have a public voice and to fall in love with someone who wasn't her husband. It's time to reassess the Victorian woman, what she was really like and what she really did; we need some other stories to balance the ones that have so far set the tone.

Being with Emily for the last year, her noisy appearance in my life from beyond the grave, has been inspirational – how could it not be? Her lesson: to just do it, just say yes; if not me, then who? To choose independence over respectability, experience over security. It's hard for a life lived like that not to be inspirational. She is not just a hero, but better than that, a flawed hero. Emily is still of her time, in the language she uses and at times her attitude to other races, her interesting approach to motherhood, her use of both her own and other young women's sexuality for her own financial gain, her support for the system of patronage of women by men, her lack of support for women's suffrage. At times Emily did manage to shock me. But that has been outweighed by my admiration for who she was, how she moved through the world, what she achieved in spite of her disadvantages. She was willing to stand up for what she thought was right, speak her mind, to point out the hypocrisy of social conventions and Victorian sexuality. More than that, I like her. Her voice comes through the years clear, liberal, clever, funny, mischievous and, at times, cutting about others, but also winningly self-deprecating. She has a rare talent in her writing for taking you with her, for writing as if it were you there, for being a surrogate pair of eyes. She is never patronising to the reader. She is one of us.

As a final unlikely postscript, as I was finishing writing this book I made a discovery – I came across the Lady de Vries that my nanna used to talk about, or Lady de Frece as her real name was (it was the spelling that had confused me). Vesta Tilley or Lady de Frece, as she became later, was the highest-paid music hall star of the 1890s. In *Tipping the Velvet* style, she made a fortune dressing up as a man and singing mischievous songs, although not in breech roles. She was more of a cheeky young soldier, or a mannered masher in a dress suit – Burlington Bertie was her most popular incarnation. Like Emily, her big break was playing at the Canterbury Music Hall. Emily must have known her and seen her perform. At the age of fifty she retired and married a leading theatre impresario who was eventually knighted. Vesta Tilley thus became a real Lady (Nanna was wrong) and lived the rest of her life in luxury in Monte Carlo. I may be related to her, not through my maternal grandmother as with Emily, but through my maternal grandfather. Perhaps she was the famous actress that Nanna was talking about? Perhaps there were so many music hall artists around, that there are all sorts of performing ancestors we could reclaim if we just looked hard enough.

Acknowledgements

I am deeply indebted to musical historian, Kurt Gänzl, for introducing me to Emily and sending me his biography, *Emily Soldene: In Search of a Singer*, which I highly recommend if you want to know more about Emily and the world of opera bouffe. I'm also grateful to Kurt for letting me plunder his collection of photographs and Philip Wray author and contributor to the Preston History website (www.prestonherts.co.uk).

Dr Helen McCarthy of St. John's College, Cambridge, gave me excellent advice on researching the lives of women in the Victorian era and an invaluable reading list. As did Kimberley, Simon and Samantha at the London Library who kept suggesting and sending me books throughout the pandemic. Thanks also to Professor Derek Scott of Leeds University for his introduction to the world of opera bouffe. I'm profoundly grateful to the late Dr Peter Linehan of St. John's for his support, kindness and humour over the years, but in particular when I started writing these improbable adventures. I know he'd rather I'd been writing about an obscure medieval Castilian monarch.

I'm so sorry he won't read the finished book – he would have appreciated Emily's hutzpah.

Thanks to my agent Lisa Moylett, and Zoe Aphostolides for believing in Emily and their help with her return to the public stage. Also my unofficial editors Judith Pearson and Sally Floyer for their wise advice with the early drafts, and just generally Kim Shillinglaw, Emma Jones, Alison Noon, Aimee Kimbell and Alison George for their unfailing encouragement and light relief through the long days of lockdown writing.

Lastly my daughters Amber, Scarlett and Daisy for putting up with my endless chatter about the antics of this ancient relation, and David Thompson, for being Emily's greatest cheerleader, coming up with the title, and generally being the most entertaining company.

Bibliography

Belina, Anastasia and Scott, Derek B. *The Cambridge Companion to Operetta*, Cambridge University Press: 2020

Davis, Tracy C. Actresses as Working Women: Their social identity in Victorian culture, Routledge: 1991

Flanders, Judith *The Victorian City, Everyday Life in Dickens' London*, Atlantic Books: 2012

Gänzl, Kurt *Emily Soldene, In Search of a Singer, Vols I and II*, Steele Roberts Ltd.: 2007

Inglis, Fred *A Short History of Celebrity*, Princeton University Press: 2010

Kay, Alison C. *The Foundations of Female Entrepreneurship: Enterprise, Home, and Household in London, c. 1800-1870*, Routledge: 2009

Luckhurst, Mary, Moody, Jane eds., *Theatre and Celebrity in Britain 1660-2000*, Palgrave Macmillan: 2005

McCarthy, Helen *Double Lives, A History of Working Motherhood*, Bloomsbury Publishing: 2020

Morton, William H., Newton, Henry Chance *Sixty Years Stage Service: Being A Record of the Life of Charles Morton, The Father of The Halls*, Kessinger Publishing: 2009

Mullin, Katherine *Working Girls : Fiction, Sexuality, and Modernity* Oxford University Press: 2016

Onslow, Barbara, *Women of the Press in Nineteenth-Century Britain*, Macmillan Press: 2000

Reitano, Joanne R. *The Restless City: A Short History of New York from Colonial Times to the Present*, Routledge: 2010

Richards, Sandra *The Rise of the English Actress*, Macmillan: 1993

Rowe, Dorothy *My Dearest Enemy, My Dangerous Friend: Making and Breaking Sibling Bonds*, Routledge: 2007

Senelick, Laurence *Jacques Offenbach and the Making of Modern Culture*, Cambridge University Press: 2017

Soldene, Emily *My Theatrical and Musical Recollections*, Downey & Co: 1898

Soldene, Emily *Young Mrs Staples*, Downey & Co: 1896

Sutherland, Gillian *In Search of the New Woman: Middle-Class Women and Work in Britain 1870-1914*, Cambridge University Press: 2015

Tomalin, Claire *The Invisible Woman, The Story of Nelly Ternan and Charles Dickens*, Viking: 1990

Walkowitz, Judith *City of Dreadful Delight, Narratives of Sexual Danger in Late-Victorian London*, The University of Chicago Press: 1992

Waters, Sarah *Tipping the Velvet*, Virago Press: 1998.

HELEN BATTEN is a bestselling writer who lives in London and works as a psychotherapist. After reading history at Cambridge, she studied journalism at Cardiff and worked in television, producing and directing documentaries for the BBC. Helen has previously published three non-fiction books: *Confessions of a Showman*, *Sisters of the East End* and *The Scarlet Sisters*.